D0571761

ANCIENT TECHNOLOGY

Greenwood Guides to Historic Events of the Ancient World

The Peloponnesian War
Lawrence Tritle

The Reign of Cleopatra
Stanley Burstein

The Decline and Fall of the Roman Empire
James W. Ermatinger

The Trojan War
Carol G. Thomas and Craig Conant

The Emperor Justinian and the Byzantine Empire
James Allan Evans

The Establishment of the Han Empire and Imperial China
Grant Hardy and Anne Behnke Kinney

The Emergence of Buddhism
Jacob N. Kinnard

ANCIENT TECHNOLOGY

John W. Humphrey

Greenwood Guides to Historic Events of the Ancient World
Bella Vivante, Series Editor

GREENWOOD PRESS
Westport, Connecticut • London

Library of Congress Cataloging-in-Publication Data

Humphrey, John William, 1946–
   Ancient technology / John W. Humphrey.
     p. cm. — (Greenwood guides to historic events of the ancient world)
   Includes bibliographical references and index.
   ISBN 0–313–32763–7 (alk. paper)
   1. Technology—History—To 1500.   I. Title.   II. Series.
   T16.H86   2006
   609.3—dc22   2006007915

British Library Cataloguing in Publication Data is available.

Library of Congress Catalog Card Number: 2006007915
ISBN: 0–313–32763–7

First published in 2006

Greenwood Press, 88 Post Road West, Westport, CT 06881
An imprint of Greenwood Publishing Group, Inc.
www.greenwood.com

Printed in the United States of America

The paper used in this book complies with the
Permanent Paper Standard issued by the National
Information Standards Organization (Z39.48–1984).
10 9 8 7 6 5 4 3 2 1

CONTENTS

SERIES FOREWORD

As a professor and scholar of the ancient Greek world, I am often asked by students and scholars of other disciplines, why study antiquity? What possible relevance could human events from two, three, or more thousand years ago have to our lives today? This questioning of the continued validity of our historical past may be the offshoot of the forces shaping the history of the American people. Proud of forging a new nation out of immigrants wrenched willingly or not from their home soils, Americans have experienced a liberating headiness of separation from traditional historical demands on their social and cultural identity. The result has been skepticism about the very validity of that historical past. Some of that skepticism is healthy and serves constructive purposes of scholarly inquiry. Questions of how, by whom, and in whose interest "history" is written are valid questions pursued by contemporary historians striving to uncover the multiple forces shaping any historical event and the multi-layered social consequences that result. But the current academic focus on "presentism"—the concern with only recent events and a deliberate ignoring of premodern eras—betrays an extreme distortion of legitimate intellectual inquiry. This stress on the present seems to have deepened in the early years of the twenty-first century. The cybertechnological explosions of the preceding decades seem to have propelled us into a new cultural age requiring new rules that make the past appear all the more obsolete.

So again I ask, why study ancient cultures? In the past year, the United States' occupation of Iraq, after it ousted that nation's heinous regime, has kept Iraq in the forefront of the news. The land base of Iraq is ancient Mesopotamia, "the land between the rivers" of the Tigris and the Euphrates, two of the four rivers in the biblical Garden of Eden (Genesis 2). Called "the cradle of civilization," this area witnessed the early development of a centrally organized, hierarchical social system that utilized the new technology of writing to administer an increasingly complex state.

Is there a connection between the ancient events, literature, and art coming out of this land and the contemporary events? Michael Wood, in his educational video *Iraq: The Cradle of Civilization*, produced shortly after the 1991 Gulf War, makes this connection explicit—between the people, their way of interacting with their environment, and even the cosmological stories they create to explain and define their world.

Study of the ancient world, like study of contemporary cultures other than one's own, has more than academic or exotic value. First, study of the past seeks meaning beyond solely acquiring factual knowledge. It strives to understand the human and social dynamics that underlie any historical event and what these underlying dynamics teach us about ourselves as human beings in interaction with one another. Study of the past also encourages deeper inquiry than what appears to some as the "quaint" observation that this region of current and recent conflict could have served as a biblical ideal or as a critical marker in the development of world civilizations. In fact, these apparently quaint dimensions can serve as the hook that piques our interest into examining the past and discovering what it may have to say to us today. Not an end in itself, this knowledge forms the bedrock for exploring deeper meanings.

Consider, for example, the following questions: What does it mean that three major world religions—Judaism, Christianity, and Islam—developed out of the ancient Mesopotamian worldview? (In this view, the world, and hence its gods, were seen as being in perpetual conflict with one another and with the environment, and death was perceived as a matter of despair and desolation.) What does it mean that Western forms of thinking derived from the particular intellectual revolution of archaic Greece that developed into what is called "rational discourse," ultimately systematized by Aristotle in the fourth century B.C.E.? How does this thinking, now fundamental to Western discourse, shape how we see the world and ourselves, and how we interact with one another? And how does it affect our ability, or lack thereof, to communicate intelligibly with people with differently framed cultural perceptions? What, ultimately, do we gain from being aware of the origin and development of these fundamental features of our thinking and beliefs?

In short, knowing the past is essential for knowing ourselves in the present. Without an understanding of where we came from, and the journey we took to get where we are today, we cannot understand why we think or act the way we do. Nor, without an understanding of historical development, are we in a position to make the kinds of constructive changes necessary to advance as a society. Awareness of the past gives us the resources necessary to make comparisons between our contemporary world and past times. It is from these comparisons that we can assess both the advances we have made as human societies and those aspects that can still benefit from change. Hence, knowledge of the past is crucial for shaping our individual and social identities, providing us with the resources to make intelligent, aware, and informed decisions for the future.

All ancient societies, whether significant for the evolution of Western ideas and values, or developed largely separate from the cultures that more directly influenced Western civilization, such as China, have important lessons to teach us. For fundamentally they all address questions that have faced every human individual and every human society that has ever existed. Because ancient civilizations erected great monuments of themselves in stone, writings, and the visual arts—all enduring material evidence—we can view how these ancient cultures dealt with many of the same questions we face today. And we learn the consequences of the actions taken by people in other societies and times that, ideally, should help us as we seek solutions to contemporary issues. Thus it was that President John F. Kennedy wrote of his reliance upon Thucydides' treatment of the devastating war between the ancient Greek city-states of Athens and Sparta (see the volume on the Peloponnesian War) in his study of exemplary figures, *Profiles in Courage*.

This series seeks to fulfill this goal both collectively and in the individual volumes. The individual volumes examine key events, trends, and developments in world history in ancient times that are central to the secondary school and lower-level undergraduate history curriculum and that form standard topics for student research. From a vast field of potential subjects, these selected topics emerged after consultations with scholars, educators, and librarians. Each book in the series can be described as a "library in a book." Each one presents a chronological timeline and an initial factual overview of its subject, three to five topical essays that examine the subject from diverse perspectives and for its various consequences, a concluding essay providing current perspectives on the event, biographies of key players, a selection of primary documents, illustrations, a glossary, and an index. The concept of the series is to provide ready-reference materials that include a quick, in-depth examination of the topic and insightful guidelines for interpretive analysis, suitable for student research and designed to stimulate critical thinking. The authors are all scholars of the topic in their respective fields, selected both on the basis of their expertise and for their ability to bring their scholarly knowledge to a wider audience in an engaging and clear way. In these regards, this series follows the concept and format of the Greenwood Guides to Historic Events of the Twentieth Century, the Fifteenth to Nineteenth Centuries, and the Medieval World.

All the works in this series deal with historical developments in early ancient civilizations, almost invariably postdating the emergence of writing and of hierarchical dynastic social structures. Perhaps only incidentally do they deal with what historians call the Paleolithic Age (Old Stone Age), the period from about 25,000 B.C.E. onward, characterized by nomadic, hunting-gathering societies; or the Neolithic Age (New Stone Age), the period of the earliest development of agriculture and, hence, settled societies, one of the earliest dating to about 7000 B.C.E. at Çatal Höyük in south-central Turkey.

The earliest dates covered by the books in this series are the fourth to second millennia B.C.E., for the building of the pyramids in Egypt, the examination of the Trojan War, and the Bronze Age civilizations of the eastern Mediterranean. Most volumes deal with events in the first millennium B.C.E. to the early centuries of the first millennium C.E. Some treat the development of civilizations, such as the volume on the rise of the Han Empire in China, or the separate volumes on the rise and on the decline and fall of the Roman Empire. Some highlight major personalities and their empires, such as the volumes on Cleopatra VII of Ptolemaic Egypt, and on Justinian and the beginnings of the Byzantine Empire in eastern Greece and Constantinople (Istanbul). Three volumes examine the emergence in antiquity of religious movements that form major contemporary world systems of belief—Judaism, Buddhism, and Christianity. (Islam is being treated in the parallel Medieval World series.) And two volumes focus on technological developments, one on the building of the pyramids and one on other ancient technologies.

Each book examines the complexities of the forces shaping the development of its subject and the historical consequences. Thus, for example, the volume on the fifth-century-B.C.E. Greek Peloponnesian War explores the historical causes of the war, the nature of the combatants' actions, and how these reflect the thinking of the period. A particular issue, which may seem strange to some and timely to others, is how a city like Athens, with its proto-democratic political organization and its outstanding achievements in architecture, sculpture, painting, drama, and philosophy, could engage in openly imperialist policies of land conquest and of vicious revenge against anyone who countered them. Rather than trying to gloss over the contradictions that emerge, these books conscientiously explore whatever tensions arise in the ancient material, both to portray more completely the ancient event and to highlight the fact that no historical occurrence is simply determined. Sometimes societies that we admire in some ways (such as ancient Athens for their artistic achievements and democratic political experiments) may prove deeply troublesome in other ways (such as what we see as their reprehensible conduct in war and brutal subjection of other Greek communities). Consequently, the reader is empowered to make informed, well-rounded judgments on the events and actions of the major players.

We offer this series as an invitation to explore the past in various ways. We anticipate that from its volumes the reader will gain a better appreciation of the historical events and forces that shaped the lives of our ancient forebears and that continue to shape our thinking, values, and actions today. However remote in time and culture these ancient civilizations may at times appear, ultimately they show us that the questions confronting human beings of any age are timeless and that the examples of the past can provide valuable insights into our understanding of the present and the future.

Bella Vivante
University of Arizona

PREFACE

THEMES

This volume in the series Historic Events in the Ancient World is rather an anomaly. Its cousins treat one (albeit often fragmented) momentous event like the building of the pyramids or the evolution of the political system of the Han Empire. In *Ancient Technology* you will find a series of six topical essays, each devoted to the evolution of a set of related technologies during the Greek and Roman periods, with frequent glances back to the empires of the Bronze Age, and even to the Stone Ages, to set in context the remarkable accomplishments of the Greeks and Romans. To give a sense of the depth as well as breadth of the field, some of these chapters focus in more detail on either a related revolutionary invention (of the Greek alphabet or coinage) or on a technological "state of the art" moment in the ancient world (the urban water system of imperial Rome); it is hoped that these will give the reader greater insight into how scholars of ancient technology pursue their work, as well as of the limitations imposed on them by the available (and often contradictory) evidence.

The most difficult part of writing this book was the selection of what to present. The evolution of western technology presents a myriad (the highest number in ancient Greek numerical vocabulary!) of influential developments and inventions, from which I have chosen only those within six broad categories. But those six, either directly or indirectly, touch on all the common elements of ancient technology: agriculture and food processing; hydraulic engineering; mining, metallurgy, and metalworking; ceramics and textiles; transportation by sea and land; coinage; writing; timekeeping; construction engineering; and military technology.

The final chapter is a retrospective essay that examines some of the reasons underlying the technical achievements of antiquity, tries to put into context the limitations that often prevented these advances from being widely adopted, and considers the impact of ancient technological achievements on the modern industrial world of the eighteenth century onward.

Technologies are, in the first instance, simply extensions of the human body, allowing us to overcome the physical limitations with which we are born, and to adapt the natural environment to our own needs. So it may strike some readers as strange that this volume includes inventions, not only of those *physical* tools by which we tend to identify "technology," but of more amorphous *concepts* like writing, elements of which, like the alphabet, are indeed tools, and in that specific case one that made subsequent technological progress possible. The first indulgence I would request of the reader, then, is to keep a broad view of what qualifies as a tool.

As a second favor, I would ask that we blur the modern distinction between the practical (technology) and the decorative (art). The origin of the English word "technology" is enlightening in this regard: it derives from the Greek word *techne*, referring to the gamut of art, skill, and craft. The Roman equivalent is *ars*, so from the beginning we see in antiquity a relationship between the utility of technology and the beauty of art. This is a theme that was important enough to the ancients that it is reflected in Greek mythology, with the marriage of Hephaistos, the god of smiths, to Aphrodite, the goddess of beauty. The Greeks and Romans, at least, understood the inseparable relationship between the two.

Finally, I think it is unproductive and even misleading to study mechanical technologies in isolation from the societies that produced them. Without a sense of why cultures spent so much effort in developing new techniques, we would have no real understanding of the momentousness of their inventions. It is true, if simplistic, to say that the principal motivation behind technological development is to make life safer and easier, the necessity of survival and the penchant for laziness being the twin mothers of invention. But there is more to progress than that. What are the social deficits that prompt technological remedies? What are the cultural traditions that inhibit change? And what momentous influences do new technologies have on the societies that produced them?

SCOPE

The field of ancient technology straddles a number of different disciplines. First, the study of technology in general is very broad in itself, and no modern engineer or craftsman has a field of expertise this diverse. In addition, the meaningful study of ancient technology requires knowledge of ancillary disciplines like ancient literature, history (both cultural and political), art history, and archaeology. Furthermore, the time frame and the geographical range under investigation are generally very large. So an inevitable danger inherent in broad surveys of ancient technology is superficiality in an attempt to cover as much ground as possible, and I am aware that I have not always succeeded in overcoming this.

For reasons of length, I have consciously limited the material in this volume both chronologically and geographically. The technologies presented all developed significantly between the Archaic Age in Greece and the height of the Roman Empire, a period of 900 years that witnessed a combination of cultural and technological energy and productiveness unequalled until the eighteenth century. That said, it proved necessary to present some earlier historical background to each case, to give the reader a sense of the long period of gestation for a particular invention or culmination of development. While I have not hesitated to delve back into the Bronze Age and even the Neolithic to set the stage, I have had to treat this earlier material so superficially as at times to be almost misleading. I have tried to mitigate this problem by giving one or two suggestions for further reading that encompass prehistory as well as historical antiquity.

I regret that this volume perpetuates the Mediterranean emphasis of traditional classical scholarship. There is much that should have been included from the ancient cultures of Asia in particular. But I admit with a mixture of self-reproach and embarrassment that I am not the person to do it. My scholarly and archaeological life has been limited to the Mediterranean world, and for me to include the remarkable technological history of, say, early China (movable type, gunpowder, the compass), while already claiming to be an expert on two other ancient civilizations would rightly test the reader's credulity.

ACKNOWLEDGMENTS

This work owes much to many colleagues and friends. I am especially indebted to two scholars who qualify in both categories: John Oleson of the University of Victoria and Andrew Sherwood of Guelph University, who have inspired me for longer than I can remember, who were my partners in an earlier work on the literary sources of Greek and Roman technology, and who have generously allowed me to reproduce here some of our translated documents from that volume (see below). Among my many former students who have suffered through my passion for things technological, I must single out two who helped me with this volume: Yvette Haakmeester, archeologist and world traveler (Chapters 5–6), and my friend Milo Nikolic, now a doctoral candidate with Oleson in Victoria (Chapter 8): their persistent enthusiasm, good humor, and support have carried me through more difficult times than they realized, and I am proud to have made some contribution through them to the next generation of scholars.

I am deeply grateful both to Bella Vivante, Editor of this series, who asked me to participate and has, despite my negligence, been a tolerant and supportive colleague; and to Michael Hermann and Mariah Gumpert of Greenwood Publishers, who have cut me more slack in the preparation of this volume than I have deserved. My student Binh Tran, who created most of the diagrams for this volume, worked tirelessly to translate complex written descriptions into accurate and comprehensible graphics; and Alison Jeppeson, a doctoral candidate in my Department, generously supplied me with a list of classically themed websites, from which I have added a sample to the bibliography.

To my temporary colleagues in Continuing Education at the University of Calgary, where I have just ended a refreshing if hectic two-year term as Dean and Director, I offer my thanks for your friendship, encouragement, and tolerance as I struggled to balance university administration with the writing of this book.

And to my wife, Laura McLeod, I acknowledge my perpetually boundless gratitude for every kind of support. This book, like my last, is dedicated to her.

SOURCES OF THE TRANSLATED DOCUMENTS

The 54 translated documents presented in this volume are all taken, with only a few minor changes, from John W. Humphrey, John P. Oleson, and Andrew N. Sherwood, *Greek and Roman Technology: A Sourcebook* (London and New York: Routledge, 1998), with the permission of my co-authors and the publisher. The following list indicates, for each document, the specific passage number of each in the *Sourcebook*:

1–3.43; 2–3.58; 3–3.29; 4–3.33; 5–3.35; 6–3.8; 7–4.2; 8–4.13; 9–9.25; 10–9.55; 11–9.53; 12–9.58; 13–8.25; 14–8.27; 15–8.30; 16–3.22-23; 17–8.13; 18–8.16-17; 19–8.38; 20–7.13-14; 21–12.21; 22–12.23; 23–12.25; 24–12.26; 25–12.29; 26–12.31; 27–10.57; 28–10.87; 29–10.90; 30–10.93; 31–10.96; 32–10.1, 24; 33–10.7; 34–10.45; 35–10.18; 36–10.105; 37–10.107; 38–8.7; 39–11.14; 40–11.17; 41–11.17; 42–11.23; 43–11.5; 44–11.4, 6; 45–11.11; 46–5.21, 26; 47–5.18; 48–6.26; 49–9.81; 50–13.6; 51–13.10; 52–1.6; 53–13.22; 54–1.1.

CHRONOLOGY OF EVENTS

The following superficial outline gives a sense of the gradually increasing speed of cultural development, as one significant discovery or technological invention leads to social advances, which in turn foster new inventions. For the purposes of this volume, the periods from the Mesolithic onward reflect the cultures of the Near East, the Mediterranean, and Europe.

PREHISTORY

Eolithic (ca. 2.5 million years ago)
Australopithecus made occasional use of improvised tools

Early Lower Paleolithic (ca. 1.8 million years ago)
Homo habilis occasionally flaked pebble tools

Middle Lower Paleolithic (ca. 500,000 B.C.E.)
Homo erectus (e.g., Pekin Man) practiced regular tool making without standardization of form

Late Lower Paleolithic (ca. 400,000 B.C.E.)
Homo presapiens: regular making of tools with standardized forms, but without any specialization of function

Middle Paleolithic (ca. 170,000–40,000 B.C.E.)
Homo neanderthalis: elementary standardized tools with some specialization of function

Upper Paleolithic (ca. 40,000–10,000 B.C.E.)	*Homo sapiens* (Cro-Magnon Man): specialized tools with composite forms; cave paintings
Mesolithic (ca. 10,000–8000 B.C.E.)	*Homo sapiens sapiens*: hunting now supplemented by more gathering and fishing; beginning of permanent settlements
Neolithic (ca. 8000–3000 B.C.E.)	The development of true agriculture allows settled life and specialization of labor
ca. 10,000	Foundation of Jericho in Palestine, perhaps the first permanent settlement in the world
ca. 8000	Foundation of Çatal Höyük just north of the Taurus Mountains in central Anatolia (modern Turkey)
Chalcolithic (ca. 5000–3000 B.C.E.)	A period within Neolithic: initial use of metal (copper), but stone tools still predominate
ca. 5000	Discovery of the simple working of native copper in the Near East; by 3500, Cyprus enters the Chalcolithic period (and the island later takes its name from its abundant supplies of copper)

BRONZE AGE

ca. 3000–1000 B.C.E.	First major civilizations (Egypt, Mesopotamia, Minoan Crete, Mycenaean Greece); beginning of urbanization, extensive trade, and writing
ca. 3100	Unification of Upper and Lower Egypt; origin of writing in Sumeria
ca. 3000	Invention of wheel in Near East
ca. 2700	Construction of the pyramids at Giza
ca. 2200	First palace built at Minoan Knossos on Crete
ca. 2000	Invention of spoked wheel in Syria
ca. 1950	First Hellenes (Greeks) enter the Greek peninsula from the north

ca. 1900	Beginning of Greek settlement at Mycenae and Tiryns
1600–1400	The cultured Minoan Cretans, through trade by sea, influence the less developed Mycenaean Greek mainland; Cyprus borrows and adapts the Cretan writing system
ca. 1450	Destruction of the Minoan palaces on Crete, except Knossos, which thereafter seems to be controlled by Mycenaean Greeks; Linear B tablets there are earliest form of written Greek

IRON AGE

| ca. 1000 B.C.E.–500 C.E. | Iron becomes the predominant material for tools and weapons; the civilizations of classical Greece and imperial Rome. |

Dark and Archaic Ages

1050–950	Colonization of the west coast of Asia Minor by mainland Greeks who have been displaced by Dorian Greek invaders
814	Traditional date for the foundation of Carthage in North Africa (near modern Tunis), by Phoenician traders from the eastern shores of the Mediterranean
753	(April 21) Traditional date of the foundation of Rome in Italy
ca. 730	Composition by Homer of two epic poems, *The Iliad* and *The Odyssey*, perhaps in Ionia (the central west coast of Asia Minor)
before 700	Greeks adapt the Phoenician alphabet to their language
ca. 700	The Assyrian king Sennacherib builds a palace at Nineveh, complete with an arcaded aqueduct to water the gardens

650–600	Earliest coinage in Lydia and Greece; first codifications of law in the Greek *poleis* (city-states); rise of tyrannies in many cities
ca. 600	Resurrection of stone architecture in Greece; in Italy, the Roman Forum is laid out as a public meeting place
540–530	Earliest dated coins from Athens
510/509	Cleisthenes expels the tyrants and establishes the world's first democracy in Athens; traditional date for the expulsion of the kings from Rome and the creation of the Roman Republic

Classical Greece

483	Silver is discovered at Laurion in Attica: beginning of Athenian prosperity
449–429	Pericles is leader of the Athenian democracy; dedication of the Parthenon on the Acropolis of Athens
431	Beginning of the Peloponnesian War between Athens and Sparta
404	Defeat of Athens and her surrender to Sparta
ca. 350	The Ionian alphabet used by Athens becomes the universal Greek script

Hellenistic Age

| 335–323 | Alexander the Great of Macedon attacks the Persian Empire under Darius III: he conquers Asia Minor and the Middle East; Aristotle (Alexander's tutor) teaches in Athens |
| 312 | The Roman censor Appius Claudius builds the Appian Way and Rome's first aqueduct |

283–246	Ptolemy II of Egypt establishes the famous Museum and Library in Alexandria: beginning of Hellenistic research
ca. 275	Ctesibius, an inventor in Alexandria, develops the piston pump and the water clock with variable hours
211	Death of Archimedes of Syracuse, inventor of the water screw and compound pulley
ca. 200	Philo of Byzantium active as an inventor in Alexandria
197	A barrel-vaulted wharf-side granary in Rome is the first datable structure made of structural concrete
153	Rome formally replaces 1 March with 1 January as the beginning of the civil year
46 B.C.E.	Julius Caesar reforms the calendar, bringing the civil year into line with the solar year

The Roman Empire

46 C.E.	Construction of Claudius' harbor at Ostia, at the mouth of Rome's Tiber River
ca. 60–70	The engineer and inventor Hero is active in Alexandria
ca. 65	Columella publishes his manual on agriculture
67	Nero participates in the Olympic Games, and starts construction of the Corinth canal
79	Eruption of Mt. Vesuvius near the Bay of Naples kills thousands (including the Elder Pliny) and buries the cities of Pompeii, Stabiae, and Herculaneum
80	Dedication of the Flavian Amphitheatre (Colosseum) in Rome
97	Frontinus becomes curator of Rome's water supply, and writes a manual titled *On Aqueducts*

330   Constantine's new city, Constantinople (modern Istanbul), is dedicated on the site of the old Greek colony of Byzantium, and becomes capital of the Roman Empire; beginning of the transition from pagan antiquity to the Christian Byzantine world

CHAPTER 1

HISTORICAL AND TECHNOLOGICAL OVERVIEW

The human race is the wisest of all living creatures because it has hands.
Anaxagoras *Fragments* 59.A.102

Technologies are inventions of humans that have allowed us to survive, and have enabled our cultures to advance. They are for the most part material objects: tools, for example, are simply detachable additions to the body, the manufacture of which generally distinguishes humans from animals. Since humans alone can conceive of past and future, so too we alone can make tools for an imagined eventuality. Tools at first enabled our ancestors to adapt themselves to their environment; only in the last 10,000 years have we used our technologies to adapt the environment to our own needs.

We begin with a brief outline of human history and technological development from the earliest times to the end of the Roman Empire, to set in chronological context the topical chapters that follow. We then survey some of the aspects of antiquity that influence what we know about tools and processes (Sources of Information), and what basic resources the ancients had at their disposal (Energy and Machines in Antiquity).

THE CULTURAL AGES OF HUMANKIND

The following outline gives a sense of the gradually increasing speed of cultural development, as one significant discovery or technological invention leads to social advances, which in turn foster new inventions. For the purposes of this volume, the periods from the Mesolithic onward reflect the cultures of the Near East, the Mediterranean, and Europe.

Prehistoric Times

Paleolithic Age. By 500,000 B.C.E., in the Lower Paleolithic, humans had made two important discoveries: how to control fire and how to fashion stone tools; eoliths, or small fractured pieces of flint, are the earliest surviving human-made tools. Pekin Man at Choukoutien fashioned unstandardized, unspecialized tools from stone for immediate use; they also used (but probably did not make) fire; they lived in caves and hunted large game in groups, the earliest form of social organization. Their pebble-tool culture evolved into the hand-axe culture of the Abevillians and Acheulians, whose axe was the first standardized implement, though it still served many different functions (that is, it was unspecialized); the regularity of this tool shows a tradition of education, and probably some form of developed speech; their hunting society made irregular use of fire, lived mostly in the open, and perhaps wore skins; and their fine workmanship shows a sense of aesthetics as well as utility.

The Middle Paleolithic Age was a period of specialized tools devised for various functions. The prepared-core technique of manufacture allowed many flake tools to be struck from a single piece of flint, thus saving time and material. Neanderthals were the major species of the period: they used skin clothing, ate mostly meat, lived in caves, and perhaps made fire; while they showed little concern for art or decoration, their remains do exhibit some signs of spirituality.

In the Upper Paleolithic, ca. 40,000 B.C.E., Cro-Magnon man (*Homo sapiens*) supplanted the Neanderthals through events that are still not understood. This more advanced culture was partly the result of leisure time, since game was more plentiful, and resulted in important new techniques, particularly the production of narrow blades with parallel sides and the invention of composite tools like the spear-thrower. The economy was still based on hunting in groups, and people still lived in caves where available; but they also began constructing shelters in the steppes: these are the first settlements, though temporary since humans were still nomads following the wild herds. Burials from the time show that these people decorated themselves with jewelry; and their carvings and cave paintings, prompted perhaps by a desire to influence magically the wild herds, show for the first time the inner feelings and desires of our primitive ancestors.

Mesolithic Age. Before 10,000 B.C.E., humans had existed for half a million years as nomadic hunters of roaming herds and gatherers of wild plants, their simple tools flaked from flint. But around twelve millennia ago, a fortuitous coincidence of natural events and human ingenuity allowed the nomadic hunting economy of the Paleolithic Age to be replaced in some areas by the hunting–gathering–fishing cultures of the Mesolithic that preceded actual agriculture. The Natufians of the Near East, for example, began an economy based on the harvesting of (probably) wild grains; and in the forested areas of northern Europe the Maglemosians or Bog-Peoples developed new tools to cut and work trees, and nets, hooks, and boats for fishing.

Neolithic Age. The change from a hunting–gathering economy to one based on agriculture occurred in the Near East around 8000 B.C.E. Now, with an assured food supply, settled life replaced a nomadic existence, and the temporary settlements of the Mesolithic grew into permanent agrarian villages, whose surplus farm products were protected from marauders, often by extensive fortifications. This period is called the Neolithic Revolution because of the radical changes that took place in humans' lifestyle, from new technologies to a new social organization that now included specialists. The primitive farmer's need for water, for example, led him to develop large social units around a natural water supply, and to organize this group for the construction and maintenance of complex irrigation systems that involved the finding, lifting, conduction, and conservation of water. By 5000 B.C.E., agriculture was spread throughout the eastern Mediterranean.

New forms of stone tools needed to be developed for working the soil, planting seeds, and harvesting the produce (the most obvious examples are the hoe, sickle, quern, and mortar and pestle); pottery was developed for the carrying and storage of foodstuffs, and textiles for both clothing and domestic purposes (both technologies, at first, almost certainly the realm of women); there was some nascent specialization of labor; and the surplus food supply caused trade to evolve between villages (hence the evolution of boats and primitive wheelless vehicles).

Early permanent settlements were established at places that offered some necessary element for the agricultural revolution: Jericho in an oasis that provided irrigation water for the fields; and Çatal Höyük on the Anatolian Plateau of Asia Minor (at a relatively immense 35 hectares, among the largest Neolithic sites yet discovered), its prosperity guaranteed by easy access to obsidian from a nearby volcano. In some fortunate places—Cyprus was one of them—native copper was easily accessible, and was tentatively hammered and sometimes cast for the last 2,000 years of the Bronze Age (a period we term the Chalcolithic after the Greek word for copper), though the limitations of pure copper meant that stone, flaked or polished, was still the predominant material for tools and weapons.

The Bronze Age

Despite its advances, the Neolithic Age was still a period of relatively primitive cultures. It was not until ca. 3000 B.C.E. that true urban civilizations were established, beginning in Mesopotamia and Egypt and quickly spreading to Asia Minor, Crete, and mainland Greece. This period, encompassing the third and second millennia B.C.E., is termed the Bronze Age in the eastern Mediterranean, since bronze was at that time predominant in the manufacture of tools and weapons.

The Bronze Age is the period that witnesses the development of large political units; of highly specialized occupations and the resulting class divisions; and of monumental public architecture. Among the new and developed technologies of the Bronze Age were metallurgy, including the mining and smelting of ores, and the annealing and casting of bronze; new developments in construction (elaborate public, royal, and religious buildings erected to impress the peasants with the might of their rulers, and to store and protect the great agricultural surpluses); writing, a natural requirement of the centralized bureaucracies of these large empires; and the wheel, used both for pottery making and for transportation.

The Bronze Age ended quite suddenly, with the invasion by peoples often with less highly developed cultures, under pressure from other migrating tribes to the north: the Mycenaean Greeks sacked Troy on the Dardanelles, the Phrygians displaced the Hittites in Anatolia, and the Greek-speaking Dorians descended into the Greek peninsula ca. 1100 B.C.E., their iron weapons proving superior to the bronze ones of their Mycenaean cousins.

Mesopotamia and Egypt. This is the era best known for the pharaohs' pyramids in Egypt and the huge temple cities in the equally agriculturally blessed area of Mesopotamia (modern Iraq), both areas favored for early development because their soil was annually regenerated by the flooding of the Nile and Tigris–Euphrates rivers, and so was fertile enough to support very large populations.

By 3100 B.C.E., the Sumerian civilization was formed in southern Mesopotamia, the north being controlled by Akkad. The Babylonian leader Hammurabi united the two areas, but by ca. 1600 B.C.E. this kingdom was largely replaced by the empire of the Hittites, the first people extensively to use iron. In the dynastic period of the Bronze Age, in the meantime, Egypt too was a unified country comprising Upper (south) and Lower (north) Egypt, ruled by the pharaohs: here, as in Mesopotamia, a centralized form of government inevitably encouraged the development of new technologies.

Anatolia, Greece, and the Aegean Islands. But important things were happening in the Mediterranean lands adjacent to the Near East as well. After the arrival of the Hellenes themselves into the Greek peninsula ca. 1900 B.C.E., there were four prosperous cultures in the northeastern Mediterranean: the Indo-European Hittites dominated central Asia Minor until the collapse of their empire ca. 1200 B.C.E.; trade between the Black Sea and the Aegean was from time to time controlled by the Trojans from their fortified city on the south coast of the Dardanelles; the mysterious Minoans, particularly on the island of Crete, reached a high level of civilization from 1700 to 1450 B.C.E. thanks largely to their control of maritime trade in the Aegean; while the Mycenaeans, ancestors of the classical Greeks, also depended on trade to support their highly developed material culture from 1600 to 1200 B.C.E., and their heavily fortified citadels are proof of both their wealth and general insecurity. The last two centuries of the Bronze Age witnessed widespread and destructive economic wars (the Greek siege of Troy is dated to about 1240 B.C.E.) and movements of large populations (like the raids of the Sea Peoples along the eastern Mediterranean coasts) that undermined the security of the large urban-based empires. The eventual collapse of the Hittites ca. 1200 B.C.E. led to the diffusion of iron working and the beginning of the Iron Age.

The Iron Age

In many areas the Bronze Age was followed by a "dark age" of two or three centuries, from which we have no written records and few physical remains. After ca. 700 B.C.E., we find the Assyrians and Persians controlling much of the Near East; their complex system of communications by road encouraged the spread of new ideas and technologies. The Phoenicians, a merchant people who lived on the coast of Lebanon, were the major traders of the early Iron Age, and so were responsible for spreading these new technologies throughout the Mediterranean; their most notable contribution to Western culture was the alphabet.

According to some scholars, Iron-Age societies shared the benefits of progressive inventions more widely than their predecessors, as seen in three new technological advances that eventually would benefit all social classes: iron gave peasants better and cheaper tools; the alphabet encouraged the spread of literacy; and coinage made commerce easier and allowed the poor to save for the products of an advanced technology. At the same time, Greece was the first society to approach an "industrial" economy: lack of agricultural land made the peninsula dependent on manufacturing and trade to obtain a supply of food in return. But there was really no ancient industry as we think of the term: shops were small and depended largely on slave labor; there was little incentive for capital investment; and the manufacturing of goods came to be considered disreputable, so there was no desire to improve technologies.

The Dark and Archaic Ages (1000–490 B.C.E.). With the collapse of the Hittite Empire and Troy, and the arrival in the Greek peninsula of the relatively backward Iron-Age Dorian Greeks, we enter a period often called the Dark Ages since the art of writing in the area was temporarily lost. By ca. 950 B.C.E. in Greece proper, aristocracies (literally, "rule by the best," that is, by the well-born) had replaced most of the old Mycenaean kingdoms, and the *polis*—the city-state—emerged in the form of an urban center (Athens, for example) surrounded by agricultural land (Attica). During this same time, many Greeks migrated across the Aegean to the west coast of Asia Minor, an area called Ionia, and there founded cities like Ephesos and Miletos. It is a period of political and social changes: revolution and overpopulation prompted the Greek cities of the Aegean basin to send out colonists to the Black Sea region and to southern Italy (which thereafter was called Magna Graecia, "Great Greece"); and in many cities the aristocrats were replaced by tyrants. The period also witnessed the true beginning of Greek culture: writing developed again under influence from the Phoenicians; western literature began with the formation (if not the actual publication) of the epic poem *The Iliad* by Homer; coinage was invented in the lands of the Aegean Sea; stone architecture and monumental sculpture first reappeared at the beginning of the seventh century B.C.E.; the decoration of pottery reached unequalled heights with the development of Athenian Black-Figure and Red-Figure vases; and the seeds of philosophy and the sciences were sown in the Greek cities of Ionia in Asia Minor.

In the west, meanwhile, Indo-European invaders called the Villanovans (whom some scholars think were indigenous) introduced the Iron Age into northern Italy. These Villanovans were supplanted in the eighth century by the Etruscans, a mysterious people whose origin, like that of the Minoans, is still debated and whose language is still largely indecipherable. Many of their attributes would connect them with the inhabitants of Lydia in western Asia Minor, and their culture in Italy seems to explode almost overnight. They were much influenced by the Greek colonies of south Italy, and some of the finest painted ceramics in the Greek mode originate in Etruria. They were in many ways the middlemen between the Greeks and the Latins: they passed on the Greek alphabet to the Romans, together with their own considerable accomplishments in engineering and divination, all of which played an important role in the development of Rome itself, traditionally established as a village in the eighth century, and ruled by kings until a Republic was established in 509 B.C.E.

Classical Greece (490–323 B.C.E.). The remarkably short but culturally stunning period from 490 to 404 B.C.E. understandably bears the title of the Golden Age of Greece, and particularly of Athens. Their successful opposition to two dangerous invasions of their peninsula by the Persians had temporarily unified many of the hitherto fiercely independent Greek city-states and in part stimulated the great cultural achievements of that century. Fortunately for Athens, in 483 B.C.E. a plentiful supply of silver-bearing ore was discovered at Laurion in Attica, and the wealth from its exploitation was the foundation of Athenian prosperity and dominance.

Under its great democratic leader Pericles, Athens outshone the rest of the Greek world politically, militarily, and culturally. Thanks largely to its superior naval power, based on the effectiveness of its fleet of triremes and the security of its harbors, Athens also dominated the Delian League of Greek states that had been formed in 479 B.C.E. to expel the Persians from the Aegean, eventually transforming the League into its own empire. This overt imperialism brought on an inevitable clash with Athens' rival, Sparta, which ended with the humiliation of Athens in 404 B.C.E. But in less than a hundred years that city had given the world tragic and comic theater, the "science" of historical writing, and an architectural and sculptural heritage whose effects are still with us.

Though Athens was forced to give up its empire and lost its political (but not cultural) prestige, no other Greek state was able to take its place for long. Sparta's predominance lasted only until 371 B.C.E., after which Thebes in Boeotia held a temporary hegemony over much of the mainland. But it was left to the Macedonians, more militaristic Greeks (and, some Athenians said, less cultured ones) from the northern part of the peninsula, to bring about the first political unification of the independent Greek *poleis*, under Philip II and his son, Alexander the Great. With his remarkable conquests and foundation of cities in lands previously tribal (many of which were named after him, including Afghan Kandahar), the young Alexander spread Greek culture throughout the eastern Mediterranean and as far eastward as the Indus River: and the benefits were reciprocal, as contact with new cultures as far away as India brought innovations and improvements to the technological level of the classical world. Alexander's untimely death caused the disintegration of the largest empire the western world had yet seen, though its influence was to endure in a new world order fostered first by his Macedonian successors and then by a new power rising in the western Mediterranean: Rome.

The Hellenistic Mediterranean (323–146 B.C.E.*).* Following the premature death of Alexander in Babylon, several of his Macedonian generals gradually gained control of large portions of his conquests: the Ptolemies established a new Greek dynasty of pharaohs in Egypt; the family of Seleucus ruled in Syria and parts of Asia Minor; and the Antigonids controlled the old Macedonian kingdom in northern Greece. There arose as well several small and independent states, such as Rhodes and the city of Pergamon in western Asia Minor, while in Greece proper the various *poleis* sometimes formed loose leagues primarily for religious and military reasons. This was a time of considerable advances in mechanical theory and practice, largely because of Ptolemy II of Egypt (283–246 B.C.E.), who established the famous Museum and Library in his capital, Alexandria, which became a productive state-sponsored research center that produced inventive scholars like Ctesibius and Hero.

But there was little hope that such a politically fragmented and competitive region could long survive: the smaller states like Rhodes and Pergamon made defensive treaties with the Romans, who by now were recognized as a world power following their successful wars against Carthage in the West.

Thanks largely to its geographical position—surrounded by easily defensible hills, at the head of navigation on the Tiber, with a midstream island that made it possible to ford the river, and in control of the salt beds at the river's mouth—Rome prospered and gradually acquired control of surrounding territories and, by the mid-third century, most of the Italian peninsula. By borrowing freely from their neighbors (in particular the Etruscans to the north and the Greeks to the south), the Romans quickly advanced their artistic and technological condition: in 312 B.C.E. the Roman censor Appius Claudius commissioned construction of the Appian Way and of Rome's first aqueduct; coinage was extended to the western Mediterranean; and the first surviving prose work in Latin—a handbook on agricultural techniques—was written by the dour Elder Cato.

Though initially uninterested in overseas conquests, Rome was first challenged by Carthaginian control of trade in the western Mediterranean, and a series of three wars brought it the grain-rich island of Sicily and then Spain with its productive silver mines. Later Rome became actively embroiled in Greek disputes when the Macedonians and Seleucids threatened its weaker eastern allies: four times in just sixty years the Romans imposed peace on the quarrelling Greek states, and three times they quickly withdrew their legions. But in 146 B.C.E., weary of their role as peacemaker and prompted by a new belief in their grand military and political destiny, the Romans destroyed the troublesome mercantile city of Corinth and brought the Greek peninsula under their protection. It is ironic—though it was probably inevitable—that the old and highly developed civilization of the Greek East took the relatively uncultured Romans by storm: as the poet Horace observed, Rome the conqueror was conquered in turn, by Greek art, architecture, literature, and customs.

The Late Roman Republic (146–27 B.C.E.). Though the Romans by this time controlled most of the lands along the north coast of the Mediterranean Sea, there was little peace at home: social and economic divisions among the citizens of Rome led to a period of internal conflicts, sometimes breaking out into full civil war. This was the age of the great and powerful generals of the Roman Republic—Marius, Sulla, Pompey the Great, and Julius Caesar—and of one of Rome's greatest statesmen, philosophers, and authors, Marcus Tullius Cicero; it was also a century of rapid Roman expansion throughout the eastern Mediterranean, where it annexed as provinces Syria, Egypt, and several states of Asia Minor. But with Caesar's assassination in 44 B.C.E., another fourteen years of tension and strife preceded the return of peace under his great-nephew and posthumously adopted son Octavian (later called Augustus), the one general who managed to eliminate all his rivals and become Rome's first Emperor. The peace that Augustus brought to the world, albeit at the expense of individual freedoms, was to last for two centuries, and gave the inhabitants of the empire—Romans, Greeks, Syrians, Gauls, Africans—an unprecedented opportunity to benefit from the economic, social, and cultural achievements that were rooted in the practical advances of Roman engineering and technology.

The Mediterranean Under the Roman Empire (27 B.C.E.–330 C.E.). The first two centuries of our era were the most peaceful and prosperous the world had yet experienced; according to Edward Gibbon, writing in the late eighteenth century, even up to his own time there had not been a more settled or happier period in human history. Emperors came and went, sometimes violently, but the imperial administration first established by Augustus managed to preserve the social and economic stability of the Mediterranean world. The Graeco-Roman cities and culture of the eastern empire flourished, and the art and architecture of the period show a fine, eclectic combination of the best from both the Greek and the Roman traditions that reached its apex during the reign of Hadrian, Rome's philhellenic and peripatetic emperor.

Not surprisingly, this is the period during which many of our literary descriptions of technology were written: the earlier agricultural manuals of Cato and Varro had been fair reflections of the rural interests of many Romans in the late Republic, but now we have the great engineering handbooks of Vitruvius and Frontinus, and the extensive if not always reliable encyclopedia of the Elder Pliny. Civil engineering in particular was at its zenith with the perfection both of massive stone arches and vaults that gave us the Colosseum and the soaring arcades of aqueducts, and of structural concrete that made possible the perfect semispherical dome of antiquity's most remarkable building, the Pantheon.

But internal dynastic and administrative squabbling, combined with pressures from the northern warlike tribes that lived beyond the empire's fluvial boundaries (the Rhine and the Danube), caused such great civil disruption and economic decline in the third century that military Emperors like Diocletian and Constantine were compelled to clamp rigid regulations on the lives of their subjects, as the Roman world was gradually transformed into the feudal system of the Middle Ages in the West. By the beginning of the fourth century the empire had been formally divided into the Latin West and the Greek East: the ancient world effectively came to a close in 330 C.E., when the capital of the empire was transferred from Rome to Constantinople (Istanbul), heralding the start of the Byzantine Christian world in the eastern Mediterranean.

Especially for those of us living in an age that sees rapid technological developments in the blink of an eye, it is difficult to comprehend the extraordinarily slow changes in early human history. This was due, at least from the advent of *Homo sapiens*, not to any mental deficiency among our early ancestors, but to a combination of very tiny populations and the absence of any technological base. Since one invention often has many new applications, development increases exponentially, not linearly; thus, we are what we are today not so much because of our own originality or cleverness but because of the inventiveness of those who preceded us, even by half a million years.

The long gestation of early technologies may be more comprehensible if we were to condense all of human history into the span of a single year, with each hour of that period representing about 60 actual years. If we begin some 500,000 years ago: on 16 January *Homo erectus* practiced regular tool making without standardization of form, but it took until 2 December for *Homo sapiens* to create specialized tools with composite forms. Agriculture and settled life began early in the morning of 25 December, and the Bronze Age appears just after noon on 28 December.

The Greek alphabet was introduced at 01:40 on 30 December, the great inventor Archimedes designed compound pulleys about noon that day, and Mount Vesuvius erupted at 15:15. Columbus did not sail to the Americas until 15:28 on the last day of our year; the atomic bomb was invented at 23:00, and humans reached the moon at half an hour before midnight on New Year's Eve.

SOURCES OF INFORMATION

There are four major sources of information about technologies from various periods of antiquity: contemporary pictures such as wall paintings and decorated pottery; the comparison of contemporary primitive societies to those of antiquity; ancient written records such as histories and technical reports; and the excavation of ancient sites. All four of these sources are used in this volume to introduce you to Greek and Roman technologies and their relationship to ancient society: ancient written records are presented in the Documents section; the other sources are shown visually as drawings or photographs within the text.

Contemporary Pictures

Graphic depictions of people's activities in antiquity form one of our major sources of information about their technologies, from the cave paintings of the Upper Paleolithic, to Athenian vase paintings of the classical period and frescoes from Pompeii. Fortunately for us, our Greek ancestors delighted in decorating their pottery and their Roman successors the walls of their houses, favoring depictions of daily activities as much as loftier mythological scenes. It is from pottery that we learn much about the armament of hoplite soldiers, the vessels used in *symposia* (literally, drinking parties), the styles of Greek household furniture, and theatrical and athletic competitions. Roman wall paintings and mosaics are equally informative: depictions of country houses, farms, and agricultural tasks; of recent events like a gladiatorial riot in Pompeii's amphitheater; of religious ritual; and of family activities like buying bread or dining in the *triclinium*.

It will come as no surprise that these ancient representations must be used with care. They are, first and most importantly, works of art, not engineering drawings, and the artists quite naturally emphasize the personal and emotional aspects over the technical details. The space available, too, often affects the accuracy of the image: pottery and coins in particular gave the artists little room to include all elements of a scene, and inevitably they would eliminate those they thought extraneous to the impression they were conveying. So it is risky to deduce the number of frontal columns from a small coin that shows a temple, or the hoplite panoply from the traditional depiction of semi-nude warriors.

Comparative Anthropology

Comparative anthropology can be a useful tool to fill in the gaps in our knowledge of some aspects of ancient technology and society. In the twentieth century, for example, many cultures in the Middle East still practiced techniques and used tools that were remarkably similar to those of their predecessors in the ancient Near East. My own experience from archaeological work in Turkey spanning three decades has shown that this is especially true in fields like agriculture, metalworking, transportation, and construction. The ox-drawn plow, iron hand-sickle, and wooden threshing sledge are still a part (albeit a rapidly fading one) of farming on the south coast; a smithy for working iron in the Anatolian town of Yalvaç could be taken straight from nearby Antioch in Pisidia, its Roman predecessor (see Figure 22); handmade carts with three-piece solid wooden wheels can still be seen in the mountains of eastern Turkey, persisting since the beginning of the Bronze Age because the simplicity of their manufacture means that farmers themselves can construct them during the otherwise unproductive months of winter; and the surviving mud-brick conical houses of Harran, ancient Carrhae, though now abandoned in favor of soulless cinder-block structures, are pretty much identical to those when Abraham lingered in the same village more than three millennia ago.

But the scholar must be careful with this type of evidence, for there are many factors that can affect what might appear as an unbroken line of transmission from the past to the present. Most obvious are the changes, not in materials or processes, but in cultural assumptions. The largely Islamic Middle East of today, for example, shows techniques and attitudes toward technology that can be very different from those of the farmers of antiquity. Still, ancient literary descriptions of long-lost tools or processes can often be confirmed and even modified by the study of modern artifacts and techniques.

Documentary Sources

Written records are available from Bronze-Age Mesopotamia onward, but it is not until the classical period of Greece and Rome that the works are valuable for a study of the technologies of the ancients. Even then, these sources—though primary evidence—must be approached with a great deal of caution, for a variety of reasons:

- The authors of ancient texts are, with insignificant exceptions, men—and upper-class men at that—whose principal concerns are agriculture (as absentee landlords rather than farmers, of course), the military, and politics. Their interest in and knowledge of the lives and efforts of women, commoners, and slaves is very limited. Thus there are many aspects of our study for which we have little written evidence: ceramic production and textiles are two good examples. And even when our authors do tackle technical subjects that interest them, they sometimes show a surprising ignorance of their own machines and processes. Still, they are often our only source of comprehensive information about certain technologies.

- Especially among the Romans, texts reflect an urban rather than rural perspective. The poets Horace and Juvenal, and the admirable Younger Pliny may sing the praises of the quiet, private country life, but they all persisted in living in Rome. "Civilization" was practically (as well as etymologically) related to cities, though the great majority of the population lived in the country.

- The ancients were almost always ethnically biased, and usually saw little of interest or usefulness in the ways of foreigners. So our Greek sources dismiss the achievements of their eastern neighbors and predecessors, though they were often more technologically advanced; and the Romans, who had all the benefits of a world empire, still found their ideal in the traditional Italian landscape.

- The ancients were, it seems, pessimistic by nature. From the eighth-century B.C.E. poet Hesiod onward, they viewed the past as a glorious age for humankind, and railed against the mores of their own time. So iron is base and common when compared to gold, despite the significant advantages it bestowed on Hesiod and his descendants. The encyclopedist Pliny the Elder reflects the same attitude three-quarters of a millennium later: "our ancestors lived the proper life, our contemporaries are corrupt."

- Only a relatively small portion of everything published in antiquity has survived today. Fortunately, most of what we do have is the best (or at least the most popular and uplifting), reissued frequently enough to ensure that at least one copy has come down to us. But the study of antiquity is hobbled by the loss of so much. To appreciate how little we have, consider the Loeb Classical Library series of ancient Greek and Roman authors: with the exception of papyri and inscriptions, it includes almost all written texts from Homer to the end of the Roman Empire, contained in 495 small volumes (including both the original Greek or Latin text and a facing English translation) that can be accommodated in two standard six-shelf bookcases. Little wonder, then, that scholars spend their careers mining every nugget out of these precious texts, turning even to the poets for material on technological subjects.

Historians. The Greek Herodotus of the fifth century B.C.E., for example, gives us information on the building of Egyptian pyramids; Thucydides from the next generation is a valuable source for the tactics of naval warfare; and the Roman general and politician Julius Caesar included many useful descriptions of military technology in his accounts of his own campaigns.

Encyclopedists. Compilers like Pliny the Elder of the first century C.E. preserve many useful if often misunderstood facts; his *Natural History* in thirty-seven volumes treats such subjects as physics, geography and ethnology, human physiology, zoology and botany, and metallurgy and metalworking.

Geographers. The Greek travelers Strabo and Pausanias have left us accounts of their journeys in the Mediterranean during the period of the Roman Empire, and offer detailed descriptions of important buildings and artifacts.

Agricultural writers. Since farming was the basis of the ancient economy, and since it was considered one of the few honorable occupations for citizens, it is not surprising that we have three Roman monographs on the subject, written by Cato (second century B.C.E.), Varro (first century B.C.E.), and Columella (first century C.E.), and treating cultivation, livestock, farm equipment, and so on, generally from the viewpoint of the absentee landlord.

Technological monographs. Vitruvius' book *On Architecture*, from the late first century B.C.E., discusses construction in general, as well as specific building types, water supply, and machines; Frontinus a century later wrote a work *On Aqueducts* and another *On Stratagems* (of which Book 3 deals with sieges); and the latter topic is supplemented by a military treatise by Vegetius (fourth century C.E.).

Poetry. Even ancient poets cannot be neglected: in his epics *The Iliad* and *The Odyssey* Homer provides detailed descriptions of shipbuilding, house and farmstead construction, and orchard planning; half a century later the Greek poet Hesiod, in his *Works and Days*, described the harsh life and primitive equipment of an archaic farmer; and the Roman epic poet Vergil wrote a poem in four books, the *Georgics*, about agriculture in the first century B.C.E.

Archaeological Excavation

Archaeology is perhaps the most productive source of information about the technologies of the ancients, since it is through archaeology that we can study the physical activities of the ancients through the built remains of their cities and villages, as well as obtain actual samples of the products created by them.

Though the recovery and study of ancient artifacts is centuries old, the early collection of ancient sculpture taken indiscriminately from random and unrecorded exploration of ancient sites like Italian Pompeii has little to do with the modern "science" of archaeology. The first serious archaeological excavation in the Mediterranean began in the second half of the nineteenth century, when pioneers like Heinrich Schliemann, inspired by the surviving literary evidence from antiquity, began in some controlled and documented way to reveal the physical remnants of the Bronze Age and the classical period at sites like Mycenae and Troy, Athens and Corinth. As a result of their early work, we have learned more about antiquity in the past 130 years than ever was added before. Our knowledge of the Bronze Age, for the most part not the beneficiary of useful documentary evidence, has been especially advanced by excavation, though there are as well many elements of classical antiquity to which archaeology has introduced us: inscriptions that reveal the taxation system of the Athenian Empire or the traffic-calming regulations in Rome; the evolution of town planning; and the skeletal remains of ships almost miraculously preserved by the Mediterranean waters that claimed them.

Archaeology has also been a useful antidote to the aristocratic male perspective that dominates our written sources. The *agora* (marketplace) of Athens has been revealed as the center of an Athenian citizen's life, much more than the Acropolis that towers above it; and the *insulae* (apartment blocks) discovered in the excavation of Rome's port city of Ostia give us a better sense of the domestic life of an urban Roman than even the cynical poet Juvenal could reveal. And—while the unearthing of an intact marble statue or hoard of gold jewelry might still attract the public's attention—archaeologists for the past few generations have been exploring as well the "minor" crafts and previously discarded relics of more common life: ceramic fragments, called the "wastepaper of antiquity" because of their abundance on almost every site, giving us clues to both domestic and commercial processes, some fragments with a provenance so identifiable that they allow us to reconstruct trade routes; small articles—metal broaches and belt buckles, terracotta votive figurines, and bronze crosses—by which we can trace the evolution of such disparate matters as clothing and religion; petrified seeds that help us track the diet of the ancients; and human bones that, through scientific analysis, provide data on life expectancy, illnesses, and causes of death.

ENERGY AND MACHINES IN ANTIQUITY

Contrary to what is often believed, the ancient Greeks and Romans—and to a lesser extent the earlier Egyptians and Mesopotamians—possessed a great many mechanical devices: by the classical period they were familiar with levers, pulleys, rotary systems, steam and hydraulic power, gears and gear trains, and even complex pumps and valves.

Sources of Energy

One of the most severe restrictions on technological progress in antiquity was the use of a very limited variety of energy sources: human power and animal power were the most significant, while water and the wind were used for only a few specific applications.

Human power was employed either alone in a great number of tasks (hauling two-ton blocks for the pyramids), or in connection with various mechanical devices like the winch or lever (propelling warships by oars, for example). These devices allowed people to transmit power over a short distance, to change the direction of the power, or to multiply it through mechanical advantage. But humans in fact can produce only a small amount of usable power: it is estimated that a single person on a treadmill can put out about 0.1 hp.

After animals had been domesticated in the Neolithic Age first as a food supply, they later came to be used as a source of energy, either as beasts of burden and draft animals or to power mechanical devices. In the Mediterranean region oxen were most commonly used for such purposes, since they were economical if slow; the horse (always considered a noble beast) was used only for transporting light loads (like cavalrymen); while donkeys and mules were assigned to pulling carts and turning rotary mills.

Moving water as a source of energy was never widespread in the ancient world: such a power supply requires a year-round and regular flow of considerable speed and quantity, something that is not common in most of the Mediterranean region. Waterwheels, for example, were apparently seldom used until about the first century B.C.E., when Vitruvius described the wheel used to raise buckets on a chain and—through toothed gear wheels—to grind grain. It was hardly more efficient than man-power: depending of course on its size and the speed of the stream below its vanes, it could produce 0.05–0.50 hp; the more efficient but costly "overshot" wheel could put out perhaps 2 hp.

Neither wind power nor steam power was taken seriously in the ancient world. The former was used almost exclusively for propelling ships; and, though Hero of Alexandria described a windmill connected to an air pump designed to blow an organ, there is no evidence for the existence of any rotary windmills before the tenth century C.E. Hero also designed a workable steam engine, but it had a low torque and was very inefficient (it has been estimated that the machine required 25,000 BTU/hour to produce 0.1 hp, the output of a human). One of its principal limitations was the absence of a cheap, efficient, and portable source of heat: though coal and petroleum were recognized in antiquity, only charcoal was extensively used, in pottery kilns and smelting furnaces, for example.

Mechanical Devices

It is seldom possible to determine exactly when a particular mechanical device was discovered or invented, but in general the chronological development was as follows.

The principle of the lever was certainly known as early as the Upper Paleolithic Age, when it was employed in such composite tools as the spear-thrower; at the same time the concept of rotary power is evident in the use of the bow drill. The lever, the inclined plane or wedge, and the cylindrical roller were all used to great advantage by the Egyptians in the construction of their pyramids at the beginning of the Bronze Age. The lever was later to be applied to other devices, such as the beam-press of the classical period.

With the invention of the pulley came two important advantages: the ability to change the direction of a force, and the multiplying of the available power. The pulley, together with its attendant devices such as the windlass, is not mentioned in literature until the fourth century B.C.E., but it was certainly used much earlier: even the Egyptians had discovered the usefulness of changing the direction of a force by passing a rope over a fixed horizontal bar, but it remained for the Greeks to devise a pulley system that increased mechanical advantage as well; and we credit the Greek scientist Archimedes with the invention of the compound pulley.

We are told, perhaps with some justification, that it was Archimedes, too, who, in the Hellenistic period (late third century B.C.E.), applied the concept of the screw (really just an inclined plane wrapped around a shaft) to practical uses like the raising of water and crushing of olives. He is also credited with the invention of the toothed gear, a revolutionary device that could change the direction of power and increase or decrease the speed of movement.

It was in part thanks to this device that in the Hellenistic and Roman periods the water wheel was used both as a lifting device and to power other kinds of machines like mills and (at the end of the ancient world) even saws. It was the Hellenistic Greeks, too, who invented the water pump with automatic inlet and outlet valves. Still, it remained for humans and animals to power most of the machines of antiquity: animal-powered mills, for example, are always more common than their water-powered cousins.

Perhaps the single most remarkable example of the ancients' skill in designing machines based on these basic mechanical principles is the now-famous Antikythera mechanism. Just over a hundred years ago, sponge fishermen working in the waters off an islet near the Greek island of Kythera discovered an ancient shipwreck, and hauled up from it (among other things) an encrusted mass of bronze. This unprepossessing discovery was to prove to be a late-Hellenistic instrument that, through an intricate system of gears and dials, allowed complex calculations of data apparently related to the solar and lunar calendars. Understandably, this bit of ancient high technology is often identified as the primitive ancestor of our modern computer. This is a bit of a simplification, since the gears of the mechanism bear a greater relationship to Renaissance mechanical astrolabes and clockworks than to the binary system on which our computers are based. But the device remains one of the most intriguing and advanced applications of mechanical theory in antiquity.

CHAPTER 2

FOOD AND CLOTHING

For the first 98 percent of the 500,000 or so years of truly human existence, small bands of nomadic hunters and gatherers kept themselves nourished and clothed by stalking herds of wild animals and gathering wild fruits and nuts. This simple and mobile life produced few technological innovations, but those few were of enormous significance, not just for the survival of the tribes but for the evolution of human societies: the flaked stone tools for killing game, cutting meat, and scraping hides for warmth; the later composite hunting devices like spear-throwers and bows and arrows; and the mining of pigments and invention of lamps for the production of the remarkable cave paintings of the Upper Paleolithic. At the same time, this nomadic existence saw little advance in the production or processing of food and clothing, and did not foster the creation of implements that we would normally associate with even the more primitive forms of human endeavor. Take pottery as one example: though Cro-Magnon artists produced molded clay figurines of the animals they hunted, any attempt to manipulate that plastic material into the form of watertight containers would be thwarted by the very fragility of the vessel when carried from kill site to water source to protective cave.

Some 10,000 years ago—that is, a short 500 generations past—there occurred the first real revolution in the course of human existence, when people's desire for a permanent and assured food supply prompted them to begin manipulating the natural course of plant and animal reproduction, beginning in the Near East and northern Europe, where the variety and abundance of wild plant and animal species had already been harvested for a millennium or two by seminomadic groups to supplement their diet: the Maglemosians of the Danish coast found a semipermanent food supply in the fish of the sea, which they harvested with newly invented bone hooks and rush nets; and the Natufians of the Near East developed saw-like sickles to cut the wild grain and simple stone grinders to process it into flour. It seems likely that domesticated animals' need for fodder meant that the cultivation of plants occurred first, perhaps an extension of the presumed role of women in Paleolithic gathering, just as men's experience in hunting evolved into the herding of cattle and other animals.

But the true agricultural life demands more than a handy supply of tamable plants and animals. It is equally dependent on a regular supply of water, which often presents a severe challenge in areas of the Near East where the spring runoff is torrential but the riverbeds are parched and cracking by summer, when the water is needed most to irrigate the crops. So it was natural that people settled around the few constant sources of water: oases with natural springs like that at Jericho, arguably the first large human settlement, or along rivers like the Nile and Tigris–Euphrates, where annual spring floods would eventually be manipulated to the advantage of farmers, allowing more than one crop a year and, by the beginning of the Bronze Age, ushering in the first true urban civilizations of Egypt and Mesopotamia.

Some would argue that the agricultural revolution was more of an evolution, since it took more than a millennium to control plants other than grains, and even longer to domesticate higher-order animals like the horse. But that seems almost like the blink of an eye when we compare the relatively snail-like progress of human ingenuity in the previous 500 millennia.

CULTIVATION AND DOMESTICATION

Early Neolithic farmers could not have imagined the impact that the cultivation of plants would have on the future of humankind. Possession of a stable food supply was the primary motivation, but by tying people to the soil for the first time, it also revolutionized society more dramatically than perhaps any subsequent technological development. A surplus of grain first allowed for the domestication of animals, then the development of trade with less favored areas, and the invention of devices for transporting materials between villages; it required new tools for the cultivation, storage, and processing of food (sickles, pottery, and mills); and it promoted permanent settlement in villages, and the almost simultaneous erection of defensive walls and other military innovations to protect that surplus from theft.

Of cultivated crops, cereals were of the greatest economic importance in the Mediterranean region in antiquity, just as rice was the staple in East Asia, and maize and quinoa in the Americas. Since wild plants were necessarily self-seeding for their survival, the early Neolithic farmers favored individual plants that had developed suicidal mutations that prevented the pod from opening naturally and scattering the seed. Thus they were able to harvest their crops without losing grains, and could later separate the seeds from the pods. Similarly with animals: those that exhibited juvenile characteristics were favored over the strong, and bred to eliminate their wild characteristics. This—the earliest form of genetic manipulation by humans—was eventually to make a significant portion of Mediterranean flora and fauna dependent on human assistance in reproduction and survival: at least as sobering an innovation as the genetic modification of foods that is being debated at the beginning of the twenty-first century.

Food Plants

Cereals were the first cultivated food plants, and can be credited with making settled life possible. Of these wheat, developed from the wild varieties that we know were present in the Near East, was the most important grain in Mediterranean antiquity, although barley was also grown, and rye in the cooler or harsher climates like the high Anatolian plateau of Turkey. Grains were usually eaten in the form of unleavened biscuits or gruel; when the latter was fermented, as it almost certainly was early in the Neolithic, it produced a simple beer.

Green vegetables such as cabbage, lettuce, and spinach are found from the Neolithic onward. Root vegetables included carrots and radishes, but not of course the potato, a seventeenth-century importation into Europe from the New World. Beans, peas, and lentils were more popular in antiquity than in many cultures today because they were common, were easily stored, could be ground into flour as a substitute for cereals, and had a high protein content that could compensate for the absence of meat in societies with limited means to preserve foods.

The cultivation of fruit trees occurred comparatively late, since it required more work and time to produce any yield (Document 1). Nuts and oil-bearing seeds like the opium poppy and olive were of great importance in cooking, lamps, medicines, cosmetics, and for industrial uses. We know from the mythological stories told of Dionysos that the vine was imported into Greece from the Near East, probably by the early second millennium, and viticulture became so widespread in a mountainous land unfriendly to cereal crops that wine was soon being exported by Greek city-states in exchange for basic foodstuffs like grain. The cultivation of the olive, still an essential element of the Mediterranean diet, is something of an

anomaly in the history of the diffusion of technologies: while most originated in the east of the Mediterranean and gradually spread westward, the
olive appears to have been cultivated first in Spain, and did not reach
Greece until the late Bronze Age.

Industrial Plants

Plants were used for various industrial purposes as well. Timber, though
not cultivated in antiquity, was the principal material for the construction
of buildings, furniture, and boats (the more plentiful reeds in the Near East
were used for many of these same purposes); so necessary was it that, by the
end of antiquity, whole regions of North Africa and the eastern Mediterranean had been denuded of their natural forests, leading to erosion and
the loss of arable land to encroaching deserts. Fiber plants were used for
textiles, including flax, hemp, and, much later, cotton, which may have
been imported from India into Egypt as late as the fifth century C.E. And
papyrus was cultivated in Egypt for use as a writing surface, and was one
of that region's most important exports.

Domestication

The domestication of animals involved the subjugation of one species
to the requirements of another, in this case of humans. While some
animals like dogs and reindeer were individually tamed during the Mesolithic period, the concerted domestication of other animals, requiring
a regular supply of fodder, almost certainly followed the introduction
of primitive cultivation (Document 2). As a rule, domestication of a
species can be determined archaeologically by morphological changes in
bone structures, like the persistence of juvenile skeletal characteristics.

In general, domestication evolved in four distinct stages: first, animals
were attached loosely to human society; then there occurred the complete subjugation and captivity of the weaker animals; this was followed
by interbreeding with the wild forms to increase the size of the domesticated variety; and finally the stock was completely domesticated and
separated from their wild cousins, which are thereafter seen as a threat
and exterminated. By this last stage animals, like cultivated plants, had
become largely dependent on humans for their survival.

Greek and Roman farms supported almost all of the animals that we
make use of today. For pulling plows and carts, and for carrying loads
from sacks of grain to cavalrymen, there were oxen, donkeys, mules, and
horses (the latter, then as now considered a nobler beast, was used almost

exclusively for riding or pulling war and racing chariots). Meat was supplied by pigs, sheep, goats, and rabbits; and by chickens, geese, ducks, pigeons, and more elegant birds like pheasants and thrushes. Cattle were kept principally as draft animals, their meat being marketed only after long service in the field: little wonder, then, that in the fourth century we know that it was priced with goat and mutton, considerably cheaper than pork, lamb, and venison. Chickens doubled as a source of eggs, and sheep and goats as sources of milk and cheese. Bees, though not domesticated, provided the principal ancient sweetener.

AGRICULTURAL IMPLEMENTS

Working the Soil

The plow was one of the most important inventions of the Bronze Age, since it was more efficient than the simple Neolithic hoe: by cutting deeper into the earth it helped prevent the exhaustion of the soil. The typical plow of antiquity consisted of a stock with a horizontal point to break the ground, attached to a draft team by a pole and yoke, and with a handle for the farmer projecting from the end of the stock (Document 3). The earliest plows, depicted in Bronze-Age Egyptian tomb paintings, were pulled by the farm workers themselves; the first yokes for harnessing draft animals were fitted around the animals' horns; only later in the Bronze Age was the chest collar developed to harness the power from the sturdiest part of the ox. In lands adjacent to the Mediterranean Sea, where soils were dry and friable, the share was small, almost horizontal to the ground, and cut a very shallow furrow (the scratch plow), whereas the denser soils of Europe required more robust shares. By the Roman period, then, iron was often used to sheath the stock, and splaying bars were developed to lay the cut sod up on one side of the plow, a process that is reflected in the myth of the foundation of Rome, when Romulus drove a plow around the limits of his future city, cutting a furrow (the symbolic moat) and throwing the soil up to one side (the wall).

Harvesting

Harvesting in the Neolithic Age was done with small, straight sickles grooved to hold flaked flint blades; subsequently curved blades were made of bronze or iron, but it remained for the Romans to invent the properly balanced sickle that we are familiar with today, which replaced the old sawing or hacking motion with a more efficient sweeping technique that was also easier on the harvester's wrist (Document 4). Though the Elder Pliny describes a kind of automated reaping machine from the Roman Empire, for which there is also some sculptural evidence, it was likely used only in the dense crops typical of northern areas outside the Mediterranean basin; true mechanization of harvesting would not occur until the Middle Ages.

Threshing and Winnowing

Once harvested, the grains needed to be extracted from the seed pods by threshing the sheaves (Document 5). This was usually accomplished in one of two ways, both making use of the farm animals on hand for other purposes: the harvest was first spread out on a circular, hard-packed threshing floor, and animals either were driven over it to crush the pods with their hooves and release the grain, or pulled a threshing sledge whose undersurface was studded with flint or metal blades that chopped the harvest and cut open the pods, a technique that can still be witnessed in some areas of the eastern Mediterranean. Then, to separate the seed from the chaff, farm hands could sieve it in baskets, but more often would toss the grain into the air using forks, shovels, or oar-like wands (a technique called winnowing) so that the lighter chaff would be blown away and the heavier seeds would settle back onto the threshing floor.

Other Implements

Other necessary agricultural implements (Document 6) included hoes, ironclad spades to break the soil and trench around trees and vines, hafted iron picks for heavy working of the soil, two-pronged iron forks, wooden forks for tossing hay, various metal knives and hooks for pruning, grafting, and harvesting vines and trees, and specialized tools like shears for animal husbandry.

THE PROCESSING AND PREPARATION OF FOOD

The Implements of Food Processing

All three of the important foods of the ancient Mediterranean—grain, grapes, and olives—needed some preliminary processing before they could be made into bread, wine, and oil.

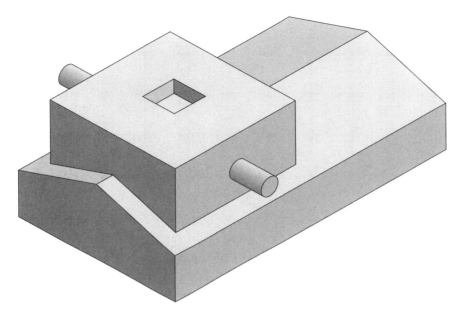

Figure 1. Push mill

Mills. At first grain was ground into flour between two flat stones (often termed a saddle quern), or in a hollow stone mortar with a pestle. From the former there developed first a pushing mill with a hopper in the upper stone to feed the grain, which allowed continuous milling (Figure 1), and later the rotary quern of two superimposed, flat, circular stones, the upper one with a vertical wooden handle for turning (a breakthrough in energy efficiency, since rotary motion is more productive than reciprocal motion) (Figures 2 and 3). By the Roman Empire the hand mill had evolved into the large, hourglass-shaped rotary quern powered by men or animals and capable of milling sufficient grain for a relatively large population; in this, the hollow upper stone was carefully balanced on a central wooden pivot to keep its inner surface slightly above the grinding surface of the lower stone, and was fitted with horizontal wooden beams to which were harnessed the animals or slaves that would turn it unceasingly as grain was fed into the upper hopper and emerged as flour beneath (Figure 4; Document 7). Finally, we have literary and archaeological evidence from the later empire that water was harnessed to turn grain mills through a series of geared wheels, a procedure that persisted through history and can still be seen in operation today.

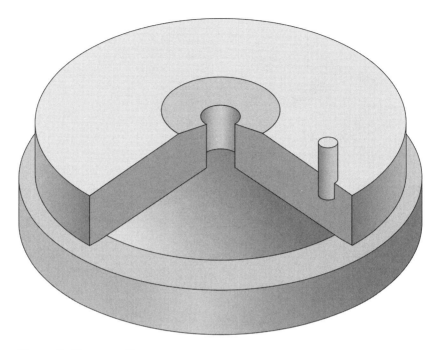

Figure 2. Rotary mill

Before extracting their oil, olives were first crushed, originally beneath a flat stone rotated over a trough of the fruit, and their pits removed before pressing. The Romans developed an olive mill called a *trapetum*, a vessel fitted with two vertical semispherical stones turning about a pivot, crushing the olives against the inner surface of the container (Figure 5).

Presses. Olives were then squeezed to extract the oil, with implements similar to those for pressing grapes (Document 8). The beam-press was a form of lever: a horizontal beam was hinged at one end, weighted with stones at the other, and a bag of grapes or olives placed under the middle. Hero of Alexandria was said to have used rope wrapped around a kind of ratcheted drum to draw down the beam-end. By the first century C.E. even greater pressure could be applied to the bag of pulp with the introduction of the screw, either to pull down the beam-end or, placed immediately above the fruit with a board between, to apply direct pressure (Figures 6 and 7). This last design, also attributed to Hero, would reappear fourteen centuries later in the early printing presses: just one of many ancient examples of a technique developed for one function that would later revolutionize another.

Figure 3. Rotary mill (Tunisia)

Food and Drink

Since most of our documentary record reflects the habits of the small wealthy class, and since native foods varied locally throughout the Mediterranean region, it is impossible to reconstruct a diet typical of the time and place in general. In this regard, our only cookbook surviving from antiquity, attributed to a certain Apicius who probably lived in the first century C.E., can be compared to the rustic recipes found in Cato's *On Agriculture* from two centuries earlier, to give us a good lesson in separating aristocratic from plebeian dishes: while Cato stresses the healthfulness of cabbage and root vegetables, Apicius includes recipes for stuffed dormice and trussed flamingo. Despite this, it is clear that the diet of most people in antiquity included bread or porridge, supplemented by vegetables and fish but little meat, all consumed along with a fermented beverage. Bread was usually made of coarse whole-grain flour in the classic pita style, with leavened bread appearing after ca. 500 B.C.E., baked in large domed ovens of the communal sort still to be found in some remote Greek villages.

Olives supplied most of the cooking oil in antiquity, and a bottle of the finest first pressing could fetch as much as a bottle of the most expensive wine.

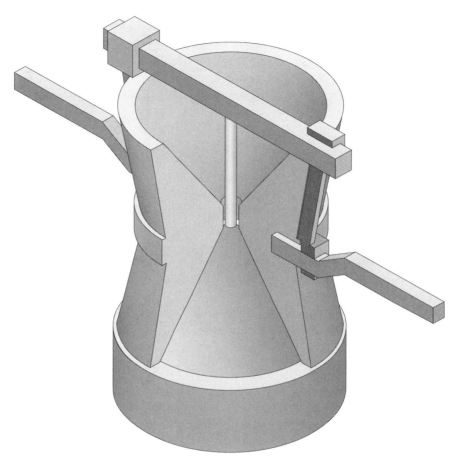

Figure 4. Donkey mill

After the fall vintage, the wine was fermented for half a year in large clay vats sunk into the ground (some of them apparently lined with pine resin to avoid leakage, popularly assumed to be the origin of modern *retsina*); it was then filtered into large clay amphorae for local sale or export, and served always mixed with water, which helps explain the Greeks' ability at a symposium (literally, a "drinking party") to carry on clever and sensible philosophical discussion while consuming many cups of wine. Beer, by the way, was popular in areas of the eastern Mediterranean like Egypt, where grain was more common than vines, but never among the Greeks and Romans, who considered wine a necessary element of civilization itself. The distillation of alcohol was a medieval development unknown in antiquity.

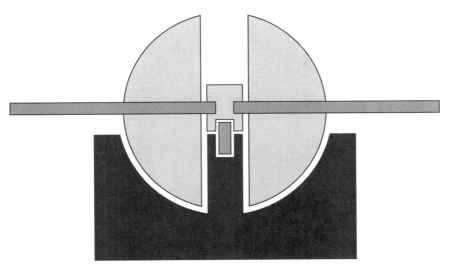

Figure 5. *Trapetum*

BASKETRY AND TEXTILES

The manufacture of textiles and of vessels for the storage and transportation of goods, both of which today we associate with large-scale automated production, in antiquity was carried out either in the home (textiles) or in small shops with a handful of artisans (pottery). Though we strongly suspect that both crafts were first the responsibility of a society's women, the production of pottery seems to have fallen to men when it became more technical with the Bronze-Age inventions of kilns and the pottery wheel, while spinning and weaving remained largely in the realm of women within the household (Document 9). We shall consider the fabrication of pottery later, along with other "industrial" crafts like metalworking; but the manufacture of basketry and fabrics, which is an essential element of human survival, and which relies on the products of agriculture, is a suitable matter for discussion here.

Woven fabrics are found from the Neolithic period on, probably having been developed from Mesolithic fishing nets and lines, as well as from early basketry; but textiles are so perishable that few examples have survived. We depend for our information largely on documentary sources and on the ancient Greeks' penchant for decorating their pots with domestic scenes, both real and mythological: the wifely duties of spinning and weaving were favorite motifs in both milieus. While we do have some

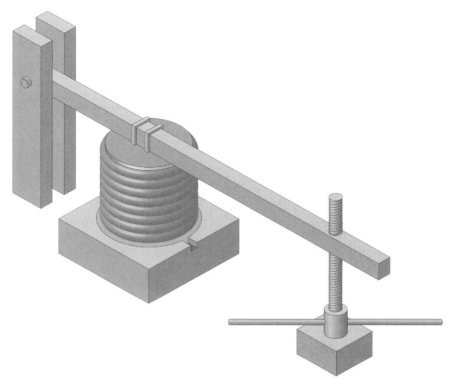

Figure 6. Beam press

pictorial evidence of men spinning thread from Egyptian tombs and Roman reliefs, it is rare. Surprisingly for a woman's task, we have many useful descriptions of ancient looms and textiles (frequently in mythological settings) that help to compensate for an almost total absence of physical remains of the end-products or the tools used to produce them.

Basketry, Matting, Rope, and Leather

Basketry began in the Mesolithic Age with the invention of fish traps by coastal people, and became common with the demands of agriculture beginning in the Neolithic Age. The earliest technique was coiled basketry, a long, spiral coil being fastened together by a sewing strip, a technique also present in early ceramic production; wickerwork developed later, and involved the weaving of strands in and out of a stake frame. Matting for floor coverings was made either by twining together

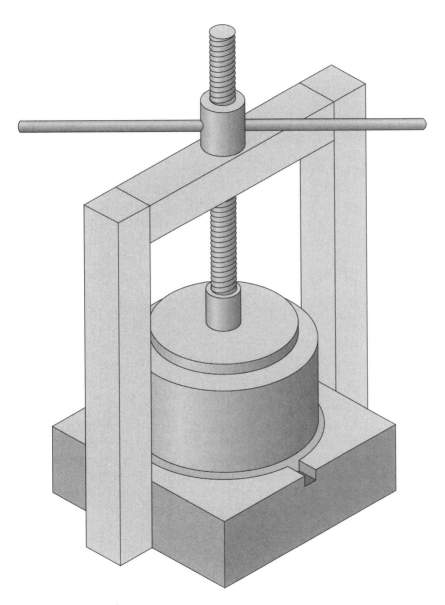

Figure 7. Vertical screw press

parallel bundles of grasses, or by weaving them on a loom; some of the earliest examples come from Neolithic sites, where the floor mats were destroyed by fire but left "ghosts" impressed into the soft dirt floors.

To judge from its depiction in cave paintings, rope was manufactured as early as the Upper Paleolithic Age, and its technique changed little from the earliest surviving Egyptian examples of ca. 4000 B.C.E.: fibers were twisted together into a yarn, then several yarns were twisted together in the opposite direction; the resulting strands were then twisted back the other way into rope.

Leather too was worked as early as the Paleolithic, as the presence of flaked flint scrapers, awls, and bone needles makes clear. Its treatment was a relatively complex procedure. First, the skin was prepared by removing the epidermis and any attached flesh through a variety of techniques: salting, soaking in water or urine, or liming. Then the leather was tanned to make it water- and rot-proof, by smoking or treating with minerals that locked in the fibrous structure. Finally, it was lubricated with greases and decorated by dyeing or embossing. In the Bronze and Iron Ages leather was used extensively for harnesses, armor, belts, coverings for chairs, tents, sandals, and even as a writing surface (the "parchment" that took its name from Pergamon in Asia Minor).

Woven Fabrics

Spinning Yarn. Most natural textile fibers were used in antiquity: wool, flax, silk (always imported from the Far East), and cotton. Both wool and flax required considerable preparation before their fibers could be spun: the flax fibers were soaked (a procedure called "retting") to decompose the outer layer, then beaten and combed; wool needed to be cleaned and carded (from the Latin word for "thistle") to loosen the tangled fibers, before being combed into parallel strands. Spinning of the fibers involved drawing them out and twisting them together to form threads, a task usually accomplished by using a tapered stick (spindle) weighted at one end, fastened to the fibers, and allowed to drop and twist (Documents 10 and 11). The spun threads were then doubled by hand (or spindle) into a two-ply. The spinning wheel, so familiar to us from early fairy tales, was an invention of the Middle Ages.

Weaving. The first looms were body-looms, in which the warp was stretched between the weaver's body and a tree. In later horizontal ground-looms, the warp was stretched between two pegged beams and was divided into even and odd threads that were alternately raised and lowered by a shed-rod inserted between alternate threads and twisted to

Figure 8. Greek warp-weighted loom (vase painting, ca. 500 B.C.E.)

separate them, or by a rod-heddle to which alternate warp threads were attached. The weft, or crosswise thread, was then passed through the "shed" on a shuttle. The more developed vertical looms were of two kinds: the warp-weighted loom, favored by the Greeks, with groups of warp threads tied to pierced stones or pottery weights (weaving from top to bottom) (Figure 8; Document 12); and the framed loom with two beams, more popular among the Romans (weaving from bottom to top). In all cases, the pattern of the woven fabric was achieved by having more than two separate sets of warp threads attached to rod-heddles or shed-rods.

Surprisingly, these ancient looms are the true predecessors of our computers. The circuit boards in your PC or my Macintosh use the principle of binary language, in which there are two symbols—yes/no, on/off—a technique developed for automated looms in the Industrial Revolution of the eighteenth century, when the alternate raising and lowering of various combinations of vertical warp threads to make a pattern was mechanized by attaching them to dowels that moved in and out of holes on a rotating band of paper, similar to those once-ubiquitous punch cards that indicated to early computers the binary system of "off/on," "yes/no," or "zero-one."

How imprecisely we can predict future practical applications of a relatively simple device.

CHAPTER 3

WATER

A reliable supply of water was the most pressing need of peoples in the Mediterranean, beginning with the farmers of the Neolithic, and so the development of irrigation was almost always contemporary with that of agriculture. Then, with the rise of large urban civilizations from the Bronze Age onward, complex systems were developed to supply populous cities with water and—equally important—to aid in the removal of human waste.

ELEMENTS OF HYDRAULICS

Locating Sources of Water

Because of the lack of year-round flowing water, particularly in the Near East, both rural irrigation and village water supplies at first depended on natural springs and then wells. The most primitive method of digging for water was to make a hole with a digging stick and to erect above the wellhead a device to aid in raising the water. For a greater supply of water artesian wells were often sunk, but the time and labor involved in such work limited them to highly organized societies. Most ancient wells were public and protected by the state, since water was a necessity common to all; upkeep was a serious matter, the wells being regularly cleaned and usually lined with stone, terracotta, or wood to prevent collapse. The dangers of contamination were well understood by the ancients: they kept human and animal waste well away from their water sources, and almost always built up the wellheads with stone or terracotta to prevent the accidental poisoning of the supply by the corpses of stray animals. (We have documentary evidence of armies intentionally poisoning their enemy's water supply by surreptitiously dumping human or animal corpses into it. Even biological warfare has its roots in antiquity.) Even in large urban areas like classical Athens and republican Rome, simple wells continued to supply at least part of the water necessary for human consumption.

Raising Water

The earliest and always most convenient devices for raising water were a person's cupped hands, but their limited capacity and stretch soon prompted adaptations like a waterproof bladder and a length of rope. More efficient was a bag or jar attached to a rope that was passed over a horizontal pole above the wellhead, reversing the direction of effort to a more comfortable downward pull; the Greeks' addition of a pulley also added mechanical advantage. For field irrigation, more water could be raised by using a *shaduf* (Document 13), a vessel attached by rope to a swiveling lever beam balanced at its other end by a counterweight to aid in lifting; these devices could be used singly or in groups (as, for example, in raising water in manageable stages from the Tigris and Euphrates rivers to the higher level of the fields), and their continued use in countries of the Middle East is a tribute to their simplicity and efficiency. The Hellenistic Greeks devised various forms of the waterwheel to raise water— buckets on a chain, pots on the rim of a wheel, and a compartmentalized drum (Document 14; Figure 9)—though all were relatively unusual, in part on account of their initial cost but largely because the permanent and consistent flow necessary to justify the investment occurs surprisingly rarely in the eastern Mediterranean especially. Archimedes partially solved these problems with his invention of the water screw for the same purpose: though it had a lower output than wheels, it had the advantages of being both affordable and portable (Document 15; Figure 10).

Conserving Water

In the arid regions of the Mediterranean, water had to be stored for the inevitable dry months, both for agricultural irrigation and to supply towns and cities: a river dammed with stones could form a reservoir, or cisterns could be hollowed out of a rocky surface; to prevent natural evaporation, underground cisterns were often dug. In periods of unrest, security demanded a hidden and accessible water supply: rock-cut secret passages were sometimes dug from walled cities to underground springs outside, examples of which can be found in the Bronze-Age Mycenaean citadels of Athens and Mycenae. With the peace brought to the Mediterranean

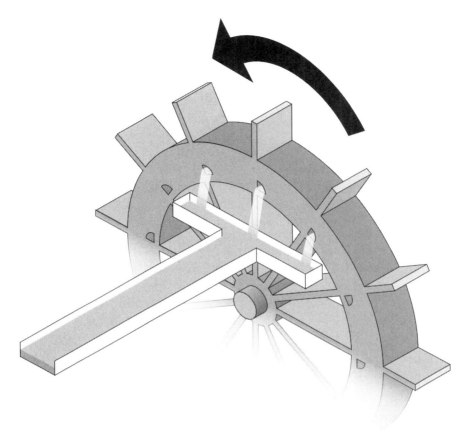

Figure 9. Water wheel, compartmentalized rim

by the Romans, masonry and concrete cisterns were more often built above ground. But the end of antiquity brought renewed dangers, especially if water conduits were exposed to an enemy, so huge underground cisterns again became a necessity for urban survival: the most impressive examples come from Byzantine Constantinople, their massive arches supported on columns reused from buildings abandoned as the city contracted in size.

Conducting Water

Since water often had to be transported long distances from its source, the ancients built long conduits or aqueducts, usually on the surface or

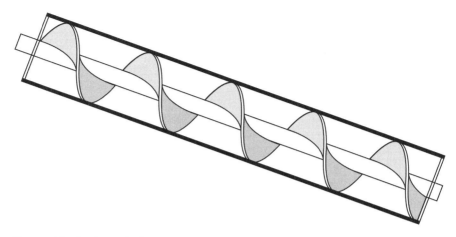

Figure 10. Archimedes' screw

underground, only infrequently elevated on arches. In desert areas, or in plains far from the source of water in the hills, the evaporation from open channels was avoided either by digging a system of underground tunnels or by covering a superficial or elevated channel. Again, only a highly organized society could provide the labor and expense of upkeep for such a project. Smaller amounts of water were carried short distances in sealed clay or metal pipes, tapered at one end to join snugly together.

To avoid the expense of long and high arcades, the Romans sometimes made use of the so-called inverted siphon, based on the principle that water in a closed pipe will find its own level; but the resulting high water pressure often required strong pipes that were either expensive or inefficient, or multiple lead pipes that divided up the pressurized flow into manageable amounts. The Romans preferred stone conduits for their aqueducts, usually running along the surface or underground, but sometimes elevated on the familiar and impressive arches.

HYDRAULIC TECHNOLOGY BEFORE THE ROMAN EMPIRE

Rural Irrigation Systems

It is no coincidence that the first true urban civilizations of the Mediterranean region developed alongside rivers whose annual floods provided a method of irrigating fields that was natural, widespread, and self-operating (though not self-regulating) (Document 16).

The annual flooding of the Nile gave Egypt a natural form of irrigation. Still, the pharaohs developed a system of basin irrigation to assist nature: a series of dikes parallel and at right angles to the river divided the valley into a checkerboard, each basin of which could be flooded independently. The Egyptians could thus control the depth of water on their fields, allow the water to be still and so deposit more silt, and transport water by canals to fields beyond the natural flood plain. They also had a complex system of measuring the height of the river with nilometers: a comparison with heights in previous seasons (which had been noted in archives) allowed them to predict the year's high watermark, and take advance precautions against either drought or flood (see Document 38).

Unlike the Nile, the flood of the Tigris–Euphrates system was unpredictable: if both rivers flooded simultaneously there was excessive inundation, and the flooding was often over when the water was most needed. So the Mesopotamian system of perennial irrigation involved the construction of a network of canals leading to all fields from the rivers; sluice gates allowed the flooding to be controlled and water to be stored for the dry season when it was needed. As in Egypt, construction and maintenance required a large labor force and a centralized authority.

Such elaborate systems were not part of Graeco-Roman field irrigation, since the rivers and streams of their lands were modest in comparison with the Nile and Tigris–Euphrates. For the most part, nature was relied on to water the crops of the Greek or Roman farmer, who usually benefited from more copious and reliable rainfall than did their Near-Eastern cousins.

Urban Water Systems

Complex systems for urban water supply predate the Romans by several centuries. From the eighth century on, the Persians built underground channels called *qanaats*, an Akkadian word that originally meant "reed," alluding to the hollow conduit, and came into Latin as *cannalis*, "reed shaped," and into English as "canal." These were subterranean channels at a slope of about 1:200 leading from the spring to the town, with vertical shafts sunk at short intervals to provide for ventilation and removal of debris, and cisterns with access stairs built at points where the water was to be drawn off. Such *qanaats* were used primarily for the irrigation of fields adjacent to the towns, and many were still in use when the Romans arrived and expanded their use. We can trace the history of true urban systems back to the Assyrian king Sennacherib, who in the early seventh century constructed 50-km-long canals from a dammed river to supply his capital at Nineveh, and another 20-km conduit to Arbela.

Most early Greek cities were established near natural springs, though as they grew it was usually necessary to bring water in from a distance, often via a gravity-fed system of terracotta pipes. More substantial hydraulic systems are rare before the Romans, but one spectacular Greek example is the 1-km-long tunnel, excavated simultaneously from both ends with only a minor misalignment, constructed on the Aegean island of Samos in the sixth century; but even here, the water was conducted in terracotta pipes laid in a channel cut into the floor of the tunnel, a technique that severely limits the volume of output. Our earliest known example of an inverted siphon, at Pergamon in Asia Minor, probably dates to the second century B.C.E., and may have influenced the Romans' later designs—though its vertical fall was relatively short, and the Romans eventually replaced it with an arcaded aqueduct.

The Athenian Agora is a good example of urban water supply and drainage in a pre-Roman public area. Water was obtained from a nearby spring and wells, and was distributed through a system of terracotta pipes and subterranean stone aqueducts, the wastewater being removed through the stone conduit of the Great Drain. Since few people could afford a private supply of water, the city, especially the Agora, was dotted with public fountain houses, where women would gather daily, carrying on their heads three-handled pots (*hydriae*) to be filled under the animal-headed spouts and carried back full to their homes, but not before the women took advantage of the temporary absence of male relatives to enjoy some lively conversation together (Figure 11).

Even after the construction of the first aqueducts into Rome, it is likely that much of the water used by the inhabitants still came from wells and cisterns. The evidence from Rome itself is sketchy, but we can make some deductions from the remains of Pompeii, where most of the public baths were originally supplied with water hauled out of wells by men using simple pulleys or more efficient chains fitted with buckets; and even after the construction of an aqueduct, the private houses relied on rainwater collected in cisterns for washing clothes and watering gardens.

ROME'S URBAN WATER SYSTEM

As in so many areas, while the Romans did not invent the concept or basic design of aqueducts, they certainly perfected their efficient application in supplying reliable water to the cities throughout their

Figure 11. Fountain house (vase painting, ca. 500 B.C.E.)

empire. The remainder of this chapter will define the various elements of an urban aqueduct system, how it was laid out and constructed (a useful example of a complex civil engineering project), and—using the city of Rome as our best documented example—how the water was distributed for various uses within the city.

Planning and Constructing an Aqueduct

In Roman aqueducts, the principle of gravity flow carried water through an enclosed conduit (*specus*) that usually ran on the surface or underground, from the source in neighboring hills to a distribution tank (*castellum*) in the city, located at the highest attainable point to allow widespread distribution. Settling tanks (*piscinae*) were usually built both at the source and along the course to settle out impurities and to aerate the water. Within the city, pipes (*fistulae*) of either terracotta or lead were tapped off the *castellum*, run below the stone pavement of streets, and fed into fountain houses (*nymphaea*) and other points of use. (On all these elements, see Document 17.)

Finding a pure and reliable source. The requirements for a suitable source were stringent: pure water, year-round flow, sufficient elevation to allow a constant gradient into the city, and yet enough distance from human and animal habitation to be uncontaminated. Vitruvius gives detailed recommendations on how to find sources of groundwater and determine its purity: an examination of the topography, the nature of the soil, surface vegetation, the presence of moisture, and even water diviners for the former; and, for purity, a study of the appearance of the water, suspended particles, and even the health of those who live nearby. Other sources, including the medical writer Hippocrates and Pliny the Elder, rank rainwater as the most pure, but acknowledge that underground springs are most commonly used for feeding aqueducts, in part because of their reliability. Despite this, at least two of the aqueducts that supplied Rome took their water directly from the Anio River northeast of the city.

Wisely, the water was first channeled into a settling tank, where it would be held motionless to allow the coarsest of sediment to fall to the bottom. From there it was led into the conduit for its journey to the city. If the water was not clear and potable when it entered the city (and several aqueducts brought muddy and even foul-tasting water into Rome), the inhabitants had a variety of techniques for purifying it: by boiling, by filtering it through porous amphorae, sand, charcoal, and wool, by desalination (evaporation followed by condensation), and—most commonly— by mixing it with wine to camouflage the taste and, at least in theory, to counteract impurities.

Surveying a route. After the location of a suitable source, a surveyor (*librator* = "leveler") would be hired to plot the line of the conduit into the city. To do this he had at his disposal a limited number of tools, but of sufficient accuracy to lay out the necessary horizontal and vertical angles that the route would follow. Most of these devices were originally developed by the *agrimensores*, state officials whose job it was to divide up public lands into regular agricultural plots, for which they needed devices that would measure angles on a horizontal plane:

- The *groma* was the most simple device: a pair of crossed horizontal arms pivoting on a vertical post and with plumb bobs hanging from the four ends to ensure that it was level. With it the *librator* could plot right angles and, with an assistant holding a leveling rod, could sight along it to determine differences in elevation, but only from a higher to a lower point.

- The same measurements could be made more precisely with the *dioptra*, which is remarkably like modern dumpy levels without the advantage of telescopic sights. A circular horizontal plate was fixed to a vertical and toothed half-plate; by turning screws aligned with the teeth the surveyor could precisely rotate the upper plate horizontally and tip it vertically. The instrument was leveled, not by plumb lines, but by an attached bent bronze tube with glass ends and partially filled with water—when the water reached the same level in both ends, the *dioptra* itself was level. Unlike the *groma*, it could determine vertical angles, and so could be used to measure elevations from a lower to a higher point.

- The *chorobates* was most useful for maintaining the proper gradient while constructing the channel, though it too could be used as a sighting tool. As Vitruvius describes it, it is a long table mounted on four vertical legs, with angled braces connecting the legs to the table and plumb lines hanging near each corner. Various angles were marked out on the braces, so the instrument could be leveled or tilted appropriately by aligning the cords of the plumb bob with the marks on the braces. For even more precise leveling, the table of the *chorobates* had a groove cut lengthwise that could be filled with water.

To begin, then, the surveyor would use the *groma* or *dioptra* to determine the difference in elevation between the source and the location chosen in the city for the *castellum*, which would need to be elevated enough to distribute its water by gravity flow. Then, using cords or chains, he would measure the distance as directly as possible between the two end points. These two figures would allow him to calculate the length of the conduit necessary to have it fall at an acceptable and fairly constant gradient to arrive at the urban distribution tank. His team would then study the intervening topography to find the best route, avoiding where possible the necessity for arcades or tunnels.

Constructing the conduit. To those unfamiliar with the details of Roman water conduction, the term "aqueduct" conjures up images of stately arches marching across the plain of Latium toward the walls of Rome. While this is not imaginary, it is unusual: both finances and security made such elegant structures relatively uncommon, though they are even now the most visible remnants of the system. In fact, most channels were by preference built along the surface of the ground or in a shallow trench, and covered with slabs to prevent evaporation; to avoid long detours around hills, the channel was occasionally accommodated in a subterranean tunnel; and only when traversing a deep gorge or a flat plain was the gradient maintained by elevating the conduit on arcades (Figure 12).

Unfortunately, our sources disagree about the minimum gradient necessary for the gravity-flow conduit: Vitruvius sets it at 1:200—that is, a fall of one-half a Roman foot over a distance of 100 feet—while Pliny the Elder prescribes a quarter inch every 100 feet (1:4,800). The physical evidence provides examples of slopes as little as 1:1,200 and as steep as 1:95, with considerable variation even along the same aqueduct. It would seem that anything less than about 1:1,000 would allow the water to flow slowly enough to drop deposits that could plug the conduit; a slope any greater than about 1:100 ran the risk of the water overflowing the sides of the conduit or damaging its walls, especially at the point of curves. If the ideal gradient was insufficient for topographical reasons, a sudden and safe decrease in elevation could be realized by building cascades, which allowed the water to fall precipitously into a pool from which the conduit continued.

Because many of the water sources were heavy with calcium carbonate, the floor and walls of the conduit would often become encrusted with lime, a deposit that archaeologists call by its German name, *sinter*.

Figure 12. Elements of a Roman aqueduct

By building settling tanks, particularly at the source, the Roman engineers tried to precipitate out most of the limestone, but regular removal of the accumulated (and remarkably hard) *sinter* was necessary to maintain the proper flow of the aqueduct.

Very occasionally and (so far as the evidence suggests) only in a few regions of the empire—southern France and Asia Minor particularly—did the Romans avoid the necessity of arcades by connecting the gravity-flow conduit to a kind of "inverted siphon" based on the principle that water in a closed system finds its own level. The U-shaped siphon would carry the water in a sealed pipe under pressure down into a valley and up the other side, to empty into an open tank at a height somewhat below that of the inlet (see Figure 12). These siphons were probably not cheaper to construct than stone arches: in many cases the water was fed into a series of small-diameter heavy lead pipes that could withstand the internal pressure, and—while the lead itself was relatively cheap, being produced as a by-product from the smelting of silver-bearing ore—the cost of transporting and fitting it must have been huge: one Gallic siphon used more than 10,000 tonnes of lead, and another had 11,000 soldered joints. If there was no financial advantage, then, why were siphons used at all? In some cases, at least, because the arcades that carried a gravity-flow conduit could not be built much more than about 40 m high, so if the valley floor were too deep, and cascades inappropriate, siphons became a necessity.

For long aqueducts, teams would normally be assigned for each segment of similar construction, and could work simultaneously at different points along the line since the surveyors had already marked at regular points the proper height or depth of the channel. The surface sections of the conduit would be cut into the ground, lined with masonry or concrete if necessary, finished in smooth cement to reduce friction and seal the joints, and covered with stone slabs to protect the water from both evaporation and (a serious threat) accidental contamination. Tunneled sections obviously required many more workers, armed with little more than picks and shovels, though some advanced mining techniques were also used. Finally, where arcades were necessary, they were generally built of large, closely fitted squared stones, the arches initially laid on temporary wooden scaffolding that rested on narrow shelves projecting slightly from the point where the arch sprang from its piers. Later, especially in the provinces, a mortared rubble core was faced with stone or brick, a construction technique that was quicker and cheaper, though generally less durable. These handsome bridges could be one, two, or even three arcades high (as in the Pont du Gard that carried Nimes' aqueduct), with a covered conduit on top; they could soar as high as 45 m on spans of 25 m, beyond which the Romans were understandably concerned about their stability.

In all cases, regular access holes from the surface allowed regular maintenance and cleaning of the channel, at least annually to remove the accumulated *sinter* and other deposits. Repairs were to be done speedily, because the regular flow could be shut off only at the source, thus temporarily depriving thousands of city folk of their water supply.

Distributing the Water

Imperial Rome required a complicated system of supplying water to its million and more inhabitants: first the transportation of water over long distances from stable and pure mountain springs, and then its distribution within the city (Document 18).

The aqueducts of Rome. When Frontinus became curator of Rome's water supply in 97 C.E., nine aqueducts had been built to feed the city, beginning with the relatively short *aqua Appia* in 312 B.C.E. and eventually totaling 438 km in length. The first two were largely subterranean; thereafter arcades were used to carry the channels across the plain that lay between Rome and the hills to the east. To save on expenses, several separate channels could be superimposed one on another, making use of the same arcade, or channels from different sources were joined together and their waters mingled.

These conduits fed elevated cisterns, from which the water was distributed through clay or lead pipes first to innumerable fountain houses (*nymphaea*) that supplied water for drinking and cooking to most of the inhabitants; public baths (the smaller *balnea* and the immense *thermae*) contributed to a relatively high standard of personal and public hygiene; and the presence throughout the city of public latrines and drains helped prevent regular outbreaks of disease. Rome in 100 C.E. boasted a water management system unequalled in Europe until the nineteenth century, with a bureau of the civil service in charge of maintenance and of ensuring equitable distribution.

Administration of the water supply. The maintenance of such an essential and complex system, and the need to supervise the fair distribution of the water to baths and industries as well as to individuals, required an equally complex bureaucracy. We are fortunate to have Frontinus as our guide to this system, a curator of the water supply who was so determined to encourage his successors to maintain his rigorous standards of maintenance and enforcement that he composed a two-volume handbook, which still survives, containing detailed descriptions of the hydraulic and engineering elements of the system, of the laws that governed the distribution of the water, and of the creative ways that Romans surreptitiously tapped into the public system to bring a private supply to their homes.

Distribution of Water

According to Frontinus, the distribution of water within the city was divided among three principal users: imperial properties, private users granted access to water by the Emperor, and public properties such as military camps, baths, ornamental fountains (*nymphaea*), and basins, of which there were almost 600 in his time. It was from the last two that the public would draw water for their personal use.

Cisterns (castella). Once the water reached the city, it was funneled into a large tank (*castellum*), designed not to store the water (the constant flow of the aqueduct would fill even the largest cisterns in a few hours, if water was not being drawn off at the same time), but to regulate the distribution of the water to various points throughout the city. Both Vitruvius and Frontinus describe the system devised by Roman engineers that regulated the flow of water to various end users and perhaps even guaranteed, without any human oversight or fallible mechanical parts, that in times of drought the pipes to private houses would be the first to shut down, then the water to the baths, and last of all the public fountains, ensuring that the inhabitants would be provided with drinking water so long as any water at all was entering the city (Figure 13).

Pipes. From these *castella*, lead workers called *plumbarii* laid pipes to the public fountains, baths, and private houses at lower elevations. Pipes of lead were regularly used in urban water distribution, even though the Romans were familiar with its unhealthy properties; in fact, because of the speed of flow and the quick buildup of *sinter*, there was little opportunity for the water to be contaminated. The pipes were manufactured in lengths of up to 3 m, and in various standard capacities, each appropriate to its function: the most common, one and a half digits in diameter, was the *quinaria*, used to limit the flow of water into private houses, for which the owner would pay a substantial fee. Simple metal taps were also used, to regulate flow or to turn the pipe off temporarily.

Fountain houses. Frontinus' figures (above) suggest one fountain or basin for every 2,000 inhabitants, though we know from mid-fourth century documents that there were 1,352 in all, more than twice as many. In smaller and more rural towns, access seems to have been easier: in

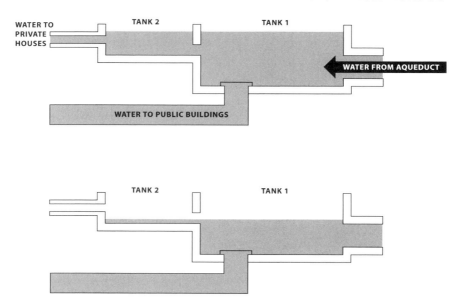

Figure 13. *Castellum* to regulate water distribution

Pompeii, where the remains are better preserved than in Rome, more than thirty public fountains have been excavated, located about every other block, each serving an estimated 600–700 people. Pipes from the *castella* fed directly into spouts, often in the form of animals' heads, from which the water ran without stop into a deep, rectangular basin; here the inhabitants would draw their water (see Figure 11). Overflow pipes channeled the excess to other installations, like the public latrines, which did not require potable water.

The imperial baths. Small, privately operated bathing houses (called *balnea*) were scattered throughout Rome. Under Augustus, they numbered fewer than 200, but by the middle of the fourth century there were more than 850. Though more plentiful, they were overshadowed in imperial times by the *thermae*, huge bathing complexes donated by the emperors to benefit the general population of the city. Three had been erected in Rome by the end of the first century C.E.: those of Agrippa and Nero in the Campus Martius, and that of Titus just east of the Colosseum; 200 years later there would be eleven, including the massive structures erected by Caracalla and Diocletian, the latter accommodating 3,000 patrons at a time. These impressive buildings were not limited to the imperial capital: all provincial cities had them, thanks to the Roman expectation of public generosity by wealthy citizens. Indeed, they became a symbol of Romanization throughout the empire, and are usually the most impressive ancient structures still visible today in the Middle East especially (Document 19).

The Baths of Trajan, constructed in Rome a decade after Frontinus was curator of the water supply, established the standard of design for *thermae* throughout the empire. The rooms were arranged symmetrically along various intersecting axes, the changing rooms (*apodyteria*) and open-air exercise grounds (*palaestrae*) in pairs flanking the central axis, along which the bathing rooms progressed: the open-air swimming pool (*natatio*), the unheated great hall (*frigidarium*), the warm room (*tepidarium*), and the hot room (*caldarium*). The heated rooms had a kind of double flooring system, called a hypocaust, the upper pavement resting on regularly spaced short pillars of brick to create a hollow between, through which circulated hot air from the adjacent furnace room. The floor was thus warmed indirectly, and even the walls gave off radiant heat from the vertical flues that carried the hot, smoky air upwards through the roof. Basins and small pools received water heated in boilers above the furnace. Traditionally, too, the *caldarium* was oriented to the southwest and protruded from the line of the baths' rear wall, to admit the warm afternoon sunlight through enormous windows on three sides: a fine example of passive solar heating in antiquity.

Elimination of waste. Many older studies of Rome's urban water systems ended with the magnificent images of aqueducts and the pools of grandiose bath buildings, ignoring the reality of removing from the city both the excess water and the human waste produced by over a million inhabitants. This is a pity, because the Romans of the empire were as ingenious and efficient in handling runoff and sewage as they were in all other aspects of hydraulic engineering.

Drains were a necessary feature of every urban area in antiquity. The Athenian Agora had its Great Drain, and the Roman Forum its Latin equivalent, the *cloaca maxima*. This stone conduit, probably the work of Etruscan engineers in the sixth century B.C.E., was constructed originally to help drain the swampy area that lay at the foot of the Esquiline, Capitoline, and Palatine Hills, and turn it into a meeting place and market common to the previously separate hilltop villages. As the forum and city expanded, other subterranean storm drains and sewage pipes were connected to the *cloaca*, with much of the city's waste dumped into the Tiber River at its outfall just downstream from the city center. Similar practical if to us unpleasant arrangements were in place elsewhere: Pompeii and provincial cities, supplemented by Roman satiric writers, give us a better sense of waste removal practices than the physical remains in Rome itself.

Since very few private dwellings were connected to the aqueduct system, it follows naturally that very few had private toilet facilities. There are some examples in Pompeii and elsewhere, located adjacent to the house's kitchen to take advantage of its grey water, and sometimes tucked under the stairs of apartment blocks. For most city dwellers, a personal chamber pot or a visit to the neighborhood public latrine was the best they could expect. The liquid contents of chamber pots could be emptied into the cesspits located behind laundry establishments, the ammonia to be extracted from the urine and used in cleaning fabrics and treating leather. So, too, with the contents of amphorae hung on the walls in narrow lanes, their tops broken off at a comfortable height to accommodate the needs of male passersby. Always looking for additional state revenue, the Emperor Vespasian in the first century levied a tax on the laundrymen who profited from this free source of chemicals, in memory of which public urinals in France are still termed *vespasiennes*.

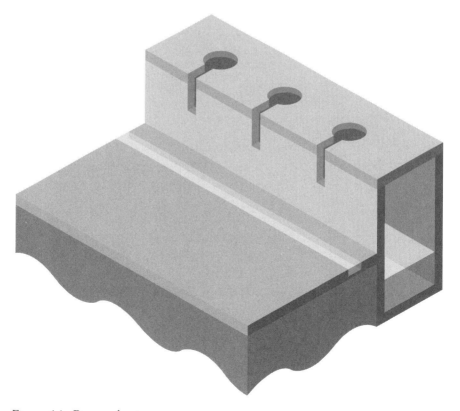

Figure 14. Roman latrine

Large public toilets, many donated by wealthy citizens, are found throughout the empire; and we know that 144 of them were scattered throughout Rome in the fourth century C.E. These were, like the bath buildings, an important element in the state's attempts to maintain a reasonably healthful environment in enormously overcrowded conditions (Figure 14). Their capacity varies, but the largest could accommodate over sixty patrons at a time, sitting on long marble benches with round holes every 50 cm or so, and a slot down the front that gave them some minimal privacy when using the ancient equivalent of toilet paper, a sponge attached to the end of a stick. Beneath the benches was a deep channel that would be flushed regularly if not constantly, using overflow or grey water from the baths and fountains to which these toilets were often attached.

The lack of privacy obviously did not distress the patrons, who were accustomed to other public activities (like bathing) that we consider private. And, while the use of communal sponges would not meet any modern country's standards of hygiene, the whole system was more healthful than anything previously devised, and clearly helped Rome and other large cities of the Empire avoid the spread of disease more effec-tively even than later societies, at least until the invention of private flush toilets.

CHAPTER 4

SHELTER AND SECURITY

The construction of artificial shelters did not begin in earnest until the Neolithic Age, the period when the development of agriculture allowed—and required—tribes to remain settled in one place over a long period. This agricultural revolution, perhaps best known from the very early walled site of Jericho, occurred in many areas of the eastern Mediterranean, but its physical remains there are perhaps best seen in the central Anatolian town of Çatal Höyük, dating mostly from the seventh millennium B.C.E.: its cubical buildings of unfired mud-brick clustered closely together around a few open public courtyards, their common walls on all sides allowing movement primarily across their flat roofs and access by ladders protruding up through holes in the ceiling, all of them together presenting blank external facades to foreign raiders now tempted by the agricultural surplus. The simple, rectilinear buildings were designed to conform both to the environment—dry and hot in summer, cold in winter—and to the materials available for construction, mostly clay and small trees. There is little differentiation among structures at this stage, and almost no specialization of rooms, though a few units have been identified as primitive religious shrines. But the construction was relatively simple, standardized, and—if the unfired bricks were elevated on a stone sockle to prevent them from being eroded by spring runoff—could last for several generations. Little wonder that the design has persisted even down to the present.

It is a sobering reminder of the basic nature of human relationships that we can trace the existence of weapons to the invention of tools themselves, and organized warfare as far back as the origin of settlements. Weapons developed in the Paleolithic for hunting wild game—the spear and spear-thrower for example—almost certainly were used with equal effectiveness against other nomadic tribes; and it is no coincidence that among the earliest permanent structures made possible by the settled life of the Neolithic were fortification walls, designed to protect the new surplus of food from the hands of neighbors who would rather fight than farm. So the two elements of shelter and security appear simultaneously, as societies struggled to cope with the twin threats from nature and from their covetous neighbors.

BRONZE-AGE CONSTRUCTION AND DEFENSE

The large and powerful empires of the Bronze Age demanded more substantial, extensive, and impressive structures than their modest Neolithic predecessors, not just for improved shelter and defense, but as symbols of their power. As in the Neolithic, the design of these monuments was still determined in each case by the local environment and the availability of workable materials, as well as by social organization and technological expertise. In Egypt the limestone pyramids satisfied the pharaohs' desire for tombs of immense size and permanence; the Mesopotamians, governed by a theocracy, constructed for their gods (and priests) large platformed temple complexes of mud-bricks harvested from the alluvial plains between the Tigris and Euphrates rivers; on rocky Crete the Minoan kings and their merchants erected complex palaces with walls of mortared rubble; and the warrior Greeks of the Mycenaean period defended themselves behind walls of stone so massive that their descendants thought them built by the mythical Cyclopes. The middle levels at Troy and the massive citadel walls of the Hittites in central Anatolia also show elements of Bronze-Age construction found throughout the eastern Mediterranean, most notably gateways protected by well-built towers and spanned by the corbelled (or "false") arch. Houses were everywhere more modestly built of mud-brick, often with wooden columns supporting flat roofs with ventilation openings above a central hearth—the same megaron hall that formed the center of Mycenaean Greek palaces.

Bronze-Age Civil Engineering

Egyptian monumental construction. Most monumental Egyptian structures were megalithic: it was easier to quarry large blocks, and the tombs were built to last forever, since the survival of the soul was thought to depend on the survival of the body. A monumental stone tomb, the mastaba, was developed early in Bronze-Age Egypt; and within 200 years there appeared the first major pyramid, the Stepped Pyramid of Zoser, in form simply a series of superimposed receding mastabas in the center of a complex of buildings. The Bent Pyramid of Dynasty IV (ca. 2700 B.C.E.) was probably modified when half-built; also in Dynasty IV were built the three great pyramids of Giza: the emphasis was by this time on processional movement from the Nile to the pyramid, and the face of the structure was smoothly finished in limestone.

Much has been written about the apparent incapacity of early-Bronze-Age Egyptian engineers to have built the pyramids, which are often described as "ancient mysteries" attributed to unknown forces, even extraterrestrial visitors. But the techniques required are, in fact, quite simple (involving inclined planes, rollers, and levers), and certainly within the ability of engineers who had at their disposal almost unlimited manpower for at least the three months of the year when the Nile was in flood, the fields submerged, and the peasants in need of some distracting work.

We know, for example, that the area of the base of a pyramid was leveled to within a few centimeters by using water channeled from the Nile to establish a flat surface from which to measure. The 2.3 million limestone blocks used in the Great Pyramid (each weighing more than 2 tonnes) were brought from the quarries along the Nile on rafts, and dragged to the site on rollers pulled by huge troops of organized labor, all of which is illustrated in Egyptian tomb paintings (albeit from later in the Bronze Age). A solid ramp was probably built spirally up the side of the monument as it rose, upon which the blocks were dragged into place. Mortar was used, not as a binding agent, but simply to ease the friction between sliding blocks; and finally, the limestone facing was applied from the top down as the ramp was being removed.

Mesopotamian monumental construction. Because of the scarcity of stone in southern Mesopotamia, the superstructures of monumental buildings were of brick (usually kiln-dried), although the foundations may have been of imported limestone; decoration was limited to buttresses imitating the appearance of earlier reed huts, and to mosaics of colored cones inserted into the mud walls. The ziggurat of Mesopotamia was a rectangular, staged temple-mound thought to represent a mountain as the god's dwelling: the Mesopotamians had migrated into the Land Between the Two Rivers from the mountainous regions to the north, bringing with them the tradition of locating temples on the tops of mountains; so in the plains of their new habitat, they simply built new "mountains" on which to elevate their shrines. These were usually built gradually over a long period, an earlier one being used as the base of a new one. The core was of mud-brick and was faced with burnt brick; the structure was approached by monumental stairways; and the architects used the optical illusion of *entasis* (the slight curving of horizontal or vertical lines) to give the impression of solidity yet lightness.

Construction in Bronze-Age Greece. The Minoan civilization of Crete in the second millennium is preserved in a series of palaces of semi-independent merchant-kings. The best is that at Knossos, partially restored by its excavator, Sir Arthur Evans. It has no fortifications, since the sea was the Minoans' defense; it is rather a continuous mass of public buildings surrounding a large open court: one wing contained the state and public rooms with storerooms beneath, another housed the royal residence, and a third was the artisans' quarter. The buildings of the palace had stone foundations, with wood-and-rubble walls, wooden columns (inverted), and roofs. The palace itself dominated a still largely unexcavated city of perhaps 100,000 people.

On mainland Greece, Mycenae and Tiryns are good examples of megalithic construction. Here, massive fortification walls were needed for protection, particularly in the confused period near the end of the Bronze Age (1300–1100 B.C.E.). These citadels contained storehouses and artisans' quarters as well as the royal palace, the center of which was the megaron or royal hall. Near the citadel of Mycenae is a group of *tholos* ("beehive") tombs, which show clearly the use of the corbelled arch/relieving triangle over the huge lintel blocks, and of the corbelled dome. These "proto-arches and -domes" did not make use of the principle of a central keystone that supported the thrust of the arch or dome (which would be used later by the Romans), but rather depended on the weight of the blocks above to secure the lower stones in place, with their angled inner sides forming the side of the arch.

Fortification walls. Impressive advances in defensive fortification walls can be seen elsewhere in the eastern Mediterranean: those found at the level of Troy VI, for example, are dated to a generation or so before the actual Trojan War. And while Homer's epic *The Iliad* owes as much to the poet's own archaic age as to the thirteenth century B.C.E., it gives a vivid and probably accurate account of the long sieges that became a part of ancient warfare by the late Bronze Age. In fact, the legendary Trojan horse, which does not appear in Homer's *Iliad* but does figure in the *Odyssey*, might well reflect an early form of wooden siege tower wheeled up to the walls of the city to disgorge soldiers over the top. In Vergil's first-century-B.C.E. Roman epic *The Aeneid*, the Trojan priest Laocoön describes the horse as "an engine built to attack our walls, to spy into our houses, and to descend on the city from above" (2.46–47); and an Egyptian tomb painting of the late Bronze Age depicts an offensive scaling ladder and a form of protective "tortoise" that would become an essential element of Roman sieges a millennium later.

GREEK AND ROMAN CIVIL AND MILITARY ENGINEERING

Construction in Squared Stone

The invasion of the Greek peninsula by the relatively primitive Dorian Greeks destroyed the architectural accomplishments of their Mycenaean cousins, and the arrival in Anatolia of rather backward invaders from the region of Thrace at the same time precipitated an architectural decline in Asia Minor as well. Until about 800 B.C.E. most construction on both sides of the Aegean was of mud-brick on stone foundations, and there was nothing that could truthfully be called monumental. By the seventh century B.C.E. more substantial structures appear, though all but the foundations and roof tiles were still made of wood. So it is not until we find buildings like the sixth-century Temple of Apollo at Corinth with its monolithic stone columns, and the original versions of massive Ionian temples of Artemis at Ephesos and Apollo at Didyma, that we can easily see the beginnings of the familiar forms of classical Greek design. By the fifth century all monumental buildings were of stone, though rather conservatively preserving in this material the elements of design taken over from the earlier wooden and terracotta structures: the triglyphs of a Doric temple, for example, have no structural function, but are recollections in stone of the original terracotta plaques protecting the cut wooden rafter ends.

The orders of classical Greek architecture. In the sixth and fifth centuries this Doric style of architecture was the dominant form in Greek cities. The column consists of a fluted and slightly tapered shaft of superimposed drums resting directly on the stylobate, the foundation of three steps. The column was crowned by a capital consisting of a circular molding like a cushion (the *echinus*) and the *abacus*, a square slab that supported the architrave, a stone beam passing from capital to capital, supporting the frieze that in turn consists of metopes (panels sometimes blank, sometimes filled with sculpture) separated by triglyphs (triple-grooved panels), the whole thing capped by a projecting cornice above which rises the triangular pediment of the roof.

A variant from the East, the Ionic order, spread from Asia Minor to Greece in the middle of the fifth century. The slender, delicate design of the column shaft, which was taller than the Doric and rested on a molded base, contrasted sharply with the ponderous and solid form of its predecessor. The small Ionic *echinus* was decorated with an egg pattern and supported, instead of the Doric *abacus*, a four-cornered cushion ending in spiral volutes. The entablature, too, was different: the architrave was divided into three parallel horizontal bands above which ran an uninterrupted (and undecorated) frieze.

After the fourth century the Doric and Ionic gradually gave way to the Corinthian order, first found in its developed form in the Temple of Zeus at remote Olbia in Cilicia: its base, shaft, and entablature are similar to the Ionic, but it has an elaborate capital designed in imitation of acanthus leaves. Though overly ornate for most modern tastes, it appealed to the Hellenistic Greeks and the Romans, so examples can be found throughout Italy and in any Roman imperial sites in the provinces.

Construction methods in stone. The basic, rectangular, post-and-lintel scheme of construction persisted in ancient architecture from the Archaic Age down to the Roman period, even though very occasionally the Greeks did make use of the true arch. Post-and-lintel design was extremely simple, requiring the skill of a mason rather than that of an architect. A basic ratio of 2:1 was used in most aspects of the planning— in the spacing of columns, for example, and, in temples, for the proportion of length to width—and this was all that needed to be plotted out before the actual building began. The rest, including finishing the exterior, could be varied and decided upon as the construction progressed, when the more ambitious and clever architects would add fine details, such as the slight horizontal and vertical curvatures in the Parthenon (*entasis* again), designed to avoid the optical illusions of divergent lines and squat massiveness.

The invention of stronger iron tools in this period had a notable effect on the building industry: iron wedges and hammers simplified the quarrying of large stone blocks, and iron chisels allowed the better shaping of these blocks. Following the seventh century stone became the chief material for monumental buildings, in the form of hard limestone, conglomerate, and particularly the marble that was commonly available throughout mainland Greece, the Aegean islands, and Asia Minor. Considerable information about the prevalent methods of construction can be derived from the remains of the buildings themselves, from the stone quarries (some of which are still in use), and from inscriptions that record expenses, contracts, and specifications.

The building blocks were first roughly worked in the quarries, and then were transported to the site in wagons. There preliminary finishing

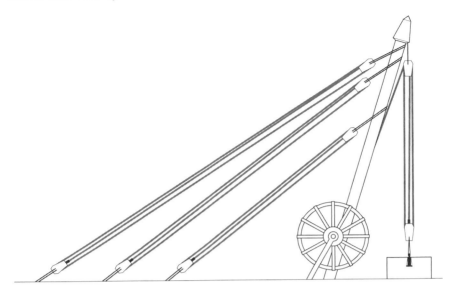

Figure 15. Roman crane (based on sculpted scene)

was carried out before the stones were lifted into position by derricks and pulleys (Figure 15); cuttings in the blocks still show the method used for lifting, usually by tongs fastened into notches, or by ropes passed through a looped hole or groove in the block. To shift the stones into position a crowbar was set in a shallow pry-hole and levered against projecting, protective bosses that had been left on the surface of the blocks (some of these were never removed and are still visible on many monuments).

No mortar was used to bind the blocks in place; instead, dowels of bronze or iron were inserted into ultimately invisible surfaces for vertical fastening, and clamps of the same metals for horizontal joints, all held permanently in place by molten lead. In order to allow the blocks to fit together as closely as possible, only the outer edges of an abutting block were finished, with the central portion of each juxtaposed face cut down and left rough (a technique known as *anathyrosis*): in this way only a small band of each invisible face of a block touched its neighbor. Once the stones were fastened into position, they were polished with smooth stones and a lubricant. In the case of columns, the separate drums were first erected one on top of another before the vertical flutes were carved along the entire shaft; in this way the eye of the viewer was drawn to the vertical fluting and away from the horizontal joints between the drums, which thus became virtually invisible.

Construction in Concrete

The Romans originally learned the art of building from the Etruscans, who in turn had been taught partially by the Greeks of south Italy: it is not surprising, then, that their early buildings in Italy resembled those of both cultures. The first revolutionary phase of Roman architecture occurred with the conquest of the eastern Mediterranean in the last two centuries B.C.E., when Romans adopted the classical and Hellenistic Greek forms, replacing the broad, squarish, and top-heavy Italian proportions with the oblong, tall, and airy Greek style. But their real contribution to civil engineering was structural concrete.

Structural concrete. Concrete, though not an invention of the Romans, was perfected by them about 200 B.C.E., and by the first century it had become the principal material for foundations and walls (Document 20). In order to obtain better footings for their buildings, the Romans were willing to alter the natural contours of the terrain and to sink deep and substantial footings of unfaced concrete. For the exposed walls above, the concrete, made of lime and volcanic sand with fragments of stone scattered through it, was poured semifluid into a wooden mould; when the planking was removed the wall was faced with stone or brick wherever it was to be seen. From about 200 to 50 B.C.E. the facing was made of small, irregular bits of stone, each with a smooth outer surface and a pyramidal tail set into the concrete (*opus incertum* = "irregular work"). For the next hundred years or so the facing stones were cut as squares and arranged corner-to-corner in rows to give a symmetrical appearance like the meshes of a net (hence the name, *opus reticulatum* = "net work"). As early as the time of Augustus the concrete was being faced with kiln-dried bricks, a method (called *opus testaceum* = "brick work") that reached its peak in the second century C.E. under the Emperors Trajan and Hadrian: hence the familiar brick facades of many of the surviving buildings throughout the Mediterranean constructed during the prosperity of the Roman Empire. Finally, as the Empire declined so, too, did methods of construction, with ever greater quantities of mortar being used between the layers of brick.

While the stone or brick facing of visible walls was not structurally necessary, the pointed ends served to bind the concrete: in fact, an early form of modern reinforced concrete. Concrete was so inexpensive and easy to use that the Romans even made columns of it: cylindrical concrete cores faced with slightly curved bricks and smoothed with liquid cement into which were set thin, prefabricated strips of fluted marble.

Arches, vaults, and domes. With their development of concrete the Romans were able to produce a whole new style of architecture based on interior spaces rather than on the Greek ideal of external beauty. As a result, Roman architecture differs from Greek design in a number of very significant ways: the true arch, for example, was substituted for the classical Greek post and lintel, and the concrete vault was used as a means of enclosing a space with a continuous curve. In town planning, too, there were innovations: rather than using buildings as central focal points in surrounding open areas, as was the usual Greek manner, the Romans used their facades to limit open central spaces; the Greek temple, for example, was now placed on a high Roman podium and positioned to form one side of a colonnade that surrounded an open central court. The curve, which had been used infrequently in Greece, became a dominant element of Roman design: the rectangular temple often became a rotunda and the square niche became a semicircular exedra. Finally, where the Greeks had used the natural landscape for the dominant setting of a temple or for the sloping seats of a theater, the Romans—whose architects were always engineers as well—created their own landscapes, by building (for one example) a free-standing theatrical structure, or by altering the natural topography to create a man-made balance and symmetry.

The use of the vault and dome in enormous structures is certainly the most memorable feature of imperial Roman engineering. This method of covering large halls was possible only after the perfection of concrete and the development of brick relieving-arches that formed the skeleton of the vault. Both the arch and barrel vault had been used long before in Mesopotamia and Egypt, and at Rome they became popular as early as the second century B.C.E. But it was principally in the imperial baths, palaces, and temples that the Romans perfected the technology of roofing great interior spaces. Stunning examples can be found in Italy (the palaces of the emperors on Rome's Palatine Hill and, most impressively, the dome of the Pantheon) and throughout the Romanized Empire. Regrettably, we have almost no documentary evidence for the construction of these magnificent vaults, so the survival of the Pantheon is doubly important, first for the breathtaking elegance of its interior space, and because it gives us an unparalleled insight into the revolutionary methods of Roman imperial architects—a perfect combination of engineering and beauty.

Domestic architecture. The Roman house or *domus*, well known from the excavations of Pompeii in southern Italy, was (like most Roman buildings) an inward-looking structure, with only one entrance and few external windows. The expensive frontage of this urban structure was let out as separate shops, with only a narrow entry between (graphically called the *fauces*, or "throat"). The first set of inner rooms, grouped around the *atrium* with its roof open above the pool or *impluvium* below, consisted mostly of small, ill-lit bedchambers or *cubicula*. A stairway led to the servants' quarters on the second storey. Through the *tablinum* lay the more private areas of the house, arranged around an open-air garden surrounded by a colonnaded portico where many members of the family, especially the women, would spend their active hours. There was often a more enclosed winter dining room as well as an open one for the warmer summer months, both within easy reach of a simple kitchen. Many houses had some form of private toilet facilities, often associated (for ease of water supply) with the kitchen or a small bathing room (*balneum*). At the rear was a vegetable garden with its attendant storage sheds.

Obviously, though, most urban dwellers of the Roman Empire, even citizens, could not afford such domestic luxury. By far the majority of city dwellers—perhaps as many as 98 percent of them—dwelt instead in tenement-like apartment buildings called *insulae*, a word that means "islands," an appropriate term for these large blocks that were isolated (*insula*-ted) from one another by the streets below. Most of these buildings were of several storeys—the tallest we know of was seven floors high—each block being made up of a large number of small apartments opening off narrow passageways and illuminated by windows in the exterior wall or opening onto a central courtyard. The cramped rental units were usually a single large room, and had no running water or private facilities, no reliable sources of heat or light, and little privacy. Though often poorly built by speculators, a few examples have been found in Ostia and Ephesos that more resemble modern, luxurious garden apartments. But, in general, it is little wonder that most ancient Romans spent most of their lives outside, enjoying the magnificent public buildings that were such a pleasant and inspiring contrast with their squalid private quarters.

Fortifications

It is a sobering sign of the success of ancient diplomacy that almost all cities from the Bronze Age to the end of the Roman Empire were fortified, though for a peaceful two centuries after the accession of Augustus as emperor the universal *pax Romana* encouraged cities to neglect their defenses and invest instead in such social infrastructure as baths and theaters. Unhappily, the military structures soon had to be shored up as the barbarian inroads began in the third century. Sobering, too, that democracy in Athens evolved in part from the formation of a citizen

Figure 16. Greek hoplite soldier (vase painting, ca. 525 B.C.E.)

army of men equipped with standardized armor and weapons, the hoplite soldiers (Figure 16),

Greek defenses. In Greece the style of fortifications was dependent on the physical conditions of a site: as we have seen, the Bronze-Age walls of Troy, Mycenae, and Athens were erected along the edge of a natural mound or cliff, forming a fortified acropolis with gates so arranged that attackers were forced to expose their unprotected right sides to the defenders, and with a carefully protected access to a water supply in the form of a spring or cistern. In the classical period, cities were protected by walls of masonry or fired brick, such as the long walls that the Athenians laid out between the fortified city and their port of Piraeus, giving them assured access to their navy and to imported supplies when otherwise confined by the hostile armies of the Spartans. In typical Greek fashion, these walls were viewed as an unfortunate necessity for survival, and were sometimes designed to be as aesthetically pleasing as they were effective (Document 21).

In the fourth century and Hellenistic period, the increasing use of siege machinery required more substantial defensive walls, fitted with strong, high towers and accommodating anti-siege catapults; a ditch was often added to deter the approach of siege towers, and small, easily protected sally ports at strategic points along the circuit wall allowed the besieged to take the battle to the enemy.

Roman defenses. Though the Etruscans favored easily fortified hilltop towns, many of which were still functioning in the Middle Ages and Renaissance and now are regularly stormed by tourists visiting Tuscany, Italians in the flatter regions like Latium took to building an artificial bank of earth (*agger*) faced in stone and fronted by a ditch (*fossa*) to discourage their enemies. As in Greece, towers were added with the spread of Hellenistic siege technology, but for the most part defensive fortifications in Italy began to be neglected after the Second Punic War, when the greatest threats to towns came from Roman generals rather than foreign invaders. Despite this, Vitruvius at the end of the first century B.C.E. devotes a long section to the construction of defensive walls (Document 22). By the middle of the third century C.E., internal disturbances and pressures on the frontiers forced the Romans again to surround their capital, unprotected since the Republic, with a new and substantial set of curtain walls, towers, and fortified gates, which were from time to time thereafter heightened and strengthened and proved a successful defensive system until the introduction of gunpowder made them obsolete. These impressive walls still largely survive, much to the frustration of Roman drivers forced to negotiate narrow stone gates that were not designed for Fiats.

In addition to their urban fortifications, the Romans also constructed ramparts, palisades, stone forts, and watchtowers along the exposed frontiers of their empire to limit incursions by hostile tribes. The most extensive and famous of these were the *limes* of the German frontier where it diverged from the Rhine and Danube rivers and required marking, themselves a deterrent to invasion; and Hadrian's Wall in northern England, to isolate the northern part of the island which the Romans considered incapable or unworthy of conquest.

War Machinery

Siege and defensive machines. We have already noted the appearance of both wheeled siege towers and battering rams long before the classical period. What the Greeks contributed, and the Romans perfected, were machines for hurling large missiles over great distances. They began to appear in Greece around 400 B.C.E., probably as imports from the east, and were greatly refined during the Hellenistic period. These devices had three constituent parts: the stretching apparatus, a groove or arm and sling for the projectile, and a sturdy wooden framework to withstand the force of impact during firing. Most of them functioned on the same principle as the bow, but the energy that was stored in the bow's bent wood was instead stored in the elasticity of twisted cords that could be temporarily stretched by pulling back an arm or rope attached to them, which was released to propel the missile in front of the string or in the sling (hence the Romans called these machines *tormenta*, from the Latin word "to twist").

Though developed initially to be used against the walls and defenders of a besieged city, all these machines were subsequently adapted to be used defensively against the besiegers themselves, though the confines of parapet walks and artillery slits necessarily restricted their size and functionality.

There were three basic designs of these *tormenta* (Documents 23 and 24). The first two, present in Greece as well as the Roman Empire, were *catapultai* that projected spear-like missiles from a groove (really an enlarged version of the crossbow) and *ballistae* that shot stones along a grooved incline of some 50 degrees. (The word *ballein* in Greek means "to throw," and was applied as well to the professional slingers who hailed from the Mediterranean islands east of Spain, which still retain the word in their modern name, the Ballearic Isles.) Surviving cannonballs for *ballistae*, many of which have been found at Carthage from the Roman siege of that city in 146 B.C.E., weigh up to 70 kg. Modern experimentation has shown that both devices could hurl missiles about 350 m, though their accuracy was inversely proportional to range. A uniquely Roman development was the *onager*, named after the wild ass because of its violent kick, which used an arm fitted with a sling rather than a grooved "barrel"; its pivoted arm was winched back against the tensile strength of the twisted cords, and when released would fly forward until abruptly halted against a cushioned board, throwing the stone projectile out of the sling to a distance of 1000 m, which made it a fearsome opponent.

The process of sieges. We have a great number of historical descriptions of sieges before the advent of gunpowder, from Bronze-Age Troy to the capture of Byzantine Constantinople by the Ottomans in 1453, all of which afford us an unusually varied suite of possible tactics. To illustrate this, I have chosen two accounts: Thucydides' description of the Spartan siege of Plataea at the beginning of the Peloponnesian War (Document 25), and—perhaps the most imaginative defensive response on record—the Sicilians' ultimately futile attempt to ward off the Romans by applying the ingenuity of Archimedes (Document 26).

Generally speaking, an invading force would first make some simple but hopeful attempts against the city's fortifications by filling in the ditches to bring towers close to the wall, by beating at the gates with battering rams, and by trying to scale the wall with ladders. When these failed (as they almost always did), they would resign themselves to an ongoing siege. Here they had a choice: either blockade the city until it was starved into submission, or make active attacks against its walls: the former would result in fewer casualties among the besiegers, but the latter usually brought a quicker end to the matter and was often thought to be more noble and courageous.

Covered battering rams (called *aries* after the horny animal) were brought up against apparently weak sections of the fortifications; a wooden framework, covered with skins kept permanently wet to avoid flaming projectiles from above, protected sappers who would undermine the walls or fill up defensive moats to give a clear avenue for wheeled offensive towers built higher than the opposing fortifications and fitted with rams below, artillery on top, and hinged bridges to be lowered onto the circuit wall; and water supplies, if accessible, were poisoned with the cadavers of dead animals or soldiers. The defenders, of course, were hardly idle during all of this: they used forks and staves to overturn scaling ladders; poured stones, hot pitch, oil, and molten lead over the sappers' tents; shot flaming arrows at the thatched roofs of siege towers; and even mined outside their walls to disable the enemy's towers and artillery.

Such was the lethal ingenuity of our bellicose ancestors.

CHAPTER 5

TRANSPORTATION AND COINAGE

Humans have always been travelers, perhaps no more so than in our nomadic hunting days of the Paleolithic. But it was, ironically, agriculture and settled life that promoted the development of transportation technology, as farmers required ever more efficient means to ship their harvests to storage or markets, as engineers devised ways of moving the large stones used for construction, and as generals transported their troops to the far-flung regions of large empires. Societies tended to develop either water-based or land-based technologies, depending on their proximity to rivers and the sea and the topography of their territory: so Persia, for example, developed as a land power while Athens relied almost exclusively on the sea. And with the improved movement of goods came international trade, regional specialization of crops or products, and eventually the invention of coinage as a reliable means of facilitating commercial exchange.

TRANSPORTATION BY SEA

The topography of the eastern Mediterranean region is generally unsuited to the easy movement of goods by land. On the one hand, areas like Greece and coastal Asia Minor are rugged, with fiord-like inlets separating the high mountains that occasionally retreat from the coast to create small plains made fertile by seasonal rivers and often accessible only by sea. Conversely, the lands of the Fertile Crescent are flat and cut through by broad, slow-moving rivers that make water transportation an easy first choice for traders.

Despite the accessibility of water travel, it remained a relatively dangerous undertaking throughout antiquity, at least on the open sea. The weather in the Mediterranean Sea is favorable for sailing in small boats for about half the year, from mid-April to mid-October; the winter months are subject to fierce storms that kept all but the foolhardy safe on shore (Document 27). But even during the normal sailing season there were dangers to be reckoned with: pirates roamed the Mediterranean almost without hindrance, until Pompey the Great was given a special command in 67 B.C.E. to sweep them from the sea; and the inability of the square-rigged ships of antiquity to sail against the direction of the wind severely limited their maneuverability and often drove them into dangerous predicaments in an age when there were no charts, buoys, or beacons to guide sailors along unfamiliar coasts (Document 28).

Early Boats

Rivers and protected coastlines, then, were the earliest highways of the Mediterranean. But while this method of travel was common to all societies, the choice of flotation material in an area depended specifically on what was available in the local environment—papyrus in Egypt, dugout logs in northern Europe, skins in Mesopotamia—from which would develop boats proper, their design in turn determined by the local material. The earliest were perhaps made of pliable bark, which is easily formed into a relatively efficient and stable shape, with curved wooden ribs added to keep the sides stiff. From that beginning, the polished stone tools of Neolithic Europe created dugouts (for which the initial hollowing was done with a controlled fire), sometimes fitted with an outrigger for balance, or joined together in pairs like a catamaran. Conical bundles of reeds also lashed together in pairs, sometimes with a third bundle attached beneath as a simple keel, were paddled or poled along the Nile and its canals, and were sometimes equipped with a bipod mast for a sail, taking advantage of the prevailing breezes to propel the vessel upstream against the current. (Bipod masts had the advantages of not requiring stays or shrouds to steady the mast, and of distributing the stress on the fragile papyrus.) In Mesopotamia, its broad alluvial plain bereft of plentiful trees and reeds, animal skins either were inflated to make floats that could carry a light wooden superstructure, or were stretched over an internal light frame of wood to form a coracle; despite their lightness, these vessels could carry a substantial load and, after floating merchandise downstream to the cities along the southern reaches of the Tigris–Euphrates system, could be dismantled and easily carried by land back home. Such local vessels, with minor improvements occasionally added, persisted throughout antiquity, and their descendants can still be recognized today in many parts of the world.

Greek and Roman Ships

In Greece and the Mediterranean coast of Asia Minor, transportation by sea was always more important than travel by land, because of the local geography. So as the city-states began to emerge from the Dark Ages, we find them using vessels apparently similar to those of their Minoan and Mycenaean predecessors, about which we have little evidence beyond a fresco from Thera showing a bustling seascape, and the sunken remains of a Bronze-Age merchantman rescued from the dangerous waters off Turkey's southwest corner. The Romans, who seem naturally to have shunned sea travel as much as possible, were more comfortable employing fleets and sailors from their provinces, and so themselves made little contribution to the technologies of shipbuilding and navigation.

Merchantmen. Greek and Roman merchant ships had a high stem and stern and a capacious hull of broad proportions (with a beam as much as a third of its length). They were propelled usually by a square linen sail on a single mast stepped slightly forward of center, and steered by one or a pair of steering oars at the stern, controlled by the steersman (Latin *gubernator* or "governor," hence the concept of "ship of state" that originated in antiquity), one of only a handful of crew members. The decks were usually planked, and the cargo stowed below directly on the keel; wickerwork was sometimes added along the gunwales, increasing freeboard to accommodate more cargo.

Warships. Warships, on the other hand, were built for speed and maneuverability rather than carrying capacity: they were designed with a shallow draft (sometimes as little as 1 m) and needle-like shape (with a ratio of length to beam of up to 7:1), and were propelled by a single sail when cruising but by oarsmen during battle. The Phoenicians were the first to add a second bank of oars above and inboard of the original oarsmen, to increase speed without lengthening the ship, since they were reluctant to use the sort of composite keel needed for vessels over 30 m or so (that is, longer than the highest tree). The Greeks followed suit, first with their pentekonter, a bireme with two rows of twelve or thirteen oarsmen on each side, and later with the classic trireme: in both vessels, each set of rowers could spell off the other to give continuous power while at sea, or were used together during an attack. The entire vessel formed a kind of high-speed torpedo, its bow fitted with an iron ram at the waterline that could pierce the hull of enemy ships, causing them to flounder (Document 29). The design and construction of these vessels prevented them from sinking when holed; though swamped, they remained afloat to be towed away by the victors. This undoubtedly accounts for our failure to discover any submerged wrecks of triremes, which has ironically deprived us of useful archaeological evidence.

So despite the extraordinary importance of the trireme in the evolution of Athenian naval power and the resulting economic domination of the Aegean Sea, we have little hard information about its design and construction: inscriptions give us some details of the costs and skilled workers necessary for its construction; scenes on pottery add a sense of its appearance; and historians like Thucydides (himself an admiral, albeit a disgraced one) describe its tactics. Recently, all these bits of information were used in the reconstruction of an Athenian trireme, the *Olympias*, launched in the summer of 1987 as a commissioned vessel in the Hellenic Navy; manned largely by volunteer crews, she has given scholars a much fuller understanding of the complexity of these ships' construction and performance.

At 30–35 m in length at the waterline, only about 5 m in width, and with a draft of about 2 m, the trireme was extraordinarily maneuverable by ancient standards, and could reach rowing speeds of about 9 knots for short periods; but the shallow draft and needle-like shape made the vessel unstable in storms. Equally challenging was the accommodation of the crew: a complement of 170 oarsmen, a dozen officers and sailors, and perhaps fifteen marines and archers left scant room for provisions, so travel was usually limited to hopping from friendly port to protected bay, where nights would be spent ashore and provisions provided locally or by supply ships accompanying the fleet. Though the task of rowing these battleships was uncomfortable, underpaid, and exceedingly dangerous, it was considered an honorable responsibility for Athenian citizens, and only occasionally were resident aliens or slaves recruited to participate; indeed, philosophers were accustomed to see the fleet as a physical symbolism of Athenian democracy itself.

The Romans adopted the trireme for their own fleets, but because they were always more comfortable on land than at sea and so preferred hand-to-hand combat, they added another 100 or so marines to the ship's complement and used large spikes attached to pivoting boarding ramps (the *corvus* or "crow/raven") to pin the enemy vessel alongside. At any rate, with the Romans' conquest of most of the lands bordering the Mediterranean Sea, and with Pompey's elimination of piracy for a couple of centuries, the responsibility of the Roman imperial fleet was reduced to minor policing activities better carried out by the light and swift galleys that were stationed at Misenum on the Bay of Naples and at Ravenna on Italy's Adriatic coast.

Construction techniques. Most ancient ships were constructed in a manner quite different from that used for wooden boats today. The keel was laid first, and the sides of the hull were then built up from it, each plank being cut with the appropriate curve in it and fastened by dowels to the one below; ribs were added to strengthen the vessel, but only after the hull had been fully formed. It is easy to see that such a method was wasteful of material, since much would be discarded to obtain the proper curvature of each plank; indeed, the deforestation of the coastal regions of the Mediterranean in late antiquity is attributed to the inexhaustible demand for wood both for building ships and for heating the ubiquitous Roman baths. It was not until the seventh century or so that the clinker method of building boats was first developed by the Arabs, who attached wooden ribs to the keel and then bent steamed planks against them to form the curve of the hull, thus using far less lumber than their predecessors.

Harbors

We have no physical evidence for the existence of man-made harbors before the first millennium B.C.E., and it is reasonable to assume that early traders anchored in the naturally formed and protected roadsteads that are relatively common in the Aegean islands and along the coastal mainland of both Greece and Asia Minor. Some, like the protected bays of Lycia, have been in use for centuries, and even now afford overnight anchorages for wooden vessels of similar size to those of antiquity but transporting tourists rather than wine, oil, and grain.

By the classical period, though, the importance of trade by sea is shown clearly by the size and complexity of ancient harbors. One of the three natural bays that formed the port of Athens, the Piraeus, could accommodate 372 warships on colonnaded and covered slipways. Carthage in North Africa (near modern Tunis) boasted a pair of harbors, one for military vessels, the other commercial. The Hellenistic harbor at Alexandria at the mouth of the Nile River was adorned with the most famous lighthouse of antiquity, a three-storey octagonal tower supporting a wood fire and metal mirrors that took its name—the Pharos—from the island the protected the anchorage behind (Document 30). And the harbor of imperial Rome at Ostia (built by the Emperor Claudius in 46 C.E. and enlarged by Trajan sixty years later) could handle at one time several hundred ships bringing grain and other foodstuffs from the provinces to the mouth of the Tiber River, where the cargo was off-loaded onto small river craft that were towed up stream to fill the warehouses and shops of

Rome. The engineer Vitruvius has concisely outlined the various elements of harbors and their construction at the end of the first century B.C.E.
(Document 31).

LAND TRANSPORTATION

Transportation by land, such an essential element of modern commerce and society, was technologically limited before the advent of the
wheel near the beginning of the Bronze Age. Previously, people relied on
themselves as their primary beasts of burden, carrying the meager pos-
sessions allowed by their nomadic lifestyle on their backs or hanging from
poles carried between their shoulders, or harnessing themselves (and
perhaps domesticated dogs) to sledges, sleds, or travois. In the millennium
or two between the domestication of beasts of burden and the invention of
the wheel, sledges with runners or rollers were used to haul heavy objects,
their movement aided by levers attached to the back of the sled, or by
water poured in front of the runners to make a muddy lubricant.

Wheeled Vehicles

The wheel for transportation was invented by the beginning of the
Bronze Age. It was originally made from a single slice of a tree trunk
stripped of its bark and cut vertically into three parts, two curved and
one almost rectangular, which were then joined together into a circle by
crossbars and mounted on a freely turning axle; versions of this design,
which was simple enough to be assembled by any farmer, can still be seen
in the seminomadic areas of eastern Turkey. The lighter spoked wheel
was developed in Syria after 2000 B.C.E. for use especially on war chariots,
and is familiar from the many tomb paintings of middle- and late-Bronze-
Age Egypt. Two- and four-wheeled carts (the former for passengers, the
latter for cargo) were common throughout the Bronze and Iron Ages,
with few changes in their design. Because the ancients never developed
spring suspension, long-distance travel by cart was a painful experience:
little wonder that the daily distance covered by carts was only forty
Roman miles, about twice that by foot.

The war chariot, familiar from Homer but never popular with the
classical Greeks and Romans, was the only vehicle drawn by horses and
usually carried a driver and a fighter, who dismounted for battle; other
societies, like the Gauls, used their chariots as weapons of war, often
fitting them out with axle blades that would terrify (and debilitate) the

opposing ranks. Lighter chariots were, of course, used for racing in the Greek games and the Roman circus, where the tactic for success was to "shave the turning post" at the unbanked track's end so closely that sparks flew from the axle—or the axle disintegrated, leaving the charioteer with the difficult choice of being dragged to death by his team or cutting himself free of the reins and being left on the track in the path of the pursuing competitors.

Horseback riding became common in the Asian steppes after ca. 1000 B.C.E., and in the Mediterranean armored cavalry replaced the war chariot in Greek and Roman armies. Though horse cloths were common in antiquity, the padded saddle was not introduced until the late Roman Empire, when stirrups, snaffle bits and reins, and horseshoes were also part of the equestrian toolkit.

Roads

While Paleolithic nomads followed in the tracks of the wild animals they hunted and Neolithic farmers trod the natural paths of their cattle and sheep, the introduction of wheeled transportation required roads with prepared surfaces to be constructed in place of those earlier tracks and paths. In the Bronze Age, Mesopotamia had rough stone roads; drier Egypt made do with hard-packed dirt roads; and Minoan Crete used stones laid in mortar for a foundation, paved with limestone, basalt, or sandstone.

In the eastern Mediterranean, only the Persians developed an extensive network of roads, a necessity for keeping military control of their landlocked empire and, not incidentally, for expediting the collection of taxes (Document 32). The state built and maintained their major highway, the 3,200-km-long Royal Road from Sardis inland from the Aegean to Susa near the Persian Gulf, including posting stations at easy one-day marching intervals of about 25 km, though a determined rider could find fresh mounts at each stage and cover the entire journey in less than two weeks.

Because of the rugged topography, most Greek roads were simply unpaved paths that followed the contours of the countryside. Land travel in remote regions was always a dangerous undertaking, and travelers sought protection from *herms*, simple stone representations of the god Hermes beside the road, especially at Y-junctions. At one of these Oedipus killed his unrecognized father in a shocking ancient version of road rage, and they were always a spot where young men with too much time on their hands would gather to watch the passing traffic and engage in frivolous discussion (the Latin for the places where "three roads" meet is *trivia*). For the most part, paved roads were found only in some wealthy

Greek cities, especially those of the Hellenistic Age after the introduction of the Hippodamian system of streets arranged on a grid and often colonnaded, and sometimes between urban areas (like Athens and Miletos) and nearby religious sanctuaries (Eleusis and Didyma, respectively). A remarkable exception was the *diolkos*, a kind of railway consisting of a stone bed with parallel grooves into which fitted the wheels of carriages that transported ships across the narrow Isthmus of Corinth, in order to avoid the dangerous sea passage around Cape Malea at the southern tip of the Peloponnese.

Of all ancient peoples of the Mediterranean, the Romans were most famous for the extensive network and durability of their highways. The system was begun in 312 B.C.E., when the censor Appius Claudius commissioned a graveled road from Rome south to the Greek colony of Capua, to help expand Roman military and commercial influence in Campania; it proved so successful that it was soon paved and extended on to Brundisium on the Adriatic coast, for the first time opening up access to the eastern Mediterranean. As with the Persians, the Romans required easy communication with their provinces, so by the time of Augustus a system of paved highways extended throughout the empire, wide enough for two wagons or chariots to pass comfortably and with regular milestones and posting stations. Mileages were usually measured from the nearest city, with markers erected every 1,000 Roman paces (that is, a double step of about five Roman feet), in Latin, *mille passus*, which gives us our word "mile." The famous Golden Milestone (*miliarium aureum*) in the Roman Forum was inscribed with the names of the principal cities of the empire and the distances to them by road, emphasizing the capital's geographic as well as spiritual role as the center of the world, and, not incidentally, asserting her political and military control at the same time (Document 33).

The construction of their rural roads varied according to the terrain and climate through which they passed, but in general a base of sand was laid first, then a layer of large gravel in mortar, and a pavement of limestone or basalt slabs or even concrete; the surface was slightly crowned to channel rainwater into ditches beside the road.

The urban road systems of the Roman Empire are equally famous, and examples can be traced in excavated cities like Ostia and Pompeii, Ephesos, and the imperial cities of North Africa, especially Leptis Magna and Sabratha, though not in Rome itself, where two millennia of subsequent occupation have pretty much obliterated most of the ancient city's infrastructure. But the obvious functionality, and even elegance, of these streets camouflages one of the decided disadvantages of ancient city life: the incessant clatter of hooves and metal wheel rims against the stone paving blocks, the shouts of wagon drivers, and the destruction and death caused by intense traffic in a very confined space. To combat these dangers, Julius Caesar as dictator proposed a law that restricted wheeled traffic in the cities of Italy to the hours between sunset and sunrise, thus turning the towns into virtual pedestrian malls for half the day—and, as the satirical poet Juvenal tells us, making insomnia the most prevalent illness in Rome (Document 34).

Bridges

Before the great cities and empires of the classical period, the crossing of a stream or river was a simple if soggy undertaking. Initially, natural fords were sought out, often where an island separated the river into two narrower and more easily crossed streams; villages soon grew up around these fords, and many would develop into important cities of antiquity: Rome itself is a good example, as is the Gallic town of Lutetia on the River Seine, the capital of the eponymous Parisii. The first constructed crossings were probably tree trunks laid across a narrow stream, or several in series resting on vertical posts driven into the riverbed. But with the advent of wheeled vehicles, a bridge the width of the road was necessary; we know that pontoons were used at first in Mesopotamia and, in Rome, wooden ones erected on stone piers. A fine example of bridge building is the temporary wooden structure erected across the Rhine by Caesar's troops (Document 35). By the time of the Roman Empire, the permanent bridges had been rebuilt completely in stone, with semicircular arches up to 20 m in diameter resting on piers hydrodynamically designed to reduce the impact of the current, and supporting a paved roadway sloping upwards from either bank and cresting in the middle.

COINAGE

The invention of coinage before 600 B.C.E., probably in Lydia in Asia Minor, was to prove a revolutionary advance: though it may have initially had little impact on either international trade or local commerce, its long-term consequences were immense. A piece of precious metal stamped by a state with a guarantee of its weight and purity greatly eased the complexity of exchange that had previously depended largely on barter; and the later introduction of bronze coins in lower denominations brought similar benefits to farmers and the trades, allowing for the first time an easy means of saving profits in a form that would last for years. And, not incidentally, the wide circulation of coins made them an ideal medium for spreading religious and political messages, and for advertising the strength and prosperity of the issuing state—no insignificant accomplishment in a culture without modern forms of mass media.

Media of Exchange before Coinage

Incidents from the epic poems of Homer suggest that trade among the Greeks at that time (probably the late Bronze Age, but perhaps even the Archaic period in which the poet lived) was based on barter, and while tripods and bowls were given as gifts or prizes, there is no evidence of a standardized value (Document 36). Some form of money (that is, any accepted medium of exchange or method of payment) existed in most early cultures long before the invention of coinage: livestock, precious commodities, and metal objects are three common examples of this.

Revealing illustrations of this come from prehistoric Italy. First, the values of specific items were often calculated in comparison with the value of sheep and oxen; hence, the Latin word *pecunia*, which first means "property" or wealth in general and in historical times means "money," derives from the word *pecus*, the collective "herd." At the same time salt, a relatively precious commodity used by the ancients as their principal means of preserving food, was also employed as a medium of exchange: hence the importance of the Salt Road (*via Salaria*) leading inland from the salt beds near the mouth of the Tiber River, and later the money given to Roman soldiers with which to buy salt (*salarium*), eventually evolving into an annual monetary allowance or "salary."

In both the biblical Near East and on Minoan Crete, as a third example, metal measured by weight was used as a form of money, and early Phoenician shipwrecks like those at Ulu Burun (ca. 1350) and Gelidonya (ca. 1200) off Turkey's southwest coast contained bars or ingots of metals (usually silver) that were certainly intended for trade. Later, even iron spits (*oboloi*) were used for exchange, especially when iron was still a relatively uncommon metal, but they are found in Sparta and other areas of the Greek world even after the introduction of coinage, when they appear connected with public sacrifices and religious practices. Even a primitive form of banking existed before coinage: in Delphi and other Greek sanctuaries, states would deposit bullion and precious metal objects in temples and treasuries for safe storage.

This persistence of primitive, nonmonetary media of exchange even after the introduction of coinage was surprisingly common in the wider Greek world, especially for local markets and in less commercially favored areas, until they were finally superseded by what can arguably be considered the world's first universal currency: Roman coinage.

The Origins of Coinage

The specific dates of various early coin types are still a matter of intense scholarly scrutiny, but the relative chronology of the earliest forms is generally accepted (Document 37).

Lydian coinage. Herodotus is confident that coinage originated in Lydia, an area of west-central Anatolia, and the archaeological evidence described below confirms this. These earliest coins were made, not of gold or silver, but of electrum, a natural alloy of gold and silver (sometimes termed "white gold") that is found in the Pactolus River near Sardis, the capital of Lydia. The wealth of the kingdom was legendary: the expression "rich as Croesus" reflects the offerings that he made to various Greek shrines, especially the sanctuary of Apollo at Delphi where, according to Herodotus (*Histories* 1.50–51), he dedicated four ingots of pure gold weighing 142 pounds each, 117 of electrum, a golden lion of 570 pounds, and enormous silver and gold bowls.

The dating of the introduction of these first Lydian coins relies in part on a hoard discovered beneath the foundations of the original Temple of Artemis at Ephesos, an important sanctuary on the Aegean coast some 90 km southwest of Sardis, first sacred to the indigenous goddess Cybele and reconstructed by Greek colonists for the first time in the seventh century B.C.E. A hoard of nineteen electrum coins was recovered from a pot buried beneath the foundations of the original Hellenic shrine, and must have been deposited as a votive offering before the generally accepted date of the shrine's construction, 650–600. So it is likely, but not yet certain, that the first electrum coins were minted no later than the second half of the seventh century B.C.E.

Aeginetan coinage. Aegina is a rugged island in the Saronic Gulf, lying some 30 km south of the coast of Attica. With land barely suitable for agriculture, and a location on the major trade routes between central Greece and the Aegean, the island naturally developed into one of the dominant commercial powers in the Archaic period: it was one of the founders of the Greek trading colony established at Naucratis in Egypt in the last quarter of the seventh century, and owed much of its prosperity to the carriage of goods and materials between the Peloponnese and the coast of Ionia. Thus it is a prime candidate for the adoption of the concept of coinage from Lydia, and the minting of the first coins in silver.

Evidence from hoards suggests that the earliest silver coins were minted on Aegina shortly after 550 B.C.E. Ancient writers attribute the invention to King Pheidon of Argos, who is said to have exchanged his silver coins in return for the old iron spits (*oboloi*), which he then dedicated in the sanctuary of Hera at Argos. In 1894 a bundle of spits was found at the Argive Heraeum, fixed upright in a base of lead, and attributed by the excavators to Pheidon. But his reign is convincingly dated sometime in the late seventh and early sixth centuries, thus preceding the earliest archaeological evidence of silver coins by two generations; and it is not even certain that he ever controlled Aegina from his base at Argos. It may well be that the tradition reflects Pheidon's introduction of a system of weights and measures, including the ratio between iron spits (*oboloi*) and silver bullion, which was later to be adapted to the relative values (and names) of silver and gold coins.

Early Athenian coinage. The earliest reliable dates for coins minted in Athens fall between 540 and 530, and can be associated with the Peisistratid dynasty that ruled the city then, rather than with Solon (as Aristotle believed): at the beginning of the sixth century, Athens had lagged behind most of her neighbors commercially at least, and almost certainly will have issued her first silver coinage after Aegina.

Fortunately for the Athenians, silver had been mined at nearby Laurion since the late Bronze Age (see Crafts, p. 107–108). The new mines that they developed, whose shafts and galleries can still be seen today, would provide Athens with much of the wealth it used in the fifth century to finance the beautification of the city, the construction of a naval fleet that would dominate the Aegean, and the pursuit of costly wars with the Persians and Spartans. So it was really from these mines that the Golden Age of Athens would be born.

The first Athenian silver coins were stamped with the insignia of powerful individuals and families: obverses included impressions of amphorae and the heads of gorgons and horses, but had no actual indication that they were minted in Athens. These simply decorated coins were apparently recalled in the last quarter of the sixth century, probably by the tyrant Hippias, who then restruck them with the image of an owl on the reverse and a helmeted head of Athena on the obverse. The most common standard of the "archaic owls" was the *tetradrachm*, which replaced the earlier *didrachm*. This type became the dominant coinage of the Greek world, and was to persist almost unchanged until the second century B.C.E.

Why Was Coinage Invented?

It is often assumed that coinage was invented to facilitate commerce, both foreign and internal, but from the evidence that we have already seen this cannot be true. In fact, coins would have little effect on trade and local economies for at least the first century after their introduction.

First, extensive and long-distance trade had been carried out long before coinage appears, by such maritime powers as the Phoenicians, the Egyptians, and the Aeginetans. The first two clearly did not see the necessity of such currency for their trade, and were slow to adopt archaic coinage even when it became common. Second, coins dating to the sixth century are not found dispersed throughout Greece and the Aegean, but only in pockets like Miletos, Aegina, and Attica; in fact, most of the powerful states of that time used no coinage at all, their own or foreign. Judging by hoard evidence, the earliest coins were limited to the areas in which they were minted, or at most within the political sphere of influence of the issuing state. And finally, there are no small denominations for the early electrum, gold, and silver issues, and bronze coins were not introduced until the second half of the fifth century. The value of the first electrum coins was considerably higher than what was useful for internal or even foreign commerce: even the smallest denomination (one-eighth of an obol) was too large for daily transactions.

So it seems clear that coinage was not used for international trade or in daily transactions, at least until the fifth century, and that the earliest coins were acceptable only in the realm of the issuing authority, which guaranteed their intrinsic value and would receive them back at that value. If invented not for commerce, then for what purpose? Scholars generally agree on the following motivations, either singly or in combination, for the first production of coins that were of such high intrinsic value that they were available only to a small number of the highest social class: to store accumulated wealth in a reliable, convenient, and permanent form; to give rulers the opportunity to win prestige through religious offerings (for which Croesus, mentioned above, is a good example); to facilitate the giving of gifts among the wealthy, often in political contexts; to pay the armies and build the navies required to meet increasing foreign threats; to fund the more complex forms of administration and government, including the collection of taxes and payment of substantial tribute; to fund the monumental public works that begin to appear in the late seventh century; and to make a profit from the very minting of coins, since the charge for the precious metal in the form of coins was higher than the cost of the metal in its bullion state.

So the initial minting of coins was conceived of for the advantage of the state and its wealthy citizens, and only afterwards would it become a medium of commercial exchange. From the late seventh century onward, there was a significant increase in trade in the eastern Mediterranean, especially in goods and commodities like amphorae and other ceramics, and wine, olive oil, and other foodstuffs. Although not the principal motivation for creating coins, trade would be greatly facilitated by the invention, with light and handy coins replacing formless lumps of bullion or bars that had to be weighed for every transaction. And, by Hellenistic and Roman times, coinage would take on yet another role as an invaluable medium of political propaganda.

Minting Technique

All Greek coins were struck with dies. Cast coins, created by pouring metal in molds, were quite rare, appearing in some areas outside the Greek world, in central Italy ca. 300 B.C.E., and later in Roman times. For early coins, on which only the obverse was decorated, the bronze die was made by engraving a small mold with the desired "device" or emblem and was set into an anvil. A precisely cast disc-shaped blank of predetermined weight and quality was heated until soft and placed on the anvil; a short bar was placed on it and hit with a hammer, pressing the soft blank into the mold set in the anvil. Thus the blank became a coin with a device in relief on the obverse, and on the reverse a depression (called an "incuse") caused by the hammered rod, usually a welling up of the flan's sides. By the close of the sixth century the end of the bar as well was fitted with a device in negative, to produce a two-sided coin, though—unlike modern coins—the images of the obverse and reverse were usually on irregular axes since the bar would twist in the minter's hand. Experiments indicate that one obverse die (set into the anvil) could produce as many as 15,000 coins, but that two or three reverse dies would be needed for the same output, since they were subjected to the direct blow of the hammer and thus wore out more quickly.

CHAPTER 6

RECORDKEEPING AND TIMEKEEPING

The first records and measurements of the passage of time can be traced back at least to the Upper Paleolithic period. Just why nomadic hunters in southwest France spent uncomfortable hours in the dark recesses of caves creating elaborate paintings of their hunting experiences is not entirely understood, but one motivation must have been the desire to leave behind a record of themselves: perhaps the handprints that accompany some of these creations are signatures, witnesses of people's earliest attempts at immortality. And it cannot be coincidental that, from the same region, a contemporary stone relief of a nude woman—whether or not an earth goddess—displays a crescent moon with thirteen notches: the thirteen months of the lunar year, which mark the menstrual cycle and female fertility. The desire to keep track of time and of our own existence is, it seems, as old as we are.

THE IMPORTANCE OF SPEECH AND WRITING

While speech itself was arguably one of the two most significant inventions of humankind (the other being the ability to generate fire), it was only when that speech could be written down that any significant intellectual progress, even civilization itself, was possible. Imagine yourself for a moment in the absence of written records: whatever advances your ancestors had made could be conveyed to you through time only orally, from generation to generation, the reliability of the tradition depending both on the memory of its witnesses and the skill of its practitioners; and inventions made in one area could be spread geographically only with the migration of the craftsmen who had developed the skill. But by committing speech to written form, humans could overcome temporal and spatial limits. Knowledge for the first time was transmitted accurately over time and space, a revolutionary development that made possible relatively quick progress in the invention and evolution of other technologies, and in the development of human social organization.

Such marvels inherent in the technology of writing gave its early practitioners special, almost mystical, powers. Many societies believed that their scripts had divine origins, and the few people who, before the invention of the alphabet, could read and write were especially respected and powerful.

PRE-ALPHABETIC WRITING

The history of the development of written scripts before the Greek classical period remains somewhat controversial, but the following chronological stages are generally accepted.

Iconography

Humans, like children, began with picture writing, present since the cave paintings of the Upper Paleolithic Age, which depicted geometric symbols and conventionalized figures hunting wild herds. But not all iconography was so elaborate: some is as modest as a series of dots and lines inscribed on pebbles. If we can "read" these symbols, it is only because many (like the cave paintings) were more a work of art that portrayed a scene important in the life of the hunter who created it, rather than the record of an idea or train of thought. This early relationship between drawing and writing persisted into historical times, most obviously in Egyptian hieroglyphs, but even in classical Greece, where the word *graphein* means both "to draw" and "to write."

Pictograms

Pictograms evolved from iconography by the end of the Neolithic period, and because their symbols are standardized and stylized, they are really the first forms of true writing. It is no coincidence that these scripts evolved first in Mesopotamia and Egypt toward the end of the fourth millennium B.C.E., since the annual flooding of the great river valleys of the Tigris–Euphrates and the Nile not only created an agricultural surplus that needed to be recorded and tracked, but also brought vast numbers of people together in one place—the first cities—which made the development of conventionalized symbols practical (Document 38).

In pure pictographic writing (of which we have few surviving examples), each symbol represents a physical object, an action, or an attribute (and sometimes a combination of these). The system is almost cartoon-like in its simplicity, and in theory at least can be read by anyone anywhere, since the symbols are initially representational and can be recognized whether or not the reader speaks the language of the writer. But this very simplicity is its principal deficit: while nouns, verbs, and even adjectives can be fairly clearly expressed, more complicated concepts suggested by prepositions and adverbs cannot.

Ideograms

Hence, pure pictograms quickly evolved into ideographic scripts, a more highly developed form of picture writing in which the symbols represent not just the physical objects or simple actions, but also the ideas associated with those objects and actions: a circle, for example, first depicts the sun, and later, by association, the more complex ideas of heat, light, day, and even god. The advantages are obvious: more detailed and complex information can be transferred over time and space, and the script is still largely "universal" in that there is no connection between the symbol and the spoken name for it in a particular language. But the attendant disadvantages are intimidating: more symbols were required to convey the complex content, and often arbitrary marks were invented to distinguish among various ideas associated with the objects: the task of memorizing the "dictionary" became enormous. As a result, only a few highly trained scribes (generally priests and bureaucrats) could read and write, giving them a real advantage over the illiterate farmers who associated the mystery of writing with divine powers. The two best examples of ideographic scripts illustrate the problem.

Cuneiform. Cuneiform, originally a pictographic script and probably the oldest form of writing, was being used by the Sumerians in Mesopotamia before 3000 B.C.E., to record the agricultural contributions of the farmers to the gods' temples (and, not incidentally, to their priests). The earliest texts, from Ur, used primitive pictograms scratched into the clay that is so abundant in the lower reaches of the Tigris and Euphrates Rivers, then hardened in the sun or a kiln. Later, for the sake of speed the symbols were simplified and conventionalized, written linearly, and rotated 90 degrees when impressed into hand-held clay tablets with a reed stylus, now forming wedge-shaped symbols (*cunei-forma* in Latin) that bore little resemblance to the original picture writing.

Fewer than a thousand symbols could convey fairly detailed lists, but because ideograms cannot represent pronouns, inflections, and the like, some cuneiform symbols came instead to be used for sounds, and the script eventually tended towards a phonetic syllabary. The script died out ca. 500 B.C.E., when it was replaced by Aramaic, and was deciphered only in the nineteenth century.

Hieroglyphs. The Greeks called Egyptian writing hieroglyphic ("holy writing") since it was used mostly for lapidary inscriptions on temples and tombs (Document 39). It appears when the first pharaoh united lower and upper Egypt sometime before 3000 B.C.E., perhaps under the influence of the Mesopotamian script; but, unlike cuneiform, its limited use as a monumental script meant that it changed little in 3,000 years. When less formal documents were written quickly on papyrus with brush pens, the script inevitably became more conventionalized and cursive; called hieratic, this form of Egyptian writing was used mostly for religious texts. An even more cursive form, demotic (from the Greek word for "popular"), was the script of daily business and private letters after ca. 600 B.C.E.

With hieroglyphs, too, it was difficult to express abstracts like adverbs, and so the Egyptians introduced symbols called determinatives that, when used with the ideograms, clarified their meaning. At its fully developed state, there were about 600 pictographic symbols, a few dozen determinatives, and another hundred or so syllabic signs that scholars think were adopted to help express names and words foreign to the Egyptian language. All three Egyptian scripts became incomprehensible by the end of antiquity (demotic endured until the fifth century C.E.), and were not deciphered until after the 1799 discovery in the Nile delta of the Rosetta Stone, which recorded a taxation document of 197 B.C.E. written in hieroglyphs, demotic, and Hellenistic Greek.

Syllabaries

In the late Bronze Age there occurred a change in the technique used to express language in written form. Instead of symbols created to express whole words or ideas, the new scripts used symbols that represented the various sounds in the spoken language. The evolution of this remarkable change is still shrouded in mystery, but its impact is obvious: a script tied to a certain spoken language requires the reader to speak that language (which, at least in theory, was not necessary in simple pictographic scripts), but that was a small price to pay for the attendant simplification of the script: instead of thousands of symbols needing to be memorized, now the language can be expressed in written form with fewer than a hundred.

Linear B: The first written Greek. Linear B is a script of Crete found in archival records from Knossos dating around 1400 B.C.E. and from Pylos on the mainland 200 years later. Some scholars, noting the oddity of a script that does not change over two centuries, have suggested that Arthur Evans, the excavator of Knossos, falsified the dating of the tablets found there in his attempt to attribute them to the Minoans rather than the Mycenaean Greeks of Pylos and elsewhere. Such suspicion seems misplaced, since the limited use of the script for palace accounts would hardly promote any sort of literary evolution.

Inscribed on small, elongated clay tablets that were subsequently stored in the palace archives, the documents were fortuitously preserved when baked hard by the fires that destroyed the palace complex toward the end of the fifteenth century B.C.E. Two young British scholars deciphered the script, comprising roughly eighty symbols, by applying to the Linear B documents their training as cryptographers during the Second World War. Beginning with a Cypriote syllabary system from the second millennium that had been deciphered in the nineteenth century, and assuming that Linear B was itself a syllabary script expressing Mycenaean Greek as it would have been spoken around the time of the Trojan War, Michael Ventris and John Chadwick managed to translate about 70 percent of the tablets they studied. Many still doubted that the language was Greek, until the discovery of a previously unread tablet that contained the pictogram of a tripod preceded by the four symbols representing, according to Ventris and Chadwick's schema, the four open syllables *ti-ri-po-do*. Case proved.

Syllabic writing was the first stage of this evolution from drawing pictures to transcribing the sounds of a language: the symbols are now the graphic counterparts of the spoken word, and for the first time there is a physical connection between the spoken language and the written word. A phonetic script can be used to represent any spoken language, and the relatively small number of symbols allows almost anyone to learn it; but one now must speak the particular language in order to read the script.

THE ALPHABET

The Development of the Greek Alphabet

The last, and most highly developed and convenient, form of written script is the alphabet, a system in which the number of symbols (each of which represents either a consonant or a vowel) is reduced to about two dozen: this is an extraordinary advance that brought reading and writing within the competence of even the most basically educated person, who no longer was faced with the impossible task of memorizing the hundreds and sometimes thousands of symbols needed for the ideographic scripts of the Bronze Age. The very simplicity of the alphabet has been its greatest strength, promoting widespread literacy and contributing to the survival of texts and documents that represent all aspects of human knowledge and imagination.

Though all the scripts used to represent languages of European origin are derived from the original Greek alphabet, the alphabet itself was not a Greek invention. How and when the Greeks encountered it, how they adapted it to their own purposes, and how it evolved into the Latin and Cyrillic scripts in use today, is the focus of this section.

North Semitic: The original alphabet. We know that the alphabet came into use in Europe almost certainly sometime after ca. 900 B.C.E. Although its actual origin is still debated, both ancient and modern scholars agree that the Greeks borrowed it from the Phoenicians, with whom they came into contact at the end of the Dark Ages: the shapes, names, and order of the Greek letters all reflect the earlier Semitic alphabet.

In this instance, Herodotus seems correct in his general attribution. The North Semitic script was the parent of two main writing systems, Phoenician and Aramaic. Aramaic would eventually become the progenitor of the Hebrew and Arabic scripts, while the Phoenician alphabet would be the basis of the Greek alphabet via direct adoption. The Greek alphabet, in turn, is the direct ancestor of Etruscan, Latin, and the modern Western alphabets.

While it is agreed that the North Semitic script was the model for the Greek alphabet, the time and place of the adoption is still a matter of uncertainty and dispute. Early literary sources are scant, and not always trustworthy; the archaeological evidence is incomplete, largely because of the perishable nature of writing media (papyrus, animal skins, wooden and wax tablets); and there is little epigraphic (inscriptional) evidence for North Semitic.

The Phoenicians and the Greek alphabet. According to mythology, Kadmos was the son of Agenor, king of the Phoenician city of Tyre (or Sidon). When his sister Europa disappeared, Agenor sent Kadmos with his brothers Cilix and Phoenix to find her; he was led to Thebes, where he built the citadel of the town. The Thebans honored him as their founder, called the citadel the Kadmea, and were referred to as Kadmeans (Document 40).

Thus it was that Kadmos and his Phoenician comrades introduced the Greeks of Thebes to their alphabetic script, while his brothers and the followers who accompanied them on the quest for Europa would found other eponymous places: Cilix established Cilicia, and Phoenix Phoenicia.

Historically, Phoenician culture developed in the area of modern Syria, Lebanon, and Israel, on the Mediterranean coast north of Mt. Carmel, in the city-states of Tyre, Sidon, and Byblos. The Phoenicians were great traders, and established trading posts and colonies along the entire the Mediterranean coast, including North Africa, southern Spain, and the islands of Cyprus, Sicily, Malta, and Sardinia. Their geographical spread, as well as the necessity to keep records of their trading activities, gave ample opportunity for the Phoenicians to establish their written script, if not their language, at various spots throughout the Mediterranean: a Punic version, for example, existed in their entrepôt of Carthage, outside modern Tunis, for several centuries after the area was conquered by the Romans.

We can see that the Greek alphabet was initially directly adopted from Phoenician script from the following four pieces of evidence: By the fifth century B.C.E., according to both Herodotus and inscriptional evidence, the Ionian Greeks already called the letters of the alphabet "Phoenician." The names and order of the letters of the Greek alphabet, from alpha to tau (α–τ), and those of the Phoenician script are essentially the same— aleph, beth, gimel = alpha, beta, gamma—the Greek names of the letters being given a final "a" as required by the inflected nature of the language. The shapes of the letters, originally derived from pictograms, are es- sentially the same in both phonetic scripts (aleph = ox, beth = house, gimel = camel), except that some letters have been reversed, inverted, or modified in some way, camouflaging the original pictographic origin and meaning, which of course was unintelligible to the Greeks (such as A, which upright no longer resembles the ox head pictogram that the North Semites chose acrophonically from *aleph* to represent the sound "a"). And the direction of writing is the same: in the early phases of the development and use of the new Greek alphabet, scribes wrote from right to left, as did the North Semites.

But, while it is clear that the Greek alphabet was adopted directly from the Semitic script of the Phoenicians, the identification of where and when this initial borrowing took place is far less certain.

Date and place of adoption. Proposed dates for the adoption of the Phoenician alphabet by the Greeks range from the fourteenth century to the late seventh century, with varying degrees of evidence. What is clear is that the borrowing took place when the Greeks and Phoenicians were in direct contact with each other, from the twelfth to the eighth century B.C.E.

First, we can discount a date before the eleventh century. There is no physical evidence to support such an early date, though we must admit the real possibility that the materials used as writing surfaces were all perishable and have left no physical record. Still, it is unlikely that the alphabet would have been in use alongside the other systems, like Linear B, that existed before the Dark Ages. Conversely, the latest possible date is provided by two archaic vases with painted inscriptions, the earliest known Greek texts, both of which are dated pretty securely to the late eighth century.

When attempting to determine the birthplace of the Greek alphabet, scholars generally agree on three presumptions: that the epigraphic and archaeological evidence suggests that it originated in one area, rather than independently at several points where the Phoenicians and Greeks had trading contacts; that the transmission must have occurred in a joint and relatively permanent settlement of Greeks and Phoenicians; and that the rapid dissemination of the alphabet points to a location either on a busy trade route or near major Greek commercial centers. Since there is no archaeological evidence in Boeotia for any Phoenician settlement, and since landlocked Thebes was not on an external trade route, we can discount the mythological tradition of placing the transmission of the alphabet in a Phoenician Thebes under Kadmos.

The site of Al Mina in Syria, identified by archaeologists as the ancient Greek site of Posideion, now seems the most likely candidate for the transmission of the alphabet. Archaeological evidence has indicated that this port city on the south bank of the Orontes River was the most substantial Greek settlement in Phoenician territory during the eighth century, when the borrowing likely occurred. The presence of Greek pottery from various Aegean islands supports the existence of extensive trade connections and a permanent Greek settlement in Semitic territory, both requirements for the transmission of the Phoenician alphabet. What is more, archaeological evidence confirms that Posideion was settled by Greeks from the island of Euboea, whose script is one of the closest to the North Semitic script of the Phoenicians. On this evidence alone, the Euboeans have a strong claim as the first Greeks to write alphabetically; and their traders would have had plenty of opportunity to bring the new system back to Greece proper.

Evolution of the Greek Alphabet

Greek was, like its Phoenician ancestor, originally written retrograde (that is, from right to left), then boustrophedon alternating lines of left to right, right to left ("as the ox turns" [*bos-stroph*] while plowing), and after ca. 500 B.C.E. left to right. Retrograde and boustrophedon, which occur together from the seventh to the fifth century, both require the writer to reverse the letters as well as the direction of the script; while this may seem awkward (especially for right-handed people), half of the letters of the early Greek alphabet are designed to be reversible. Boustrophedon, in fact, is a quite natural way of writing, and is more efficient for both the writer and the reader: those old enough to remember dot-matrix printers will appreciate this.

Though the Greeks' adoption of the alphabet occurred at one place and at one time, as the new script spread throughout the Greek world cities developed local variations in letter forms and even in the alphabet itself. It was not until the late fifth century B.C.E. that a common model began to be adopted: the one chosen was the Ionian Greek alphabet originally from Miletos in Asia Minor, although even it was not perfectly adapted to all the variations of dialects. In Athens, the Ionian letter system was formally adopted by a democratic vote in 403/2, and by 350 B.C.E. it became the established, universal, classical Greek script of twenty-four letters.

Thereafter, changes in the alphabet were limited to the simplification of letterforms, necessitated by the increasingly common use of writing among the intellectual and commercial classes in particular. The classical style was retained as the monumental script for use in inscriptions, especially the large, formal, official, and public documents inscribed with chisels on stone—epitaphs, boundary stones, dedicatory and honorary inscriptions, and laws and decrees—the generally straight and angled letterforms reflecting the medium used by the inscriber. But, as writing was mastered by more people for less formal documents, new media were developed that were more affordable and easier to use: first, wax tablets and, after ca. 500 B.C.E., papyrus sheets. These surfaces and the tools used to write on them encouraged the development of a more cursive and simplified script; hence the evolution of variant forms for each letter, which we think of as lowercase letters.

The Impact of the Alphabet on Greek Society

Many scholars, recognizing that even a syllabary like Linear B (to say nothing of ideographic cuneiform) was difficult to learn, emphasize that pre-alphabetic scripts were used almost exclusively for administrative purposes within the palace culture of the Minoans and Myceneans, and that writing (and thus literacy) in these societies was reserved for the upper class and (in the cases of Mesopotamia and Egypt) a scribal caste. They argue, quite convincingly, that the simpler and more natural Greek alphabet made possible widespread literacy, since anyone could learn to read or write the limited number of signs in the new alphabet. In support of this "democratizing" view of the alphabet, they point to the earliest examples of Greek writing, graffiti scratched into or painted on pottery or stones by the common man. Thus, they argue, the development of the Greek alphabet rendered obsolete the role of the scribe or official responsible for writing in ancient administrations, and, some two centuries after its adoption from the Phoenicians, directly led the way to the evolution of democracy in Athens.

Others have recently challenged this view, arguing that significant standards of literacy did not occur until the nineteenth century, and that the simplicity or difficulty of mastering a script is not directly related to literacy rates. While examples can be found to support this approach, it fails to take into account two important elements of Greek culture in antiquity: first, that the evolution of written records from palace accounts to literary genres, which began in the archaic period, proves an increase in literacy, though it was inevitably limited by the constraints of the technology of publication, since texts were written individually by hand, and were thus expensive and of limited accessibility (a limitation that would, of course, remain true until the fifteenth-century adoption of the printing press and movable type in Europe); and second, that Athenian democracy, though it involved all enfranchised citizens in debate and vote, was itself accessible only to a small number of people of the right age, sex, and parental nationality, all of whom were certainly literate.

The Alphabet after the Greeks

The Etruscans. We still do not understand the origins of the language of the Etruscans, despite its documentation in thousands of inscriptions and recognition as a non-Indo-European language. Living north of the Tiber River in Italy, they had close cultural and commercial relations with the Greek trading ports of southern Italy (Magna Graecia), and may have borrowed the Greek alphabet from the colonists at Cumae (Kyme). Certainly the Etruscan adoption of the Greek script took place at a very early period, at most within a century or so after the Greeks' initial borrowing of the Phoenician alphabet, when the original Greek alphabet probably had not yet diverged into its early dialectical branches. The oldest Etruscan document is a tablet dated to the eighth century B.C.E., the earliest abecedary found in the West and surely used for pedagogical purposes. All but two letters in Etruscan abecedaries found so far, dating down to the fifth century, have parallels in the Euboic alphabets of Kyme and Eretria on Euboea. The early texts are written from right to left, like their Phoenician and archaic Greek predecessors; and the twenty-two Semitic letters are in their traditional order, followed by four additional Greek letters.

Latin. The Latin alphabet was derived from the Greek via the Etruscans of central Italy, sometime in the seventh or sixth century B.C.E. to judge from the earliest epigraphic evidence. This period is traditionally associated with the two Etruscan kings of Rome, whose reigns may be slightly adjusted by archaeological evidence but almost certainly fell within those two centuries. An inscribed stele, buried beneath a late Republican stone pavement in the Roman Forum, dates to about the sixth century B.C.E., and uses archaic letters in boustrophedon; the text, unfortunately, cannot be precisely deciphered.

The Romans adopted twenty of the original twenty-six letters of the initial Etruscan alphabet; three other signs were adapted for numbers; the Greek *zeta* was dropped because the sound it represented did not exist in Latin; and only one *s* sound of the three Etruscan ones was retained (the Greek *sigma*). About 312 B.C.E. the letter C, used for the sound *k* and the Etruscan *g*, was given a cross bar for the latter sound, creating the new letter G. This gave us the twenty-one-letter Republican Latin alphabet up to the second century: A B C (=K) D E F G H I K L M N O P Q R S T V X.

Various additions were made during Rome's expansion through the Mediterranean: after the conquest of Greece in the second century B.C.E., Y and Z were added to transliterate Greek words into Latin (like *zephyr* the wind), giving twenty-three letters; and three new letters were devised by Emperor Claudius in the first century C.E., but were never accepted (Document 41). Finally, the medieval additions of U, W, and J were introduced to differentiate between the consonantal and vowel sounds of the existing Latin letters V and I.

The Cyrillic alphabet. The forty-three-letter Cyrillic alphabet, at root the twenty-four classical Greek letters in shape and sound but supplemented by new letters to express new sounds, was traditionally introduced into eastern Europe in the tenth century by the proselytizing St. Cyril, and would become the basis for the alphabets of Slavs, Russians, Ukrainians, Bulgarians, and Serbs. About the same time, equally enthusiastic devotees of Roman Catholicism were spreading the Latin alphabet among the Poles, Czechs, Slovaks, Croats, and Slovenes. As a result, those eastern European adherents of Orthodox Christianity today use the Cyrillic alphabet, and those of the Roman Christian faith the Latin alphabet.

WRITING MATERIALS AND BOOKS

Almost any reasonably smooth surface could be used for writing—we know, for example, that the Latin word for "book" (*liber*) derives from the tree bark that could be peeled off, flattened, and painted on—and humans had been manufacturing pigments suitable for writing as early as the cave painters of the Upper Paleolithic. But with the spread of literacy in the classical period, society required more convenient, durable, and cheap means of producing texts for a greater variety of purposes: daily commerce, public laws, private letters, and books of literature.

Writing Surfaces

Wax tablets. Among the earliest and most common new writing surfaces were wax tablets: panels of wood with raised edges and covered with smoothed wax, into which letters were scratched with a metal stylus, pointed at one end for writing, flattened at the other for erasing. There were great advantages to this system: the materials were inexpensive, the tablets were portable, and the surfaces could be reused over and over by softening and smoothing the wax with moderate heat. The disadvantages, of course, were equally important: though individual panels were often hinged together into diptychs (two) or triptychs (three), the length of a document was still severely restricted; and the wax was unsuitable for text that needed to be preserved. Still, tablets were clearly useful for small businesses and especially for students, whose teachers could correct their mistakes easily, and who could refresh their "pages" every night at home. Much of our evidence for these wax tablets comes from their appearance in school scenes painted on Greek vases of the fifth and fourth centuries B.C.E. (Figure 17).

Papyrus. Throughout the classical period the most common writing surface was papyrus, a more durable material for more permanent records, light enough to be used for letters, and able to be glued together into a long roll to accommodate more text (Document 42). The Greek name for papyrus was *byblos*, which has come into English as the Bible; and though it has also given us the English word "paper," there is no technological connection between the two: paper manufactured from wood pulp was a Chinese invention that found its way to the west, via the Arabs, around the eighth century, but did not become common until the Renaissance.

Figure 17. Writing on a wax tablet (vase painting, ca. 500 B.C.E.)

Papyrus was harvested almost exclusively in Egypt, where it grew in the shallow marshes along the Nile. The plant's stem was cut lengthwise into strips, which were laid parallel to one another and covered with a second layer at right angles; the layers were dampened, covered with glue, and pressed together into sheets about 15 inches high and 8 inches wide, which themselves were glued together into a long, continuous roll about 25 feet in length. The writing was applied with a split-reed pen, dipped in an ink of soot, gum, and oil. The text was written in a series of parallel columns about 4 inches wide, beginning at the left edge of the long roll, generally with no spacing between words and no punctuation beyond a slight stroke in the margin to indicate a change of topic (the Greek for "written beside" being *para-graphos*). Only one surface of the papyrus was written on, so a typical roll could accommodate between twenty-five and seventy-five modern printed pages. This was the length of the classic book, the *liber* or *volumen* (the latter from the Latin word for roll), and explains why ancient texts like Vitruvius' work on architecture, originally published in ten *libri* or scrolls, can be accommodated in a single modern book.

Parchment. According to tradition, the rivalry between two of Alexander's successor kingdoms—the Ptolemies in Egypt and the Attalids of Pergamon in Asia Minor—prompted an Egyptian prohibition of the export of papyrus; the Pergamenes, forced to find a new source of writing material, hit on the idea of smoothly finishing the skin of young animals (calf, lamb, or kid) to produce a surface that was both durable and double sided: named after them, it became known as *pergamene*, later corrupted into "parchment" (also called vellum). The story is probably apocryphal (we have evidence of writing on leather from much earlier), but parchment was an important invention, especially in late antiquity when the rather clumsy scroll (imagine trying quickly to find a reference near the end of a volume) was superseded by the codex, a true book of large parchment sheets (quires) folded into halves, quarters, or eighths, stitched together, and the folds cut to produce separate pages. This is the direct ancestor of our printed books, whose pages sizes are still described by the number of folds (quarto for large volumes, octavo for the common size of book).

Stone. For durable records—laws, edicts, epitaphs, and the like—the ancients inscribed their texts on finished stone *stelai* using chisels of various size and shape to form the generally angular shapes of uppercase letters. In the case of some important Roman inscriptions, cast bronze letters were inserted into the cavities, creating a brightly visible text and monumental effect.

Publishing

By modern standards, publication of literature was a modest technique in antiquity, since it was never done mechanically (hence the Latin *manu scriptum*, "written by hand"). An author would either write out his original by hand or more often dictate it to a slave, and commission a book dealer to produce copies. The dealer would then dictate the text to a group of educated slaves who would dutifully copy it down, employing a collection of abbreviations that allowed them to keep up with the reader; those who could not keep up, or who nodded off during the long and tedious hours of transcribing, might do the best they could to make sense of what they were left with; thus, no two copies of the book would be the same.

Once each roll of papyrus was complete, its edges were trimmed, smoothed with a pumice stone, and tinted black; the title was written in red ink (*rubricus* in Latin) on a tag that would hang free from the end of the roll; it would often be dipped in cedar oil to protect it from moths and worms, and finally the two ends of the papyrus were attached to wooden rollers with decorative tips, producing the classic scroll. The reader would hold the scroll in her right hand and unwind it with her left, moving from each column of text to the next on its right, until the rod in her left hand contained the entire roll, which then needed to be laboriously rewound before it could be read again.

The individual scrolls making up a complete work would be gathered together into a basket and sold in the shop of a bookseller (*librarius*); once purchased, they would be stored in wooden cases built into niches in the walls of the library (*bibliotheca*), each volume in a horizontal pigeonhole with its red title tag hanging beneath for easy browsing. Because of the small scale of production, books were bought only by wealthy individuals (Cicero, for example, had a private collection at each of his several residences) or by the public libraries that appeared in the Hellenistic and Roman periods: the library and museum at Alexandria is the most famous example, but local benefactors often donated a library to their home city, the remains of which can still be seen in excavated sites like Ephesos and Pergamon.

We should note here that the production of limited copies has two serious implications for the study of ancient literature, and of antiquity in general. First, the oldest surviving manuscripts of ancient texts come from several centuries after the original publication: the oldest copy of Vergil, for example, dates to the fifth century, and of Pliny to the eighth, while the majority of "ancient" manuscripts are products of the eleventh to fourteenth centuries. The originals have passed through several editions before these surviving copies were made, and it requires considerable expertise and patience to try to reconstruct the author's actual words uncorrupted by the hands of scribes. Second, while it is impossible for us to imagine that every copy of *Harry Potter and the Half-Blood Prince* could be lost to posterity, ancient production runs of a handful of copies could easily fail to survive one or two generations. We think that we have a substantial portion of the most important works by Greek and Roman authors—the most popular, at least, would be reissued many times, increasing their chance of survival—but it is a sobering realization that a single bookcase can accommodate all the surviving published literature from Homer in the eighth century B.C.E. to the early Christian apologists more than a millennium later.

TIMEKEEPING

Interest in keeping track of (and predicting) the passage of time varied greatly in antiquity, especially between rural farmers and urban dwellers. By necessity, farmers worked during daylight hours, and had no need to divide that period into measurable segments; what their work did require was an ability to differentiate the seasons: sowing, plowing, harvesting, the vintage, and so on. Not surprisingly, then, from the Neolithic onward they followed the rising and setting of stars and the movement of constellations to determine the appropriate timing for their work—the rising of the Dog Star (Sirius) around mid-July denoted, for example, the traditional beginning of the Nile's flood in Egypt and the hottest season in Rome—and for their agricultural festivals. The more complex urban societies of the Bronze Age and after required more precise measurements both to accommodate commerce and to organize social activities to cope with large populations in small areas. So it is no surprise that, by the early third millennium, both Mesopotamia and Egypt had devised reasonably accurate civil calendars based on a solar year of about 365 days.

Greek Calendars

In early Greece, calendars were developed independently by each city-state, and originally had a religious function: to determine the correct time for festival days. Since the regular waxing and waning of the moon is easier to observe than the slower changes of the sun's path and elevation from the horizon, lunar calendars were usually developed first, based on twelve months of 29.5 days in each cycle; and, in order to bring the lunar year into alignment with the solar one, every few years an additional few days would be added. The Athenian calendar is a good illustration of this: the year began with the first new moon after the summer solstice and consisted of twelve months named after festivals, each of twenty-nine or thirty days and beginning with the new moon. This gave a year of 354 days, so each third year an additional month was inserted in mid-year (a procedure called "intercalation").

From the fifth century on in Athens, each year was named after the city's principal archon, one of nine leaders chosen annually by lot; this is the yearly dating system used by writers like Thucydides and, though it might seem unwieldy, required little more effort than the memorization of the list of presidents or monarchs required of students today. But because there was no standard calendar among the dozens of city-states, the Greeks used one of their common institutions—the quadrennial Olympian Games—to designate years internationally, beginning from the traditional date of the first games in 776 B.C.E., and proceeding through the four years of each Olympiad.

The Roman Calendar

Since the Roman calendar is the ancestor of most yearly reckonings used in the modern world, it deserves more detailed study, both as an example of our own inheritances from antiquity and as a model of how a deep sense of tradition can prevent societies from improving their technologies. We begin here from the smallest to the longest common measurements of the passage of time.

Seconds and minutes. Neither of these units played a role in Roman timekeeping, for both technological and social reasons: their apparatus was not fine enough to distinguish them, and they were in the scheme of things insignificant to agricultural and urban life. They were introduced in the medieval period, *minuta* as a "minute" (the adjective, not the noun) segment of time, one-sixtieth of an hour, and [*minuta*] *secunda*, a "second minute," that is, the *second level* of division into sixtieths, or one-sixtieth of a *minuta*.

Hours. As was the case in Greece, the length of Roman hours was variable from season to season, since the period from sunrise to sunset was divided into twelve hours of equal length. Thus, Roman hours were of the same length as ours only twice a year, at the spring and autumn equinoxes; the hours could be as brief as forty of our minutes during the short days of winter, and as long as eighty minutes in midsummer. The difficulty that these variable hours presented in the design of timepieces and the organization of labor was enormous, and will be discussed later.

Days. The day, then, was divided into periods of light and darkness. The first hour of the day began at the rising of the sun, and the twelfth ended with its setting. The period from sunset to sunrise, being a less productive time of day, was treated more simply and was traditionally divided into four equal *vigilia*, also seasonally variable; the word derives from the night watches of the Roman army. Unlike our Mondays and Tuesdays, Roman days were not named.

Weeks. The Romans did not have the equivalent of our seven-day groupings. The closest they came was the *nundinum*, a period of eight days that reflected the rotating market days of neighboring towns, but this was not used in official calendars. Readers with some knowledge of Latin will recognize that the word *nundinum* actually means "nine days" (*novem dies*), not "eight." The Romans counted inclusively, beginning with the present day, so our "day after tomorrow" was three days away for Pliny. When they eventually did adopt a seven-day week from the Middle East, perhaps as early as the second century, the Romans followed Babylonian tradition by assigning the names of their seven planetary gods to the days of the week: Sol, Luna, Mars, Mercurius, Jupiter (Jovis), Venus, and Saturnus. These have been largely preserved in the Romance languages, but English has mostly followed the Anglo-Saxon names of deities: Sun, Moon, Tiw, Woden, Thor, Frigg, and Saturnus.

Months. There were originally ten months in the Roman year, beginning in March and ending in December, with what we assume was an uncounted gap of sixty days or so during the agriculturally unproductive time after midwinter, which reinforces the rustic origin of their calendar. Three of the first four months were named after divinities—Mars, Maia, Juno—while the fifth to the tenth were named in numerical sequence, Fifth to Tenth: Quintilis, Sextilis, September, October, November, December. Sometime after the urbanization of Rome under Etruscan influence, January and February were added, but it was not until 153 B.C.E. that 1 January was made new year's day in place of 1 March: an odd delay, when one realizes that the month of *Ianuarius* was named after the two-faced god Janus, protector of gates and doors (which is really what a "janitor" does), a perfect symbol for the passing out of the old year and beginning of the new. Of the twelve months, March, May, July (*Quintilis*), and October each had thirty-one days, February twenty-eight, and the rest twenty-nine.

The easiest way to indicate a date is to give the day of the month—we say 15 March and 16 March, for example—but here the Romans were hobbled by the same kind of impediment to change that saddled them with hours of variable length. Almost certainly preserving elements of an archaic lunar calendar (note that the Latin word for "months," *menses*, refers also to the natural lunar cycle of female fertility), they identified three days of each month as a kind of anchor, from which other days would be counted: the Kalends were the first of each month, the Nones the fifth or seventh (the latter in thirty-one-day months), and the Ides the thirteenth or fifteenth (ditto). They would then count backwards (inclusively, of course) from the next anchor day: the Kalends of March was followed by "six days before the Nones" (2 March), "five days before the

Nones" (3 March), "four days before the Nones" (4 March), "three days before the Nones" (5 March), "the day before the Nones" (6 March), and the Nones (7 March). Then all over again, counting backwards from the Ides; and, after the Ides, backwards from the Kalends of April, which means that half the days of each month were given in relation to the *following* month. Had Julius Caesar's assassins picked 16 March instead of 15 March to strike their blow against the dictator, Shakespeare's unfortunate soothsayer would have had to shout "Beware the sixteenth day before the Kalends of April!"

Years. The twelve months noted above produced a year of 355 days (not coincidentally an almost exact lunar year). As we saw in the case of the Athenian calendar, an intercalary period would be inserted in the middle of February to bring the civil calendar into alignment with the solar year. Unfortunately, the procedure was entrusted to political appointees, who could freely add days or not if they wished to help their elected friends or hinder their opponents. The result was that, by 46 B.C.E., the civil calendar was a full eighty days ahead of the solar year (Document 43).

Caesar, who was dictator at the time, resolved the problem first by creating a new and accurate civil calendar (based on an Egyptian model) to come into effect on 1 January 45 B.C.E. and then, in order to have it align with the solar year, by proclaiming that the current year, 46 B.C.E., would be 445 days long. The new "Julian" calendar was almost the system we use today: eleven months of thirty or thirty-one days each, and February with twenty-eight days except every four years, when an extra twenty-ninth day was added to bring the average solar year to 365.25 days. In honor of Caesar, and of Augustus who did some minor fiddling, the months *Quintilis* and *Sextilis* were renamed July and August.

Sixteen centuries later, the Julian calendar was revised for the last time: in 1582 Pope Gregory XIII decreed that, though all terminal years of a century would normally be leap years, only those divisible by 400 would receive the extra day (hence 1600 and 2000 were leap years, but 1700, 1800, and 1900 were not): this recognized that the solar year was not actually 365 and a quarter days, but rather 365.24. Some countries, unwilling to follow the lead of the Catholic Church, retained the Julian calendar for two or three centuries; now it is principally the Greek and Russian Orthodox churches that use it, for establishing their traditional religious festivals.

Finally, like the Greeks the Romans had two systems for designating their years: either by the names of the two annually elected consuls (compare the Athenian archon), or by counting from the commonly accepted date of the founding of Rome, our year 753 B.C.E.

Centuries. One would expect the Romans, who prided themselves on their decimal system and who commonly organized things into groups of a hundred (centurions commanded 100 men, and centuriation was their system of marking out regular plots of land), also to have noted the passage of a hundred years. Their equivalent of a century was a *saeculum* (the French *siècle*), a period that reflected the longest human life, originally 100 years, but after Augustus 110. The reason once again points to the religious origin of their calendar, and to their determination to preserve tradition over simplification. The celebration of a *saeculum* could be held only after all those who were alive at the beginning of the last one were now dead; and, since at least by the beginning of the empire a very small percentage of Romans lived past their 100th birthday (or at least claimed to have), from Augustus onward it was thought prudent to celebrate the festival every 110 years.

CLOCKS

In the first century B.C.E., the astronomer Andronicus built an elaborate timepiece and weathervane in the Roman Agora in Athens. The Tower of the Winds contained two distinct timekeeping devices that were the commonest means of telling time. At the top of the octagonal structure were eight sculpted panels symbolically representing the principal winds; beneath each relief was a *gnomon*, a metal rod that extended from the face of the building and cast its shadow on the sundial inscribed below. Such devices were reasonably accurate clocks, but their use was restricted to the daytime, and only when there was little cloud cover. To resolve this limitation, inside the building Andronicus built a water clock, the details of which we can only partly piece together, since the only substantial part of it that survives is the reservoir attached to the outside of the tower, kept filled by the nearby aqueduct and supplying a continuous flow of water to the clock inside.

Sundials. We observed earlier that it was primarily urban dwellers in antiquity who felt any need to calculate and record a passage of time less than a day. For those who did care, the position of the sun with respect to some fixed object or the varying length of a person's shadow could give a rough estimate of the time of day. The fixed sundial was an elaboration of the simpler shadow clock, a flat piece of metal with one end bent up at right angles that could measure the length of the shadow cast by the vertical lip. In the case of the sundial, made popular in the Hellenistic period, a fixed vertical spike or post (the *gnomon*) cast a shadow onto a flat, hollow, or conical "dial" on which were inscribed the hours (Document 44). The matter of seasonally variable hours, of course, together with the differences resulting from different latitudes, made the format of the "dial" more complex. One of the notable surviving examples is the great sundial erected by Augustus in the Campus Martius north of Rome's city center, for which he used an obelisk imported from Egyptian Heliopolis as the gnomon; it, and the metal hour markings inset in the pavement, can still be seen.

Water clocks. Sundials were the only ancient mechanisms that could indicate with some accuracy the real time of day; but they were useless on overcast days, at night, and indoors. The Greeks and Romans never satisfactorily overcame this shortcoming, but they used all their ingenuity

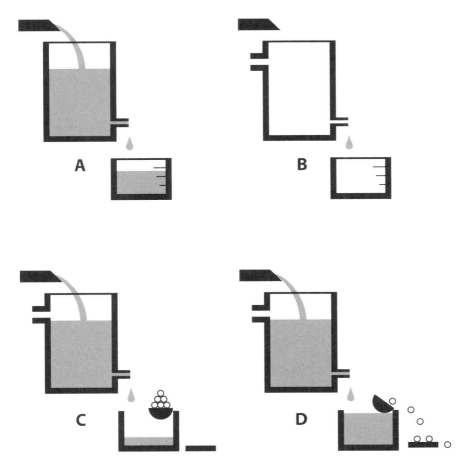

Figure 18. Water clocks (*klepsydrae*) and an early alarm clock

to try. First, they devised a simple machine for measuring a period of time, but not real time: the *klepsydra* (Greek for "water thief") was a clay vessel of a certain capacity, with a small hole at its base; once filled with water and the plug removed, it would empty in a consistent period of time that could be endlessly repeated. The *klepsydra* worked well in places like law courts or assemblies, where it was important that each speaker be given the same length of time to make his case; but, because the water flowed more slowly as the vessel emptied (because of the diminishing pressure of

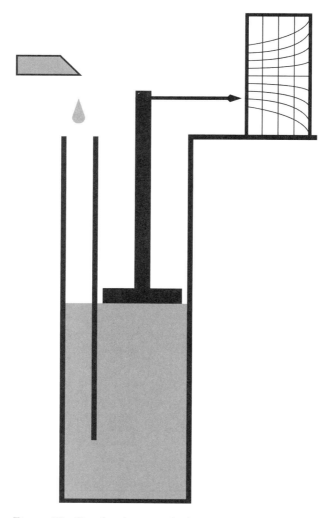

Figure 19. Ctesibius' water clock

the remaining water), it was almost impossible to divide the period of flow into equal segments—it was all or nothing. This restriction was solved, if not (as some suggest) by Plato in the early fourth century, then by Ctesibius in the third, with the invention of a "stationary flow" system: with the insertion of an overflow pipe near the top of the vessel, and the provision of a steady supply of water into the vessel, the level of water remained constant, as did the pressure, producing a consistent flow through the outlet and allowing that flow to be calibrated (Figure 18, A–B).

We have descriptions of a pair of "alarm clocks," again sometimes attributed to Plato but probably from a century later. In one (see Figure 18, C–D), a steady flow of water drips into a hollow cylinder; the gradually rising column of water eventually tips a saucer in which are placed marbles; as these tumble out of the saucer, they land on a metal disc and ring out the time to arise.

Finally, it was Ctesibius who devised the most advanced form of mechanical clock that could, at least in theory, indicate the passage of hours, and even accommodate the seasonally changing length of them (Document 45). By providing a stationary flow of water into a cylinder, he could calibrate the rising water level in the cylinder; and by floating on the surface of that water a small figure holding a horizontal pointer, he transferred the calibrated segments of passing time to another cylinder on which were inscribed the hours. To account for the different lengths of those hours, he used the overflow water to turn a series of reducing gears attached to the inscribed cylinder, causing it to rotate once every year; and the lines on the cylinder indicating hours were curved rather than parallel, making them gradually wider apart as the year progressed from the winter to the summer solstice, and narrowed for the next six months (Figure 19). Short of replacing variable with fixed hours, that was as advanced as ancient clocks could become. Little wonder that a character in one of Plautus' comic plays bemoaned the invention of timepieces, and longed for the old days when a person's stomach was the only clock he needed.

CHAPTER 7

CRAFTS

Here we survey two of the most important technical crafts of antiquity: the working of metals and the production of ceramic and glass vessels. Both began in the Neolithic as tasks common to many individual households, but by the time of the Roman period techniques were refined and complex enough to require highly trained sub-specialists in areas like the production of decorated jewelry, painted vases, and blown glass. To the crafts described here could be added many others: weaving, for example, belongs as much here as in association with the agricultural processes that produced its raw materials; and there are other crafts like woodworking that have regretfully been omitted because of limitations of space.

MINING, METALLURGY, AND METALWORKING

The two most significant metals in the ancient world were copper and iron, together with their alloys bronze and steel. Humans were first attracted to colored stones that they found were malleable and could be beaten into a shape by simple hammering: this was true of native copper and gold, both of which were worked as early as the sixth millennium, long before the advent of the "metal ages," just as natural or meteoric iron was collected and simply worked at least a thousand years before the advent of the Iron Age. This apparent discrepancy in chronology exists because we date the beginning of the Bronze and Iron Ages to the time when the metals were smelted from ores, and new metalworking techniques were developed to fashion them into functional shapes.

Primary Metals

Gold. When Hesiod called the oldest period of human existence the Golden Age, he chose that metal because it was the most precious; unintentionally, he got the historical order of first use of his four metals right as well. Gold was worked long before silver, copper, and bronze because it had three advantages: though rare, it often exists in its natural form, not combined with other metals, and so needs no special metallurgical techniques to extract it; it is so malleable that it can be worked without specialized tools; and its low melting point makes it easy to cast. So gold, like native copper as we will soon see, was gathered and formed into simple decorative shapes long before the true metal ages began; but its very malleability made it almost useless for the manufacture of tools and weapons.

The earliest source of gold was alluvial, as is perhaps reflected in the mythological story of the Golden Fleece, which even in antiquity was taken to indicate the use of sheep's wool in trapping gold particles suspended in rivers like the Pactolus near Sardis (Document 46). When alluvial (or "placer") deposits had been exhausted, the metal's natural alloys like electrum (a pale yellow amalgam of gold and silver) were mined and smelted by a method called cuppelation, by which the impurities were absorbed by the sides of a small, porous pot in which the ore is heated. Gold was used exclusively for precious ornaments and the like, and in the Greek and Roman periods it was an important base for coinage. The Romans were especially skilled in rolling it and beating it into very thin gold leaf.

Silver. Silver too was used early. It was usually obtained from the lead ore galena (lead sulfide), in which it was present in small quantities as an impurity, or from electrum, its alloy with gold. It too was used for ornaments, expensive tableware, and later for coinage: the common rate of exchange, one unit of gold to ten of silver, reflected the naturally occurring proportion of the two metals in antiquity.

Lead. Lead was a significant by-product of silver working, but its softness and general unattractiveness limited its applications; almost unusable for tools and weapons (except sling bullets), it was employed in weights, for pipes and solder, to fix in place the metal clamps used to bind together building blocks, and to sheath the hulls of ships to prevent sea creatures from boring through the wood.

Copper/Bronze. As with placer gold, easily obtained native and alluvial copper was being hammered into decorative objects as early as 5000 B.C.E. (hence the last two millennia of the Neolithic are referred to as the Chalcolithic, or "Copper-stone" Age). Its stronger alloy bronze was originally made accidentally, since the copper used by the Sumerians contained naturally more than 10 percent tin. Bronze is superior to pure copper because it is harder and more easily worked, and became most common after ca. 1600 B.C.E., when metalworkers discovered how to obtain its separate ingredients by smelting copper sulfides (like chalcopyrite) and tin oxide (cassiterite), ores that were found in Germany, Spain, and Britain, prompting the opening up of new trade routes to central and western Europe. Bronze, too, was used for coinage—the cheapest denominations—and was commonly cast as tools and weapons. Brass (an alloy of copper and zinc) was also manufactured in antiquity, but was never as common as bronze.

Iron. Because of the complex techniques necessary for smelting and working iron, it remained a relatively precious metal until well into the first millennium B.C.E. Even the later Greeks and Romans were unable to keep the metal at a high enough temperature (about 1,500 degrees Celsius) for long enough to produce cast iron, so it was always worked by forging in antiquity, which in fact produced a kind of natural steel, since the iron absorbed carbon from the processes of smelting and forging.

The Bronze-Age Hittites of central Anatolia were the first to use it for weapons, and they jealously protected its manufacture to give them a military edge over their neighbors. But with the collapse of their empire about 1200 B.C.E., itinerant metalworkers carried the secret technique westward and introduced it to other societies like the Dorians of northern Greece, whose subsequent migration southwards into the peninsula was made easier because of their weapons' superiority to the bronze ones of their Mycenaean Greek cousins.

Bars of iron were one of the earliest media of exchange, while the metal was still relatively rare and before the invention of coinage. But by about 700 B.C.E., it was so common as to be considered base, a fitting metal to represent what Hesiod saw as the degenerate culture of his day (see Document 54). Unattractive though it might be, iron was inexpensive and durable enough to be the Greeks' and Romans' primary metal for tools and weapons and, significantly, the first metal to benefit the large, rural, peasant populations in the form of hoes, axes, and sheaths for their plow shares. As a farmer himself, Hesiod might have appreciated this.

Mining

The best examples of Greek and Roman mines are the Athenian silver mines at Laurion in Attica and the deep Roman workings at Rio Tinto in Spain. In the latter, shafts were driven 30 m down, even beneath the water table, and were kept dry by a series of eight pairs of water wheels turned by animals on treadmills. At Laurion, the galena was hacked from the rock face using wetted wooden wedges and iron picks and chisels, in spaces too low to stand erect in; by a rope-and-pulley arrangement the ore was removed from the galleries—some of them over 100 m deep—to the surface, where it was ground to a fine powder in reciprocal mills that resembled those for processing grain, and then separated by flotation (the heavier metal being left behind) before being taken to the smelting furnaces.

To be a miner in antiquity was to be a doomed man (Document 47). Consider the hazards recounted by our ancient sources: subterranean galleries largely without artificial reinforcement; tunnels so low that miners often worked in a supine position, unless of course they were small boys; galleries beneath the water table, subject to flooding; noxious fumes from the earth; intermittent ventilation through air shafts from the surface; fires lit in the galleries to heat the rock faces, the scalding steam created when cold water was thrown on the heated face to crack it, and the shards of stone that exploded from the face; and the application of acid to the cracks, to split them further. Trauma, asphyxiation, poisoning, burns, drowning. Little wonder that life expectancy for miners was less than a year; and little wonder, too, that no free man would be willing to assume this occupation. So the mineral wealth of Athens and Rome—what was the real foundation of their cultural achievements—relied largely on the expendable lives of slaves.

Metallurgy

It was the early third millennium B.C.E. before the smelting of a metal from its ore was discovered, almost certainly through the use of the pottery kiln, which was the only source of heat that could reach sufficiently high temperatures: it may be that a copper ore used initially to produce a blue glaze on pottery was inadvertently smelted during firing in the kiln, producing droplets of pure copper that would have excited any Bronze-Age artisan. From that moment on, because smelting requires considerable skill, full-time specialists were needed, and metallurgy could be practiced only in those highly productive agricultural areas that could support such artisans.

In addition to the ores that we have examined above, the principal requirements for metallurgy are fuel, air supply, furnaces, and specialized tools (Document 48).

Fuel. Charcoal was the commonest material for fuel, since coal is not plentiful in the Mediterranean area, and it is the only source of heat that could attain sufficiently high temperatures for tasks like smelting ores and firing pottery. It was manufactured throughout the Mediterranean, not just from trees but from brush, roots, and even animal dung if these inferior fuels were all that was available. The process was simple: the raw material was piled in a heap, set alight, and covered with damp clods of earth; the slow burning over a long period concentrated the reduced material to pure charcoal, which would thereafter burn with an intense, concentrated heat.

Air supply. Since the highest temperatures could be reached only in an oxygen-rich environment, a strong and consistent supply of air was essential. Natural wind and fans may have been used early on, but the former was inconsistent and the latter inefficient. So blast air for the furnaces was produced by blowpipes (reeds fitted with a clay nozzle) and later by bellows, first in the form of skin bags with a nozzle attached to one "leg" and a simple flap valve cut into the other, later (as seen in Egyptian tomb paintings) two wooden panels joined by an accordion of skin and worked in pairs, one under each foot of the worker, who would draw the air into the pump by raising the upper panel with a string, and expel it by stepping down with his foot, thus producing an uninterrupted blast. Similar accordion bellows were used through late antiquity: note the slight figure to the right of the furnace in Figure 20.

Furnaces. Though no physical evidence has survived, the earliest furnaces were probably simple heaps of ore piled on burning wood, though it would be difficult to tap off either the slag or the desired metal from such an arrangement. Far superior were the large shaft furnaces of the Iron Age, modeled on the earlier pottery kilns, their heat source separated from the ore, fitted with bellows for blast air and taps for removing the slag or the molten metal, and capable of being operated continuously (Figure 20). They were used widely for smelting copper, lead, and iron; precious metals like gold, on the other hand, were refined in smaller furnaces where crucibles held the precious metal separate from the charcoal.

Metalworking

Casting. Casting was the preferred technique for forming into usable tools those metals and alloys with a relatively low melting point. Gold and copper were first cast in open one-piece molds made of sandstone or

Figure 20. Greek smelting furnace (vase painting, ca. 525 B.C.E.)

clay, a technique that allowed the easy and quick production of standardized designs, but unfortunately left one surface of the ornament or tool flat and (not insignificantly) produced a solid, heavy item that used much precious metal. The invention of two-piece molds corrected the first of these problems, by allowing symmetrical tools to be cast; and the later development of removable cores inserted into the molds solved the second by creating completely hollow pieces of art or tools with hollow shafts for hafting.

Such cast metal tools had several advantages over those of stone: they were thinner and sharper, were more durable, allowed a greater variety of forms, and could be reworked when dull or broken. Typical cast bronze tools included the hafted hammer; axes and adzes; and chisels, drills, saws, and files. Weapons cast of bronze included the dagger with a central strengthening rib; the sword; and spearheads to be fastened to wooden hafts.

Forging. When smelted in antiquity, iron ores produced, not a pure metal as was true of copper, but a slag-like lump of material containing many impurities. This "bloom" was then hammered while hot, to expel extraneous fragments and to combine the iron with residual carbon from the furnace, which produced a kind of unintentional steel that was much harder than pure iron. This was then forged or annealed—hammered into the desired shape while red hot, repeatedly folded and beaten out to realign its particles, then quenched in cold water and reheated—to produce a strong wrought iron especially suited to functions like wheel rims as well as the usual swords, daggers, and knives. The process of forging required new forms of tools itself: metal tongs for holding the hot iron, heavy hammers for pounding it, and anvils to support the repeated blows (Figures 21 and 22, the latter from a contemporary forge in Turkey).

Fine metalworking. At the other end of the scale were many advanced techniques for manufacturing fine and intricate metal objects as diverse as wire, embossed cups, and hollow-cast statuary. Here we must limit ourselves to cire-perdue casting.

In this "lost wax" process of casting fine objects, a layer of wax was placed over a clay core and modeled to the desired shape; another clay

Figure 21. Iron-working (vase painting, ca. 500 B.C.E.)

Figure 22. Iron-working, a forge in central Turkey

casing was placed over top and the wax was melted and removed; the resulting cavity was then filled with molten bronze. When the outer clay casing was removed and the disintegrated core withdrawn, the result was a hollow bronze object, light and sparing of metal. Variants of this technique were devised to cast objects as small as brooches and as large as hollow life-size statuary of bronze.

Both the Greeks and Romans excelled in producing works cast in metal: in the National Archaeological Museum in Athens, the noble statue of Poseidon (or is it Zeus?), his right arm poised to hurl a trident (or thunderbolt); and the life-size horse and jockey that represent the liveliness of the Hellenistic period. And, in Rome, perhaps the most remarkable cast metal sculpture of all: the Emperor Marcus Aurelius astride his horse, dominating the Capitoline Hill since Michelangelo placed him there. (The statue now on the Campidoglio is a copy, the original housed in the adjacent museum, protected from the dangers of Rome's urban environment.)

CERAMICS

Pottery has been called the "wastepaper of antiquity" because it was cheap enough to be discarded when no longer useful or appealing. The large vessels in which oil, wine, and grain were transported to the harbors of the ancient world were usually thrown out behind the warehouses once their contents had been emptied: at Rome, for example, the result is a mountain of broken pieces of pottery that still rises some 35 m beside the Tiber River. Museums throughout the Mediterranean area are similarly overflowing with ceramic displays, especially of the elegantly decorated Greek Black-Figure and Red-Figure pots produced in Athens in the late sixth and fifth centuries B.C.E.

Early Pottery

The history of ceramics is really the history of settled life and civilization: it was only the nomadic hunters of the Paleolithic Age who had no need for storage containers and no safe way of transporting such fragile objects. It is now realized that the invention of pottery does not always coincide with the beginning of the Neolithic Revolution; but the settled life of an agricultural society usually requires such vessels for the storage and transportation of foodstuffs, and they are cheap only if they are produced in the quantity required by whole villages. Fine examples of the earliest known Mediterranean pottery are the handmade and decorated vessels from sites like Hacilar (now in Turkey), dating to before 6500 B.C.E.

Because natural clay lacks porosity and often cracks when heated, it was often mixed with a tempering material (for example, powdered shell or chopped straw). The clay was then manually pulverized, levigated (purified by sedimentation, by which the heavier coarse particles settled to the bottom and the lighter impurities floated to the top), and finally kneaded to eliminate air. The earliest method of shaping it was to squeeze a ball of clay between the thumb and forefinger; the later coil technique involved the spiral coiling of a sausage roll of clay to form the walls of the pot; the walls were then thinned and smoothed by some convex tool on the inside and by a concave paddle or palm of the hand on the outside.

The pot was then left to dry in the open air until the water content was only about 10 percent of the original; a slip of fine clay and water was then applied, the surface was burnished with a pebble, and decorations were incised or painted. The technique of firing the pots hard had probably been discovered accidentally, either from the firing of clay-covered hearths, or from baskets lined with clay that were dropped in a hot fire: in fact, we still have a few very early ceramic fragments that show the "ghosts" of this basketry. Kilns were not used at first for firing; instead, pots were piled in a heap and covered with straw for fuel, a technique that often caused uneven firing and mass wastage.

Developed Ceramic Techniques

Kilns in the Bronze and Iron Ages were able to obtain temperatures above 1,200 degrees Celsius: they were usually cylindrical or beehive in shape, with a separate furnace connected by a conduit. The more elementary vertical kiln, with the pots separated from the fire by a perforated clay floor, was often difficult to load with pots, and the heat inside was not always uniform. The horizontal kiln, with the hot gasses entering from the side, at least partially solved these problems.

The potter's wheel was the first important mechanical invention of the Bronze Age: with it, pottery making became a full-time specialization. The earliest form of the wheel was a pivoted baked clay disc heavy enough to revolve of its own momentum when set spinning by a hand, stick, or strap; but it was a slow wheel, awkwardly close to the ground, and usually required a second worker to keep the wheel in motion. So Minoan and Mycenaean pottery was not "thrown," but was gradually built up on a slowly rotating disc. Decoration in the Bronze Age was either by painting or glazing (the application of a slip of powdered glass reheated until it began to fuse). Crete produced some of the finest designs and decorations of the period. It was in the decoration of these pots that the Minoans excelled: beautiful polychrome motifs of plant and marine life (particularly octopuses) were designed to flow freely with the contours of the delicate shapes.

The expansion of trade in the Archaic Age (ca. 700–500 B.C.E.) saw the development of a true pottery industry in many Greek city-states, and ceramic vessels were exported as works of art as well as containers for the shipment of products. Wares from Corinth and Athens were especially fine and popular at this time, and were exported throughout the Mediterranean and central Europe. At about the same time, production of pottery was made easier and cheaper with the Greeks' invention of the fast kick-wheel, which elevated the potter above the surface of the ground and allowed pots to be thrown and turned: smaller ones in one piece, larger ones in sections that were joined at structural points like the neck and body, body and foot, and handle and body.

Even as early as the Neolithic, potters had made decorative use of a clay's tendency to change color in firing, depending on the nature of the gasses present (either oxidizing or reducing in nature): a two-toned decoration of a pot could be obtained by covering part with ash to keep out oxygen, which would turn the clay black. By mastering a more elaborate sequence of firing the pots, Greek craftsmen produced magnificent polychrome wares, with black and red the primary colors. A preliminary sketch was made on the clay with a stylus, and the whole surface was then covered with a wash containing iron (this would stay red or change to black according to the nature of the firing). In Red-Figure pottery, which became popular after ca. 530 B.C.E., the potter covered the background and details with glaze while the figures were left (or "reserved") covered only by the iron wash. The vessel was first fired under oxidizing conditions; the vents were then closed, cutting out the oxygen and rendering the whole pot black in the "reducing" environment, and the firing temperature increased sufficiently to fuse the glaze; finally, the vents were reopened and the pot re-oxidized, a process that affected only the figures that were not covered by the now-hardened glaze: these turned back to red while the glazed, nonporous background remained black. It will come as no surprise that the ancient process is only imperfectly understood today and has never really been successfully duplicated.

Pottery Shapes

Though it is usually the decoration of ancient pottery that attracts our attention now, it must be remembered that the working of clay into ceramics was more technology than art, and the shapes of vessels were gradually perfected to fulfill specific functions; indeed, much can be learned about the economy as well as the society of an ancient culture by studying the functional shapes of their pots. Drinking cups show *symposia* scenes, *lekythoi* to hold oils offered at tombs are given funereal scenes, and so on.

The shapes of pots varied according to their use: three-handled *hydriae* with narrow mouths for carrying water; two-handled amphorae with pointed bottoms for shipping and storing grains and liquids; large kraters for mixing wine with water, the elegant *oinochoe* for serving it, and the two-handled saucer-like kylix from which to drink it; cylindrical cosmetic boxes and small perfume bottles; rather coarse, everyday cooking pots and ovens; warp weights and spindle whorls for weaving; and lamps for use with oil.

GLASS

Around 2000 B.C.E., Egyptian potters developed a method of fusing a silica sand with an alkali to produce true glass, which was then either cast in molds (like faience) or ground and carved when cold and set; but the resulting product was rarely more than a simple bead. After ca. 1600 B.C.E. rods of molten glass were coiled into the shape of a bottle; or a core of sand in a bag was dipped into viscous glass to form the vessel. These techniques remained dominant until the end of the first century B.C.E., when glassblowing began in the Levant; the blown object was often cut or engraved when cold, to add further decoration and to produce exceptionally fine objects of great value (Document 49). For obvious reasons, glass was never in common use in antiquity, and even rarer are vessels that have survived intact.

CHAPTER 8

CONCLUSIONS: TECHNOLOGY, INNOVATION, AND SOCIETY IN ANTIQUITY

This last chapter examines two important elements of technology in antiquity: first, the extraordinary if often theoretical technical innovation of the Greeks and Romans from the Hellenistic period to the height of the empire; and second, the social, political, and technical impediments that prevented them from applying much of that knowledge in a broad and useful way.

Of the many aspects of the second half of this chapter, we will discuss two themes in particular: the apparently widespread prejudice against manual labor and, by extension, technology; and the social and technical factors in antiquity that severely limited the application of new techniques that we would expect today.

HIGH TECHNOLOGY IN THE ANCIENT WORLD

There are two themes in the first section of this chapter: first, how highly evolved mechanical technology was in the ancient world; and second, how dependent our modern technological advances are on the intelligence and creativity of our Greek and Roman ancestors. The complex mechanical devices described by the Greek inventor and engineer Hero of Alexandria will give us the evidence to examine energy, machines, and high technology in the ancient world. Then we will see how many of the mechanical principles described by Hero reappeared in later eras, especially in the years leading up to the Industrial Revolution in eighteenth-century Europe.

Research and Development in Ancient Alexandria

Hero lived and worked in the Museum at Alexandria around the middle of the first century C.E., at a time when the entire Mediterranean world was under Roman authority. Of the many cities that Alexander had founded and named after himself, it was the Alexandria positioned on one of the seven mouths of the Nile River that would have the greatest impact on the future of western civilization. There, in the third century, one of Alexander's Ptolemaic successors founded the museum and its attendant library, the kind of state-supported think tank that most contemporary scholars can only dream of. Ironically, little of this great city survives in physical form, though its intellectual spirit is very much a part of our modern culture.

The unusual blend of pure science with engineering, of both intellectual inquiry and applied technology that existed in the museum was well described by Philo of Byzantium, one of Hero's predecessors: "Engineers from Alexandria achieved advances in the theory and construction of siege engines, because ambitious kings gave them large subsidies to encourage technology. Not everything can be accomplished by the theoretical methods of pure mechanics, but much can be discovered through experiment" (*Artillery Manual* 50.3).

The written history of mechanics, both theoretical and applied, can reasonably be said to have started with Aristotle in the fourth century B.C.E., though his frequent references to the "vulgar" aspects of craftsmanship have prompted many scholars to assign to other writers his works on practical applications of scientific principles (works like his *Mechanika*). At Alexandria, Ctesibius was an early pioneer, although it is only from later sources like Hero that we know of his designs of water clocks, force pumps, and a pipe organ. Philo of Byzantium followed Ctesibius in the third century, and his surviving work, *Elements of Mechanics*, includes much material on the sort of pressure mechanisms that delighted Hero 300 years later. Archimedes of Syracuse was one of the great technological geniuses of all time, whose productive life was tragically cut short during the Roman capture of his city. And, on the Roman side, we have the architectural handbook of Vitruvius, the tenth and last book of which describes many of the "practical" machines that appeared from Ctesibius to Hero.

Among the works that we know were written by Hero almost a century after Vitruvius, the two most important for our purposes are the *Automatopoetike*, on the construction of two miniature mechanical puppet theaters, and the *Pneumatika*, on pressure mechanisms that employ air, water, steam, and siphons. In the preface to the latter, Hero clearly describes a double motivation—the practical and the fantastic—for his inventions: "By the union of air, earth, fire, and water, and the concurrence of three or four elementary principles, various combinations are created, some of which supply the most pressing needs of human life, while others simply produce amazement and alarm." Though often accused by modern scholars of wasting his talents on the invention of useless gadgets and toys to amuse his royal patrons or deceive gullible worshippers, Hero in fact shared in a long tradition of fascination with humans' creation of machines that imitate living beings, a tradition that began with Homer, who in *The Iliad* described magical robots built by the god Hephaestus on Mount Olympus: "He busied himself among his bellows, for he was making tripods, 20 in all, to stand along the wall of his well-built house. He put golden wheels beneath the base of each one so that, of their own accord, they might enter the assembly of the gods and go back again to his house—a marvel to see" (18.370ff). Robots figure often, too, in descriptions of Hellenistic parades and celebrations. Athenaeus describes one such automaton in an elaborate procession mounted in Alexandria by Ptolemy Philadelphus in the middle of the third century: "A four-wheeled wagon eight cubits wide was pulled along by 60 men. On it sat an image of Nysa, dressed in a yellow cloak with gold spangles. This image stood up automatically, without anyone touching it, poured milk from a golden cup, and sat back down again" (*Deipnosophistae* 5.198e–f).

Hero's Machines

Simple machines. A few relatively simple machines devised by Hero would have a huge impact on the mechanization and automation of later cultures, especially our own.

For one of his puppet theaters, Hero devised a system of proto-cams to cause a pivoted arm to rise and fall in a hammering motion (Figure 23), a simple device that reappears in any number of modern machines.

As an illustration of the state of gearing and axle mechanisms in Hero's time, the odometer (described first by Vitruvius) used a series of cogged wheels and worm gears to decrease the revolutions of the vehicle's axle to a relatively slow rate, producing over a measured distance a gradual rotation of a

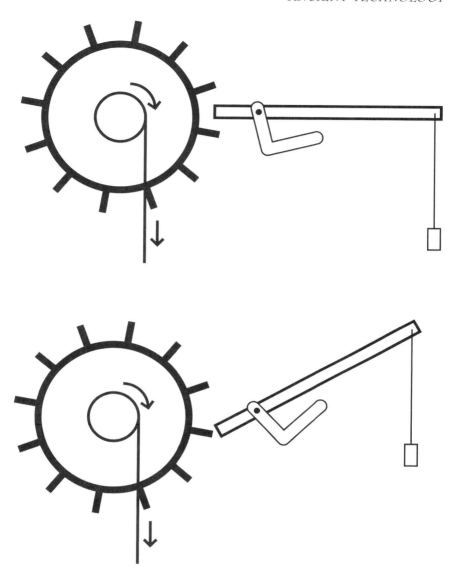

Figure 23. Early cams (Hero)

pierced upper plate, through which marbles fell into a vertical tube, to be counted later to determine the distance traveled (Figure 24). He also invented for his *automata* a combination axle that allowed wheels on the same axle to rotate at different speeds, the basis of an essential element—the differential axle—in the design of the automobile eighty generations later.

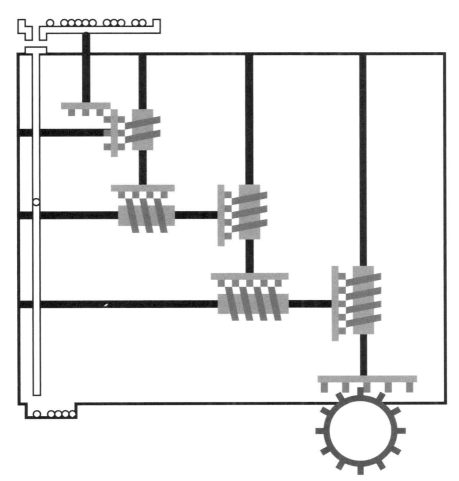

Figure 24. Odometer (Vitruvius and Hero)

A novel application of the lever can be seen in Hero's coin-operated holy water dispenser: it was not the world's first vending machine, but its basic principles are those used in many such devices until recently (Figure 25). A coin inserted in the slot strikes one end of a balance beam, lifting the other end temporarily and drawing a plug out of a pipe, allowing the water to flow. As the balance returns to equilibrium, the plug drops, seals the pipe, and the flow ceases.

One of the serious limitations on the functionality of ancient machines was the lack of an efficient and portable source of energy to power them. For his movable puppet theaters, Hero devised a technique of

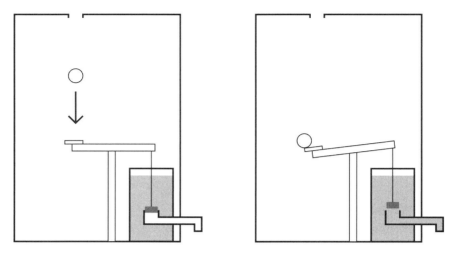

Figure 25. Vending machine for holy water (Hero)

self-propulsion that is reminiscent of an hourglass: the upper bin is filled
with grain or sand, which gradually filters through a small hole into the
lower chamber, causing the weight resting above it to descend with it,
drawing up the cord that is wrapped around the wheel's axle, which then
rotates (Figure 26). The restrictions of this form of propulsion are obvious: a very low output of energy, and a very limited period of operation.

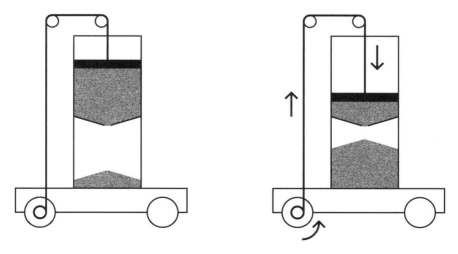

Figure 26. Automated stage machinery (Hero)

This was one technological hurdle that even Hero and his colleagues were unable to surmount.

Complex pressure machines. Hero and his fellow Alexandrian inventors took some simple machines—the screw, axle, weights, and gears—and combined them with forms of pressure—air, water, steam, and the vacuum—to construct complex mechanisms, many of no obvious or immediate practical function, but all eventually leading to the fine instrumentation necessary for the advanced technologies of today.

His bird *automaton*, operated simply by a primitive form of crank, uses gear wheels to cause the figure of the bird to rotate, and the compression of air to have it whistle (Figure 27). As the secondary spool is turned, it drops the metal bell further into the water, thus compressing the air inside and forcing it out the whistle.

Another device, which automatically refills a wine cup as it is emptied, uses a control valve to regulate the flow (Figure 28). Since a liquid

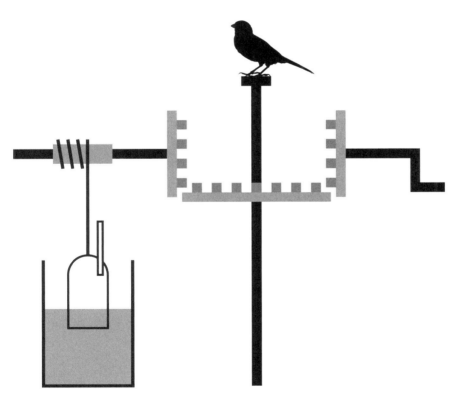

Figure 27. Automated bird (Hero)

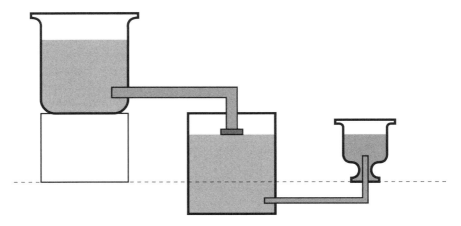

Figure 28. Bottomless wine cup (Hero)

in a closed system will find a common level, as the wine is removed from the cup, it is replaced by wine from the central reservoir to which it is attached by a pipe. While the surface of the reservoir falls, a float falls with it, opening the faucet attached to a primary reservoir and allowing wine in, sufficient to seal the faucet again when the float rises. This is a good example of a mechanism that was probably never constructed: first, it is difficult to understand how the goblet, which must remain fixed to the table, could actually be drunk from; and second, a float valve of this sort is extraordinarily difficult to construct. So, if not used to amaze spectators, why did Hero describe it? Perhaps to illustrate theoretical mechanical principles in a practical way, using a common experience of his time; to put it another way, he was perhaps interested in explaining, in an understandable way, principles that he knew were significant, but for which he could give no immediate practical application.

This is certainly not the case with Ctesibius' double-cylinder water pump that used pistons to create water pressure, and valves to regulate its flow (Figure 29). As one handle was lifted, it created a vacuum that opened the inlet valve and sucked water into the cylinder; when the handle was then pressed down, the pressure closed the inlet valve and forced the water out of the cylinder through the flap valve. By operating in tandem, the two cylinders could project a steady stream of water through a rotating nozzle added by Hero to create the world's first efficient fire pump.

Hero's most ingenious machine employed a whole series of mechanisms and physical principles to cause a pair of temple doors to open, apparently miraculously: the expansion of air when heated, displacement

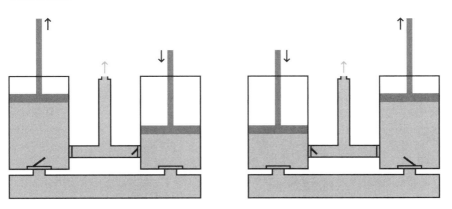

Figure 29. Dual-piston water pump (Ctesibius and Hero)

of matter, a siphon, gravity, pulleys, rotary motion, counterweights, and the principles of a sealed system (Figure 30). When the worshipper lit a fire on the hollow altar, the air within was heated and expanded, finding an exit through a pipe leading into a sealed metal sphere half-full of water. There the compressed air began to displace the water, which in

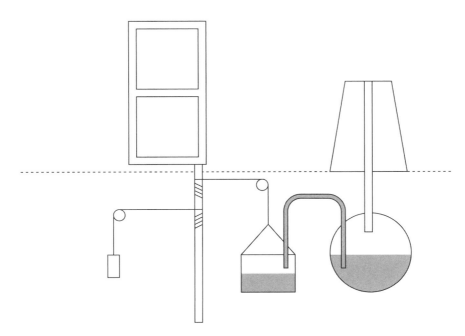

Figure 30. Temple doors that open mysteriously (Hero)

turn was forced out through a bent tube into an open bucket. As the bucket became heavier with the water, it descended, pulling with it ropes attached to the posts of the temple doors. As these were rotated, the doors opened. Now, because this is a closed system, the opposite occurs when the fire is extinguished: the air in the altar contracts as it cools, creating a vacuum that sucks air back from the sphere; this in turn creates another vacuum, drawing the water out of the pail, which becomes lighter and (because it is attached to a counterweight) rises, loosening the ropes and turning the doorposts in the opposite direction to close the doors. This seems remarkably like a Rube Goldberg device, and has about as much practical point to it; but for its time it is a remarkable display of knowledge of physical principles.

Finally, we come to what is surely Hero's best known invention: the steam-powered turbine, which foreshadows the steam engines of the late eighteenth century and the jet planes of the twenty-first century (Figure 31). Water in a closed reservoir is heated to boiling, and the resulting steam finds an escape through a pair of bent tubes that are attached to a freely rotating metal sphere. As the sphere fills with steam, it is made to spin rapidly as the steam then shoots out of a pair of bent jets. The device does work, as has been shown by a laboratory reproduction of the principles. But it is horribly inefficient: great quantities of fuel are required to heat the water, the device must be stopped regularly to be refilled, the joints are difficult to solder, especially at the points of rotation, and the contraption produces no torque, but is simply a rapidly spinning sphere that generates an estimated 0.1 horsepower and can be stopped by gently placing a hand on the sphere. The device itself is useless—but the principles on which it is designed are momentous.

Ancient Mechanisms and the Industrial Revolution

Fortunately for the history of Western technology, many of the writings of Hero and some of his predecessors were preserved after the fall of Alexandria to the Arabs in the seventh century; indeed, Arab engineers and scientists were the ones who were largely responsible for maintaining the continuity in Mediterranean engineering from antiquity to the Renaissance. Others of Philo's and Hero's treatises were reproduced during the Middle Ages, often with monkish attempts to translate the material into illustrative diagrams, which are, unfortunately, often less illuminating than the complex text. These manuscripts contained the limits of the knowledge of mechanical and physical principles through the medieval period and Renaissance, until Europeans in the seventeenth century saw

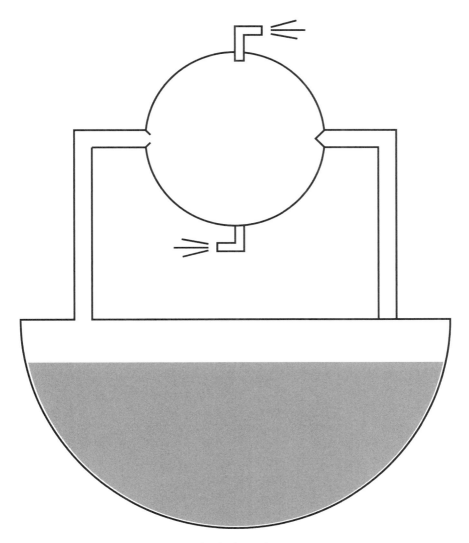

Figure 31. Steam turbine, or aeolipile (Hero)

revolutionary possibilities in them. By this time, Europe was on the verge of another technological revolution, and the mechanics of the ancients, like their literary and artistic accomplishments, were once again in vogue.

Though there is scant explicit evidence for tracing a direct link between these ancient machines and those invented from the late Middle Ages to the Industrial Revolution, a few striking examples suggest that the revolutionary European machines of the time owed their beginnings to the work of Hero and his Alexandrian colleagues. In the medieval period the rotating axle of a Vitruvian waterwheel was fitted to the sort of cams invented by Hero for his *automata*, to power both a bellows and a hammer for use in metalworking. And we have seen how the principle of Hero's screw press, which applied pressure directly on the pressing bed to crush the olives or extract the juice from the grapes, reappeared in the early Renaissance with the European development of the printing press, a machine that has probably had a greater influence than any other on the development of Western civilization and the evolution of modern democracies.

But the connection with the Industrial Revolution in Europe is even more remarkable. Hero's application of the expansion and contraction of air to motivate his miraculously opening temple doors reappeared in the design of Thomas Newcomen's atmospheric steam engine, built in 1712, which used the expansion of steam to drive the piston upward, and introduced cold water into the cylinder to condense the steam, turning it into a smaller volume of water, and creating a vacuum that draws the piston downward. All the elements of Ctesibius' piston pump appeared in James Watt's pumping engine in the eighteenth century, which combined the ancient principles of the piston and steam pressure to produce a more efficient engine than Newcomen's, and introduced the Industrial Revolution into western Europe. It was Watt, too, who was largely responsible for the development of mobile steam engines, in the form of locomotives that were quickly to replace canal boats and the draft animals that had been used to drag and carry just about everything since their domestication in the Neolithic Age 10,000 years earlier. All of the components of his engine—steam power, pistons, rocker arms, cams, valves—had been used by Hero in his "gadgets" at the dawn of the first millennium.

IMPEDIMENTS TO TECHNOLOGICAL INNOVATION

Why, then, did the ancients themselves not apply their mechanical principles to initiate an industrial revolution 1700 years earlier? In examining this complex topic, we are faced with the problem of our own industrial background. Our modern lives are dominated by efficiency, innovation, and consumption to an extent that makes it difficult for us to evaluate neutrally a culture in which these values were not paramount. The Industrial Revolution that began in the eighteenth century has instilled in us an expectation of unlimited material growth, and inevitably skews our evaluation of societies that are not so obsessed. The analysis of ancient progress by many scholars is set before the background of the Industrial Revolution, and they have often asked why there was no technological revolution in antiquity, at a time when, as we have just seen, most mechanical and physical principles were already well understood. Better, perhaps, to ask why there should have been a technological revolution. While it is certainly not wrong to use modern developments in an attempt to understand the ancient situation, it is important to beware of imposing modern values on ancient societies. Simply put, our twenty-first-century concept of progress is not applicable to antiquity.

Assessing Technological Innovation in Antiquity

The question why there was no "industrial revolution" in Greek and Roman antiquity has been widely discussed since the advent of our own, modern Industrial Revolution. Reasons that were put forward during the first half of the last century include upper-class prejudice against manual labor, widespread slavery, lack of financial resources and of raw materials, inefficient land transport, and insufficient implementation of known scientific principles. To some, the main impediment to industrial development in antiquity was the economic irrelevance of technology and the widespread investment in the purchase of agricultural land and prestigious objects by wealthy individuals. As a corollary to all of this, scholars generally list various conditions that need to be fulfilled for new technologies to be invented and widely applied. Population size, available capital, power sources, and raw materials are commonly taken as indispensable prerequisites for such development to take place.

Modern opinion on this question has undergone significant change in the past two generations. In 1965, Moses Finley argued that antiquity, and the Roman Empire in particular, was a period of technological stagnation, and his view was accepted as authoritative for three decades. More recently, scholars like Kevin Greene have questioned seriously that assumption, relying more heavily on what they see as the more reliable evidence from archaeological excavation. As one example, consider waterwheels. Some technical authors from antiquity, like Philo of Byzantium and Vitruvius, describe various designs, but the general impression is that they were relatively uncommon, because of both their cost and the general absence of steadily flowing rivers in the eastern Mediterranean. Material evidence, on the other hand, is very well preserved in an anaerobic, waterlogged environment, so these important devices tend to survive rather well in the archaeological record, especially in

northwestern Europe, and contradict their relative absence in literature. Even more obvious evidence for Roman innovation can be found
in their accomplished use of concrete and the radical change in building construction that took place between the Roman Republic and late
antiquity, and which is nowhere reflected in their surviving building
manuals.

There is another important issue in this regard, what one scholar has
called the "blind spot" of innovation. We should recognize from our own
experience over the past few generations the difficulty any society has in
recognizing gaps in its own knowledge. The Romans, for example, did not
know that they did not know electricity. So, at least until recently, societies consider that there is no need to innovate when everything works
satisfactorily and no new serendipitous discovery or change in external
conditions compels development to take a quantum leap. Such compelling factors—for example, the advent of precise time measurement, the
development of movable type, or the discovery of hydrocarbons as a fuel
source—are not the rule, but the exception. In their absence, however,
technology does not stand still; it develops in smaller, yet significant
steps that, to a modern mind accustomed to rapid change, may appear as
stagnation. This is true all the more if literature seems to suggest a general
disdain for technological innovation. While it cannot be proved, it seems
likely that it was the individuals who used tools and devices on a daily
basis who introduced these gradual improvements. These developments
were not made to be commercially "marketed" in a modern sense, but
merely to make life easier for the individual laborer, artisan, or workshop.
The dissemination of improvements was not a priority in an economy that
was traditionally based on subsistence. Technological development on
this level would explain the absence of literary evidence and the localized
occurrence of sophisticated devices such as particular watermills in the
archaeological record. What is more, technological innovation need not
be expressed only through tools and machines, but can also be perceived
in improved methods of managing existing resources such as in agriculture
or the military; and in those respects, the Romans were certainly very
expert.

Prejudice against Manual Labor

Every scholar who writes about ancient attitudes regarding technology
inevitably mentions the prejudice of our surviving authors against the
practice of what they term "mere mechanics." The Greek word for this is
banausia, which is almost always employed by classical writers with a

perceptible sneer. There are hundreds of examples from ancient literature in which the authors make dismissive comments about manual labor and the practical, physical application of knowledge, which we—albeit anachronistically—label as scientific (Documents 50 and 51). Aristotle is a prominent example, and even the highly practical Archimedes refused to record his inventions because he considered them demeaning. The causes of this negative opinion in part were the natural disdain of the wealthy elite for manual labor, but this scorn was not applied universally to all technologies. There were writers who held manual labor in high esteem, of whom one example is Hesiod from archaic Greece. And Roman senators in particular are effusive in their praise of agriculture, and attribute Rome's success to the hardy stock of republican farmers; still, they themselves were absentee landlords rather than dirt farmers. But the prejudice also had an economic basis: technology requires the investment of capital, which was controlled by the upper classes, who traditionally invested in land rather than commercial production, and so were dismissive of inventions that might improve productivity. Here, then, is one reason why technological progress was, by our expectations, extraordinarily slow and modest in antiquity. We should not feel particularly superior in this regard. Prejudices against manual labor in certain social circles are not merely an ancient phenomenon, but existed during the Industrial Revolution and persist even today. The difference then was that the prejudice was almost universal among people who had any significant influence in what we would call "research and development."

Social Constraints

Early in their history, the Greeks attributed technological innovation to the mythical Prometheus, who was given credit for introducing to humankind fire and all the subsequent technical inventions, including numeracy and literacy (Document 52). At the same time, they were aware that humans derived much of their innovation from a close familiarity with natural processes and from a motivation of necessity for survival. So there was a general acceptance that technological advance was both good (as divinely inspired) and necessary. Yet our (aristocratic) sources suggest that it was otherwise. Part of this is due to the class-based prejudices that we discussed above, but there were several other social elements that contributed to the general reluctance to adopt technological advances.

The rural life. In both Greek and Roman societies, the agricultural life was considered the only manual labor worthy of a free citizen. There were good reasons for this attitude: the fact is that, even at the height of the Roman Empire, perhaps 90 percent of the working population was actively engaged in the production, transportation, processing, or selling of food; and both cultures had early in their development relied on the simple and solid virtues of peasant farmers for their political and military successes (though this is often exaggerated by later urbane writers), to such a degree that Roman senators, for example, were legally required to invest most of their wealth in land rather than trade or industry. This is not a situation that favors promotion of innovative technology.

Urban employment. The Greek and Roman economies were based on labor-intensive production, and the state relied to a great extent on industries (if they can be called that in antiquity, when most enterprises involved household or cottage production) to keep citizens employed (Document 53). If rulers were unwilling to invest in and accept the social and financial risks of innovation, then their citizens could hardly be expected to act differently. So a shoemaker, for example, who wanted to increase production to meet increasing demand for his wares would establish a second factory employing an equal number of workers as the first, unaware that the same output might be achieved by applying new technology or efficiencies in the old workshop.

Slavery. Careful examination of literary and epigraphic texts suggests that, in any of the Roman provinces, and in rural as well as urban environments, something between a quarter and a third of the population were slaves. Though we find this difficult to comprehend now, it has been a short century and a half since slavery was abolished in the United States and only slightly longer in the British Empire. Slavery was a simple fact of life in antiquity. Though many aristocratic writers, like the Younger Seneca in the first century C.E., advocated sympathetic treatment of slaves ("It is just a matter of luck that you were born free and he a slave"), all were aware of the economy's reliance on slave labor, and not one proposed its abolition. So there was a real danger inherent in any technological innovation that would reduce the reliance on slave labor: if they cannot be kept occupied, how can we control them?

Pessimism. There is a general belief in the contemporary world that life will become better as the years advance, that progress is both good and inevitable. To many ancients, as we observed earlier, the opposite was true: the best times were in the distant past, and contemporary life is debased. The most vocal advocate of this pessimism was Hesiod, a farmer in Boeotia in the Archaic Age, who is best known for his description of the five ages of humankind, which details the progressive decline from the Golden Age, when humans and gods coexisted, to the base Iron Age of his own time, full of constant labor and sorrow (Document 54). In a culture that believes in the continuing degradation of society, there is little incentive to find relief in technological innovation.

Technical Constraints

Compounding what we have just discussed, there were real limitations in technology that inhibited progress in antiquity. Here we present just two, though they are perhaps the most significant: the lack of a portable source of high-quality fuel, and the inability of ancient methods of timekeeping to create a standardized means of producing goods.

Fuel. As we saw earlier, the principal high-intensity fuel of antiquity was charcoal, a nonrenewable resource that is as vulnerable as our modern oil reserves, but not nearly as productive. But the difficulty was not so much in the thermal value of charcoal as in its portability: the ancients were never able to devise a method of directing the energy of charcoal to operate their machines. It was this deficiency that prevented Hero's steam turbine from functioning efficiently.

Timekeeping. Again, our study of ancient methods of keeping time has revealed some serious deficiencies, not the least of which was the inability to construct a simple and regular system of recording hours. Without that kind of regulation, employment was chaotic and production of goods unpredictable. If the point of commerce is to produce the greatest number of units at the lowest cost, the ancients were hobbled by an outdated and inefficient system of time management. But from their point of view, of course, production and consumption were not the principal drivers of the economy.

So we return to the observation made earlier: that it is inappropriate to judge ancient economic and social models by modern standards and expectations. But (someone could suggest) would they not have been better off if they had had the imagination to discover modern theories of progress and utility? Perhaps. But we should give them credit for the remarkable things they did discover, and acknowledge that our apparent advances are, first, dependent on their earlier efforts, and second, not in all cases universally beneficial to our quality of life.

BIOGRAPHIES

Apart from those engineers and inventors whose written work still survives—people like Hero of Alexandria and Vitruvius—we know unfortunately little about the lives and creations of those men and (especially) women who conceived revolutionary ideas, applied new techniques to old procedures, and advanced the technological bases of human life in antiquity. In fact, in most cases we do not know even their identity. The person who first combined the elevated pottery wheel with the momentum of a foot-operated flywheel to replace the slow, awkward, and uncomfortable squat wheel contributed enormously to the welfare of humanity, and deserves recognition at least on a level with that awarded to Archimedes for his water screw, but he (almost certainly "he" in this case) remains yet another unknown inventor.

In this biographical section, I have for the most part limited entries to people who actively advanced technology, and have excluded those whose contribution to ancient technology is largely the fact that they wrote about it: so there is no Homer, Vergil, or Younger Pliny here. Nor are there any women. Though we have some record of female scientists—Hypatia of Alexandria is one good example from late antiquity—I have been unable to discover any ancient technical invention attributed to a named woman. That there were many, I have no doubt, not only in the traditionally female pursuits of food gathering and processing, textiles, and medical technology, but (if the tantalizing fragments we have about the ninth-century Assyrian queen Semiramis are any guide) even in military, civil, and hydraulic engineering.

Archimedes

Archimedes was born in the mid-280s B.C.E., in the Greek city of Syracuse on the east coast of Sicily. It seems likely, to judge from the small bits of evidence that we have for his life, that he studied in the museum at Alexandria, before returning to Syracuse under the patronage of its long-reigning king, Hieron II.

He was arguably the most learned and influential scientist and inventor of all antiquity. He wrote profusely about his mathematical discoveries in particular, and over a dozen works survive, either in Greek or in Arabic translation, describing his ground-breaking work in calculating surface areas and volumes of spheres and cylinders, the value of pi, parabolas, and a way of expressing extraordinarily large numbers, using 100,000,000 as a base (a remarkable leap of logic, since in Greek the largest named number was 10,000, a myriad).

Unfortunately, he was reluctant to commit to paper his equally significant and wide-ranging contributions to the development of machines in antiquity, thinking (like any good aristocrat) that such practical inventions were not really worthy of his attention. So we are left with a series of anecdotes recorded by others (Cicero, Vitruvius, and especially Plutarch's *Life of Marcellus* 14–19) to give us a sense of his technical accomplishments.

Perhaps the most famous story told of Archimedes relates his discovery that a solid body submerged in a liquid displaces its own volume. Hieron, it seems, had commissioned a solid gold wreath for dedication to the gods, but worried that the final product was not pure and contained lesser metals of the same weight. Archimedes, always exercising his mind even when at the public baths, noticed that, as he sank deeper in the tub, more water spilled over the edge; realizing that his body displaced, not its weight in water, but its volume, he is said to have leapt out and, without lingering to dress, rushed to the palace shouting "I have found it!" (*eureka* in Greek). By first determining the volume of the crown by submerging it in water, then calculating what that volume of gold should weigh, and finally comparing it to the weight of the wreath, he discovered that the crown's volume was indeed greater than the volume of pure gold: the metalworkers had cheated the king.

Another story describes the invention of compound pulleys, for which he was generally given credit. Faced with the dilemma of lifting an enormous ship from the dockyard into the water, he divided the weight among many ropes that were attached to pulleys—in effect, the first use of blocks and tackle—and lifted the ship easily by using mechanical advantage: the ratio of the weight to the modest force required to lift it was the same as the ratio between the small height of the lift and the long distance the rope needed to be pulled. This discovery is similar to Archimedes' observation about the principle of the lever, that if he were given a distant place to stand and a long enough pole, he could move even the earth. And his invention of the screw, which had a practical application in raising water for irrigation, was a third variation on a simple machine (see Document 15 and Figure 10): inclined planes had long been used to help lift material, and the screw is nothing more than an inclined plane wrapped around an axle and enclosed in a cylinder: in retrospect, a simple concept, but the product of an amazingly fertile mind.

Finally, Archimedes invented a dizzying array of war machines to aid his fellow Syracusans in their doomed attempt to repel a siege by the Romans in 212–211 (see Document 26). All illustrate the sort of practical application of theoretical principles for which he was renowned, and which he himself belittled. According to Plutarch, Archimedes testily rebuked a Roman soldier who, during the capture of Syracuse, had discovered him working in his study, and was killed on the spot, despite orders from the Roman commander Marcellus that the great thinker be spared.

Cato the Elder

Marcus Porcius Cato (234–149 B.C.E.) was born into a senatorial family, but one that had not attained any prominence. He was raised on a family estate northeast of Rome, where he presumably inherited the somewhat ruthless approach to agricultural economics typical of his class, and developed the strict morality that would be his defining characteristic both during and after his lifetime.

Like all young senatorial men of the time, he served in the army during the Second Punic War against Hannibal, and then entered politics, serving under the respected Publius Cornelius Scipio Africanus, whose affection for things Greek Cato found difficult to bear. He was the first member of his family to become consul (195), then went to Spain as its governor, and in 184 attained the censorship, an honored position that gave him a legitimate platform from which to attack what he perceived as the conspicuous consumption and lax morality of his fellow Romans.

In his political, legal, and personal life, Cato reflected the traditional Roman values that had long been viewed as providing the solid foundation of the Roman state: devotion to one's religion, state, and family; strict obedience to the laws; social conservatism (hence a stern attitude to women and slaves); a deep distrust of foreign influences (he was said, wrongly, to have refused until his last years to learn Greek); and a

driving passion for accumulating wealth in the form of productive agricultural estates. It was this last that prompted his most famous remark,
which he reiterated at every meeting of the Senate: *Karthago delenda est*,
"Carthage must be destroyed," an invocation prompted more by his wish
to acquire the rich farm lands of North Africa than by any fear of a
humbled Carthage as a military threat.

Cato wrote the first work in Latin prose (now lost), the *Origines*, a
study of early Roman history that he is said to have composed specifically
for his sons since all previous work in the area had been written in
Greek. But it is his surviving work, the *de Agri Cultura* ("On Agriculture"), that earns him an entry here. It is a practical handbook that, in
two volumes, gives direction to absentee landowners whose farms are run
by a mix of free and slave labor, and who are motivated principally to
make a profit: hence he pays more attention to the cultivation of olives
and vines than to grains, and advises rather callously that ill slaves be
sold off before they become a financial burden. Though he admired the
simplicity of the founders of Rome and their reliance on agriculture (his
effusive praise of the merits of cabbage is a reflection of that antiquari-
anism), he was no Cincinnatus, the fifth-century Roman farmer called
from his plow to lead the troops, and after victory immediately returning
to his plow. Still, Cato knew his agriculture, and is especially valuable for
the insight he provides to a period when the profession of farming was
undergoing revolutionary changes, as the small subsistence plots of the
traditional peasants were being bought up by the wealthy and assembled
into large plantations, and as new agricultural techniques were reducing
the reliance on free labor and causing serious social upheaval.

Columella

Lucius Junius Moderatus Columella was born in Spanish Gades
(Cadiz) sometime in the first third of the first century C.E. We know little
of his life apart from his probable service in the Roman army and his
publication, ca. 65 C.E., of a detailed, twelve-volume treatise on agriculture (*de Re Rustica*) and another short book on orchards (*de Arboribus*),
both of which survive complete.

He is the most professional of our surviving agricultural writers, and
it is clear from his text that he was very much a practitioner. Though
writing two centuries after Cato, he reiterates that pioneer's emphases
on large, slave-run plantations specializing in profitable crops like vines
and olives (and, by implication, compelling Rome and Italy to continue
importing grain from provinces like Sicily, Africa, and Egypt). But he

was no rural bumpkin: he cites Vergil repeatedly, and he composed his tenth book, on gardens, in reasonable hexameters as a continuation of Vergil's poem the *Georgics*.

Ctesibius

Though clearly possessing one of the most technically inventive minds of antiquity, Ctesibius remains almost unknown to us as an individual. Of personal details, we are told only that his father was a barber. None of his works survives, but fortuitously several of his successors make mention of him and his achievements in the evolution of mechanics.

He was active as an inventor in Alexandria in the first half of the third century B.C.E., and is credited with the invention of the piston pump with valves (in Vitruvius and Hero), the water organ (Vitruvius), the water clock with variable hours (Vitruvius) (see Document 45 and Figure 19), and the catapult (in Philo).

Daedalus

Daedalus was an important technical inventor in Greek myth and legend, his name coming to symbolize the ideal craftsman. Though some of his exploits are located in Athens, according to Homer and others most of his activities took place on Crete in the late Bronze Age, while he was in service as architect to King Minos. There he devised (among other marvels like mechanical dolls and a giant) the wooden framework that allowed Minos' wife Pasiphaë to realize her desire to copulate with a bull, and subsequently designed the labyrinth to imprison the horrible offspring of the union, the Minotaur. All this naturally aroused Minos' anger, which Daedalus escaped by inventing wings, which he attached with wax to himself and his son Icarus; Daedalus flew safely on to Sicily, but his son, like many young men heedless of his father's warnings, flew too near to the sun, which melted the wax and sent him plunging into the sea.

These intriguing tales are a good reflection of how early technologies are often fantastically represented in oral myths. We know from Columella, for example (*On Agriculture* 6.37.10–11), that Roman farmers used a specially designed wooden framework to mate the smaller jackasses with larger mares to produce tractable mules; Daedalus' contraption is almost certainly a mythical representation of this practical device for interspecies breeding. Archaeology has shown us that the labyrinth is the maze of storage rooms in Minos' palace at Knossos. Icarus' death is invented simply to explain the name of the Aegean island of Icaros in the Icarian Sea, and even Daedalus himself is a patent fabrication, his name having been invented to explain the origin of the Greek adjective *daedalos*, meaning "cleverly worked." He is, then, the personification of the Clever Artisan, and so in many ways the patron of this volume.

Frontinus

Sextus Julius Frontinus (ca. 30–104 C.E.) was born to Roman citizens perhaps in the province of southern Gaul (*provincia* = modern Provence). He followed the usual ladder of public offices and military service, becoming consul in 73 or 74 and then serving as governor of Britain, where he was involved in military campaigns and founded a new fort at Isca (modern Caerleon in Wales). In 97 the Emperor Nerva appointed him superintendent of Rome's water supply (*curator aquarum*), a responsibility he fulfilled with great energy and decisiveness. After two more consulships with the Emperor Trajan as his colleague (a sign of the great respect and trust in which he was held), he died about 104.

Frontinus used his military and administrative experience and skills to compose two handbooks for his successors, both of which survive. For *The Stratagems*, a four-volume manual for military officers, he outlines the contents in the preface to each book: "Types of stratagems to guide the commander in his necessary preparations for battle. Types of stratagems that pertain to the conduct of battle. Types of stratagems that are, to my mind, vital after the battle is over. Types of stratagems for capturing a fortified position by force. Conversely, types of stratagems for protecting the besieged." His other work, *On the Aqueducts of Rome*, in two volumes, he wrote when *curator aquarum* to set out for those who would succeed him all the details of the urban water system. In both works, Frontinus displays his practical experiences, his good sense, and his devotion to detail. He must have been considered the ideal civil servant.

Hero

We have already examined, in Chapter 8, much of Hero's contribution to the evolution of machines in antiquity, so here we will simply review what we know about his life and writings.

Though for years he was placed anywhere from the third century B.C.E. to the second century C.E., we now know that he was an active inventor at the Museum of Alexandria in the middle of the first century C.E., when he described an eclipse that we can firmly date to 13 March 62. There are many works attributed to him that are of ambiguous authorship, and there is a real possibility that part of the confusion may arise from the existence of two scientists of the same name but from different periods. Apart from his written work, we have only an anecdote that has him die from an explosion of his aeolipile; but this is nothing more than an attempt to connect him with heroes of mythology, who (like Odysseus and Jason) are killed by their own creations (in the case of Odysseus, by his unrecognized son by Circe; and Jason, by the insecure prow of the good ship *Argo*).

Hero is credited with over a dozen works in mathematics, metrology, and technology. For our study, the most significant surviving works are three: *The Pneumatics*, a study of how pressure (air, water, steam, and vacuum) can be harnessed for practical (or, in some cases, apparently impractical) purposes; *The Construction of Automatons*, on the self-propelled stage scenery that so delighted audiences of the time, but also revealed serious attempts at robotics; and *The Mechanics*, the second book of which outlines the mechanical advantage of levers, pulleys, wedges, and screws, while the third book meanders through sledges, cranes, and wine presses.

Many scholars have dismissed Hero's contributions to the evolution of machines as trivial applications with no practical basis; others have taken his models of a holy-water dispenser and self-opening temple doors as proof that he was a tool of the priests of Alexandria. Both these criticisms are nonsense. First, his written work seems more like lecture notes than prepared texts, suggesting that he was speaking and demonstrating devices to students, or at least to people who had some knowledge of what was being presented. And second, his "religious" devices have nothing to do with deceiving credulous worshippers, but are quite obviously creations to illustrate physical principles. Hero was, it seems, the consummate teacher: using contemporary situations like a drinking party (the bottomless wine glass) or a visit to the temple (the miraculous doors) to instill in his audience an understanding of basic—but seemingly strange—physical and mechanical principles.

Philo of Byzantium

Philo, originating from the Greek colony of Byzantium on the Bosporus straits between Europe and Asia (later Constantinople, modern Istanbul), was an inventor practicing in Alexandria: he seems to have been active around 200 B.C.E., so almost certainly was a student of Ctesibius, and gives us a link from that period to Hero.

His principal work, largely it seems assembled by his students, was the *Mechanical* (or *Mathematical*) *Collection*, much of which is extant in various forms. Book 4 dealt with catapults (including a compressed-air missile launcher invented by Ctesibius, but otherwise unknown), Book 5 with pneumatics (seventy-eight machines operated by air pressure or steam, preserved in an Arabic text and later translated into European languages), Book 6 with automata (not extant, but probably reflected in Hero's work of the same title), and Books 7 and 8 with offensive and defensive siege machinery. Many of his inventions clearly reappear in Hero's published works, though not always attributed to their inventor.

Pliny the Elder

Gaius Plinius Secundus (23 or 24–79 C.E.) was a Roman civil servant, whose appointment to various imperial offices gave him access to, and spawned an interest in, almost all areas of natural science and human endeavor. He was born in Comum (Como) in northern Italy, to a middle-class family. After the requisite military service—in his case twelve years, mostly on the difficult and dangerous border with the German tribes—he entered the imperial civil service, where he devoted the rest of his life. He is perhaps best known as the commander of the Roman fleet at Misenum on the Bay of Naples in 79 C.E., when Vesuvius exploded on a hot Friday afternoon in August; Pliny launched some of the fleet under his command in an attempt to rescue friends and others fleeing from the hot ash and lava flows; but—as his young nephew Pliny the Younger graphically describes in a subsequent letter to the historian Tacitus—he himself was unable to escape and succumbed to the sulfurous fumes.

Pliny is best known as an encyclopedist, whose *Natural History* in thirty-seven volumes tackles all aspects of natural history ("animal, vegetable, and mineral" as the *Oxford Classical Dictionary* defines it), with, as he himself claims, 20,000 facts and observations culled from his reading of 2,000 books.

His nephew, the Younger Pliny, not only describes his uncle's death in the eruption (*Letters* 6.16 and 6.20), but gives us (*Letters* 3.5) an unparalleled insight into the creative processes of a devoted compiler: a few hours given over to sleep; otherwise uninterrupted reading of texts; early mornings and late evenings dictating to scribes; continual revision and constant attention to new ideas, despite external attractions. Much of what Pliny has handed down to us is dubious, and his moral judgments of contemporary Rome are a constant reminder that he is a typically conservative Roman. But his was an active and searching mind, and despite his limitations he has preserved for us much that otherwise would have been lost. He is a character whom we would all like to invite for a lively and wide-ranging conversation over dinner.

Prometheus

Prometheus is a mythological figure credited with the invention of many technologies of benefit to humans, for which a jealous Zeus punished him. Among his contributions: the very creation of humans; the invention of speech and language; the gift of fire to humans (in punishment for which Zeus had Hephaistos create woman); the teaching of men to offer the gods only the useless fat of offerings; and many other technological advances. He was the sympathetic link between human and divine, and so an important element in ancient society.

Varro

Marcus Terentius Varro (116–27 B.C.E.) was born northeast of Rome, in the same rural area where Cato had been raised. As a member of the aristocracy, he was educated at Rome and Athens, followed the usual political career, and unhappily chose to fight on Pompey's losing side in the civil war against Caesar. Like many, he was later reconciled to the dictator, and was appointed to plan the first public library in the capital. Caesar's assassination intervened, however, and Varro narrowly escaped death during the proscriptions organized by his successor in Rome, Mark Antony. Wisely, Varro went into retirement, and spent the rest of his life writing treatises on a wide variety of subjects.

Varro was a true renaissance man 1,500 years before Leonardo and Michelangelo, the most learned Roman of all, according to one ancient scholar. He was an accomplished poet, wrote scholarly accounts of Roman history, law, linguistics, and applied sciences, and was a promoter of a "liberal" education (that is, the appropriate fields of study for a "free man" [*liber*]). Though most of his output is now lost, references in later writers suggest that he wrote an astounding seventy-five titles in more than 600 volumes. Of these, two works survive in more than just fragments: six of an original twenty-five volumes on *The Latin Language*, and the full text, in three volumes, of his *de Re Rustica*, on agriculture and animal husbandry, which reveals many advances in farming technology and economics in the century since Cato published his manual.

Vitruvius

Vitruvius Pollio (active in the third quarter of the first century B.C.E.) was a military engineer and architect for Caesar and Augustus, whose fame rests entirely on his ten-volume study *On Architecture*. This is a work of exceptional importance to students of ancient architecture and technology, since it is the only manual on this topic that has survived and was to prove enormously influential in the Italian Renaissance, when architects like Michelangelo and Palladio used him extensively. It contains much that today we would consider extraneous to architecture: clocks and siege engines, for example.

Vitruvius relied heavily on earlier writers, which is fortunate for us, since he provides insights into the work of important engineers like Archimedes and Ctesibius. Though he introduces contemporary Italian designs, especially for the construction of houses, his architectural examples of monumental structures come largely from the Hellenistic Greek eastern Mediterranean, where the traditional post-and-lintel construction in stone was not yet being supplanted by the revolutionary designs made possible by concrete.

PRIMARY DOCUMENTS

FOOD AND CLOTHING

DOCUMENT 1
Arboriculture

Here the Elder Pliny (Natural History 12.1–4) describes the early use of trees and plants in the history of humankind, and rightly speculates that they provided necessities of life long before the development of other technologies.

For a long time the favors of the Earth remained hidden, and her greatest gift to man was thought to be the trees and forests. From these he first obtained his food, cushioned his cave with their foliage, and clothed himself with their bark. Even now there are races that live in this fashion. . . . Afterwards trees soothed man with juices more seductive than grain—the oil of the olive to refresh his limbs, drafts of wine to restore his strength—in short, such a variety of delicacies offered spontaneously by the seasons, foods that still make up the second course of our meals.

DOCUMENT 2
Animal Husbandry

A tradition frequently associated with the opening of the American West—the conflicting interests of farmers and ranchers that often led to violence—was nothing new even to the Romans, as Columella (On Agriculture 6, Preface 1–2) makes clear.

I realize that some experienced farmers have rejected animal husbandry and have consistently shown contempt for the herdsman's role as being harmful to their own profession. And I admit that there is some reason for this attitude, insofar as the object of the farmer is the antithesis of the herdsman's: pleasure for the one comes from land every inch of which has been cleared and tilled, for the other from land that is fallow and covered in grass; the farmer hopes for reward from the earth, the rancher from his beast, and for that reason the plowman abhors the same green growth that the herdsman prays for.

Still, in the face of these discordant aspirations there is yet a certain compatible relationship between the two. In the first place, there is usually more advantage in using a farm's fodder to feed one's own herds rather than someone else's; and secondly, the luxuriant growth of the earth's produce results from abundant applications of manure, and manure is the product of the herds. Nor for that matter is there any region where grain is the only thing to grow, and where it is not cultivated with the help of animals as much as of men.

DOCUMENT 3
Instructions for Constructing a Plow

We have two detailed ancient descriptions of how to construct a plow: this selection from Vergil (Georgics 1.160–174) and a passage of Hesiod from almost 700 years earlier. Both are the product of poets who, while experienced agriculturalists themselves, have left us unfortunately obtuse texts on which to base any reconstructions.

We must speak as well of the tools available to the hardy peasants, without which the crops could not be sown and would not grow. First the plowshare and the heavy oak of the curved plow, and the slowly rolling carts of Ceres [protector of grain], and the threshing sledges and drag hoes and rakes of excessive weight. . . . Even before it is removed from the forest an elm is bent by great force and shaped for the plow beam, taking on the form of a curved plow. To this are fitted, first a pole extending eight feet from the stock, then a pair of "ears," and a bifurcated share beam. A lightweight linden tree has already been cut down for the yoke, and a lofty beech as the plow handle to turn the bottom of the device from behind.

DOCUMENT 4
Harvesting Grain

Columella (On Agriculture 2.20.3) gives a very brief description of the principal harvesting tools of antiquity, while Pliny (Natural History 18.296) describes a unique device, confirmed by contemporary sculpture, that seems not to have been widely used.

There are several methods of harvesting. Many farmers cut the stalk in the middle with a spitted sickle, either bill-shaped or toothed; many collect the ear by itself, some using a pair of flat boards, others a comb—quite an easy procedure in a thin crop but very difficult in a thick one.

On the large estates in the Gallic provinces, huge frames with teeth set along the [forward] edge and with a pair of wheels are driven through the crop by a draft animal yoked to the rear. This tears off the ears, which then fall into the frame.

DOCUMENT 5
Threshing and Winnowing

Both techniques described here by Varro (On Agriculture 1.52) could be seen in use until recently in some of the remoter areas of the eastern Mediterranean.

Some farmers use a yoke of oxen and a sledge [to separate the kernels from the ears of grain]. The sledge is constructed in one of two ways: a board with a rough surface of stones or pieces of iron and loaded down by the weight of the driver or some heavy object is dragged along by a team of oxen and severs the kernel from the ear; or the driver sits on toothed axles between small wheels and drives the oxen that pull it. . . . Elsewhere threshing is done by herding draft animals onto the floor and keeping them moving with goads; their hoofs then separate the grain from the ears.

The threshed grain should then be tossed from the ground during a gentle breeze, with winnowing scoops or shovels. In this way the lightest part, called the chaff and husks, is fanned outside the threshing floor and the grain, because of its weight, falls into the basket clean.

DOCUMENT 6
Equipment for an Olive Orchard

This list from the oldest surviving prose work in Latin (Cato's On Agriculture, chapter 10, from the second century B.C.E.) reflects the inventory for the kind of medium-sized farm probably owned by an absentee landlord and worked by a mixture of hired and slave labor; we know that the personal holdings of citizen peasant farmers were substantially smaller than this. A iugerum was an area just under 30,000 square (Roman) feet, about an acre and a half, the amount of land that the early Romans thought could be plowed in a single day by one yoke (iugum) of oxen.

For an olive orchard of 240 *iugera*:

Workers, a total of 13: 1 overseer, 1 housekeeper, 5 laborers, 3 plowmen, 1 donkey driver, 1 swineherd, 1 shepherd.

Livestock: 3 pairs of oxen, 3 donkeys fitted with packsaddles to carry manure, 1 donkey for the mill, 100 sheep.

Pressing equipment: 5 fully equipped sets of oil presses, 1 bronze vessel (capacity 750 liters) with 1 bronze lid, 3 iron hooks, 3 water pitchers, 2 funnels, 1 bronze vessel (capacity 75 liters) with 1 bronze lid, 3 hooks, 1 small basin, 2 amphorae for oil, 1 pitcher, 3 ladles, 1 water bucket, 1 shallow basin, 1 small pot, 1 slop pail, 1 small platter, 1 chamber-pot, 1 watering pot, 1 ladle, 1 candelabrum, 1 half-liter measure.

Equipment for draft-animals: 3 four-wheeled carts, 6 plows with shares, 3 yokes fitted with leather harnesses, 6 sets of trappings for oxen, 1 harrow, 4 hurdles for carrying manure, 3 manure hampers, . . . 3 saddle cloths for donkeys.

Iron tools: 8 iron forks, 8 hoes, 4 spades, 5 shovels, 2 four-pronged drag-hoes, 8 mowing scythes, 5 reaping sickles, 5 pruning hooks, 3 axes, 3 wedges, 1 mortar for grain, 2 tongs, 1 oven rake, 2 braziers.

Containers: 100 storage jars for oil, 12 receiving vats, 10 jars for storing grape pulp, 10 jars for holding the lees, 10 wine jars, 20 grain jars, 1 vat for steeping lupins, 10 medium-sized storage jars, 1 washtub, 1 bathtub, 2 water basins, separate covers for jars (both large and medium).

Milling equipment and furniture: 1 donkey mill, 1 pushing mill, 1 Spanish mill, 3 mill rests [?], 1 table with a slab top, 2 bronze pans, 2 tables, 3 long benches, 1 bedroom stool, 3 low stools, 4 chairs, 2 armchairs, 1 bed in the bedroom, 4 beds with cord mattresses, 3 beds, 1 wooden mortar, 1 fuller's mortar, 1 loom for making cloth, 2 mortars, 4 pestles (1 each for beans, emmer wheat, seeds, and cracking nuts), 1 8-liter measure, 1 4-liter measure, 8 stuffed mattresses, 8 coverlets, 16 cushions, 10 blankets, 3 table napkins, 6 patchwork cloaks for young male slaves.

DOCUMENT 7
Milling Grain

In this first delightful poem, attributed to Vergil (Moretum 16–29, 39–42), we have a somewhat romanticized picture of a poor farmer's morning task of making bread, grinding the flour with a small, portable rotary mill. The second passage, from Apuleius' The Golden Ass (9.10–11), recounts the woes of a fellow who has miraculously been transformed into a donkey, only to find himself hitched to one of the large hourglass-shaped rotary mills.

A meager heap of grain was poured upon the ground, from which he helps himself to as much as his measure would hold, amounting to 16 pounds in weight. He leaves his storeroom and takes his position beside the mill, placing his trusty lamp on a small shelf firmly fixed to the wall for just such a purpose. Then from his clothing he frees his two arms and, first putting on an apron of hairy goatskin, he sweeps the stones and hollow of the mill with a brush made of tail. He mobilizes his two hands for the task, allotting a job to each: his left is given to feeding the mill, his right to the work of turning and driving the unceasing spin of the wheel, while the left from time to time helps out her weary sister by taking her turn—and the grain passes through, braised by the stone's swift strokes. . . . Once his work of turning has made up the proper amount, he transfers handsful of the bruised meal from the mill to a sieve and shakes it. The husks remain behind in the sieve, while the flour filters through the holes and falls out clean and pure.

By chance, there passed by a baker from the next village, who had purchased a large quantity of wheat. He bought me as well, and led me off with a heavy load to the mill he ran. . . . There, a throng of mules continually went round and round turning a number of mills, not just by day but actually were kept at it even by night, producing flour through the small hours at the turning mills that never stopped. . . . Early the next day I was harnessed to a mill that seemed the biggest of all, and with blinders on I was set walking on the curved path of a circular track, so that by keeping on the same restricted circuit and retracing my steps again and again I might keep wandering around the set course.

DOCUMENT 8
Pressing Grapes

Here Pliny (Natural History 18.317) describes some presses used for obtaining the juice to make wine. His allusion in the second sentence ("Length is what counts . . .") shows he is talking here of a lever press, whose mechanical advantage improves the longer the beam extends from the fulcrum.

Some use individual presses, though it is more expedient to use a pair, however large the single presses. Length is what counts with these beams, not their thickness: the long ones press better. Our forbears used to pull down the beams using ropes and straps and by levers; but within the last hundred years the Greek system was adopted, in which the grooves of a vertical screw run in a spiral. Four turning-spikes are fitted to the screw by some. . . . Within the past twenty years we have discovered how to use small presses and a less spacious pressing shed: a shorter vertical screw projects downward onto the middle of the pressing disks, which exert a continuous downward pressure on the grape sacks set beneath.

DOCUMENT 9
Textiles Become the Responsibility of Women

In this passage the poet Lucretius (On the Nature of Things 5.1354–1360) betrays the ancient bias against women as productive workers.

Nature forced men to work the wool earlier than the female sex—for the entire male sex is far better in skill and much more clever—until the hardened farmers turned it into a reproach, so that the men willingly yielded it to female hands and at the same time they themselves undertook the hard labor and toughened their bodies and hands in the hard work.

DOCUMENT 10
The Equipment for Spinning and Weaving

Pollux (Lexicon 10.124–125) here lists most of the items used by the household's women to produce the material for clothing.

In a few words one can pull together the rest of those items that pertain to the women's quarters: woven baskets and baskets with narrow bottoms and the smaller types of both . . ., and the spindle and the circular whorls, the skeins of yarn, the weaver's shuttle and the comb of the loom; and the upright loom as well as the side beams of the loom; and the weaver's rod [to attach the alternate threads of the warp] and the beam along with the vertical beams of the loom [between which the web hangs down] and the long beams of the loom [between which the web is stretched]; and the stone weights [for the warp threads] and the loom weights, and the flat blade [to strike the weft threads home].

DOCUMENT 11
Spinning: The Three Fates

Catullus (Poems 64.310–319) describes the three mythical fates, daughters of Zeus (or Night) who spun, measured out, and cut the thread of each human's existence.

Their hands solemnly plucked at their eternal labor. The left hand held the distaff wrapped about with soft wool; next the right hand, carefully drawing out the fine threads with upturned fingers fashioned them, then twisting, the right hand twirled the spindle weighted with a smooth whorl on the downward thumb; and then with their teeth continually plucking they made the product even and smooth and bitten bits of wool clung to their dried-up lips, bits which previously had been sticking out from the smooth yarn. Before their feet the soft fleeces of the shining wool were protected in small wicker baskets.

DOCUMENT 12
Weaving: The Contest between Arachne and Athena

Myth has it that Arachne boasted openly of her weaving skills, and was challenged to a contest by Athena, the goddess representing women's tasks. Ovid (Metamorphoses 6.53–60) here describes the beginning; by the end, the insolent Arachne had won, was punished by Athena, hanged herself, and was transformed into a perpetually weaving spider.

Without delay they set up the twin looms in different places and stretch them with the fine warp. The web is bound to the beam, reed separates the thread [of the warp], the weft is threaded through the middle [of them] with sharp shuttles, which their fingers help through, and once led between the threads [of the warp], the notched teeth pound [it into place] with the hammering sley. Both hasten along, and with their mantle girded about their breasts they ply their skilled hands, their eagerness making the labor light.

WATER

DOCUMENT 13
A Shaduf

This passage, probably wrongly attributed to Aristotle (Mechanical Problems 28.857a–b), analyzes the mechanical principles behind the operation of a shaduf or "swipe."

Why do they construct the *shaduf* at wells the way they do? For they add to the wooden beam a lead weight, the bucket itself having weight whether empty or full. Is it that the work is divided into two moments (for it is necessary to dip it, and to haul it up again), and it happens to be easy to send the empty bucket down, but hard to haul it up full? There is advantage, then, in letting it down a little more slowly, in proportion to the great lightening of the load as one draws it up. The lead weight or stone attached to the end of the pole accomplishes this. For the individual lowering the bucket must overcome a greater weight than if he were to let down the empty bucket alone, but when it is full the lead pulls it up.

DOCUMENT 14
Water Wheels

This passage from Vitruvius (On Architecture 10.4.1–5.1) describes three versions of wheels designed to raise water, each of which had its advantages and limitations: the tympanum *(high volume but low lift), a wheel with compartmentalized rim (moderate volume and lift), and the* noria *(low volume but high lift). He omits the fourth common type, the* saqiya, *a wheel with clay pots attached to the rim and usually powered by animals harnessed to a horizontal cog wheel meshed with the vertical wheel.*

Now I will explain the devices that have been invented for raising water, how the various designs are contrived. First I will speak about the *tympanum* ["drum"]. This device, to be sure, does not lift water to a great height, but it discharges a great amount quickly.... Around the axle is a drum made of planks joined together, and it is mounted on beams that have iron bearings to carry the axle ends. In the interior of this drum are set eight radial partitions running from the axle all the way to the circumference, dividing the interior into equal compartments. Around its outer surface are fixed planks with 6-inch openings for receiving the water. Likewise, close to the axle there are small round holes in one side corresponding to each compartment. This device . . . is set in motion by men treading it. It scoops up the water through openings in the circumference and discharges it through the circular openings near the axle into a wooden trough connected to a conduit. . . .

When, however, the water has to be raised higher, the same principle will be put to use in this manner. A wheel will be built around the axle, of a large enough diameter so that it can reach the height that is required. Rectangular compartments will be fixed around the circumference of the wheel and made tight with pitch and wax. Thus, when the wheel is turned by men treading it, the containers will be carried up full to the top of the wheel and on their downward turn will pour out into a reservoir what they have themselves raised.

But if a supply is required at still greater heights, a double iron chain will be set up, wound around the axle of a wheel and allowed to hang down to the lowest level, with bronze buckets the capacity of 3 liters suspended from it. Thus the turning of the wheel, by winding the chain over the axle, will carry the buckets to the top, and as they are borne over the wheel they will necessarily turn over and pour out into a reservoir what they have raised.

Wheels of these same designs can also be set up in rivers. Around the circumference are fixed paddles that, when struck by the force of the river, move along and cause the wheel to turn.

DOCUMENT 15
The Water Screw

Vitruvius (On Architecture 10.6.3–4) here describes the most famous invention attributed to Archimedes. Notice that the device was rotated as a whole, whereas in contemporary versions still in use along the Nile the screw is turned independently inside the stationery wooden cylinder, usually with a crank.

[Strips of wood are stacked up to form a spiral around a wooden axle.] Planks are fixed around the circumference of the spiral to cover it. Then these planks are smeared with pitch and bound with iron bands, so that they may not be dislodged by the effect of the water. The ends of the shaft are capped with iron. On the ends of the screw beams are placed with cross pieces at each end fixed to both. In this way the screws can be turned by men treading them. The mounting of the screw will be at such an angle that it corresponds to the construction of a Pythagorean right-angled triangle: that is, so that the length is divided into five units and the head raised three of the same units.

DOCUMENT 16
Natural Irrigation in Egypt and Mesopotamia

Egypt and Mesopotamia were favored for agricultural productivity because of the silt-laden waters of their river systems. Here, Pliny (Natural History 5.57–58) describes the annual Nile flood from early summer to early fall, and Herodotus (Histories 1.193.1–3) the use of canals and water-lifting devices to bring water to the fields from the Tigris and Euphrates Rivers.

The Nile River begins to rise at the first new moon after the summer solstice, by gradual degrees as the sun passes through Cancer. It reaches its crest when the sun is in Leo, and in Virgo subsides at the same rate as it rose. . . . The amounts of its rise are determined with calibrated marks in water shafts: a rise of 24 feet is just right; if any less, the waters do not irrigate all the fields and there is no time for sowing because the earth is still thirsty; if any more, the floods delay work by receding too slowly and waste the time for sowing since the ground is sodden.

The land of the Assyrians receives little rainfall, enough to fatten the roots of the grain. But the standing crop is watered from the river, which brings it to ripeness and causes the grain to mature. This is done not as in Egypt, where the river by itself overflows its banks into the fields; here there is manual irrigation with the use of *shadufs* or swipes. For the whole countryside of Babylonia, like that of Egypt, is partitioned by canals, the largest of which is navigable: it extends southeast from the Euphrates to another river, the Tigris. . . . It is so productive of grain that it usually yields 200-fold, and as much as 300-fold in the best harvests.

DOCUMENT 17
Building a Roman Aqueduct

While Frontinus gives detailed descriptions of the individual aqueducts that supplied Rome with water, Vitruvius (On Architecture 8.6.1–11) here supplies a generic description of the components of an aqueduct system, including the (rare) construction of "inverted siphons" and the distribution of the water once it has reached the city.

Water can be conducted in three ways: by flow in masonry channels, lead pipes, and terracotta pipes. Here are their specifications. If in channels, the construction must be as solid as possible, and the stream-bed must have a uniform slope of no less than six inches in every hundred feet. The channel is to be vaulted over so that the sun does not touch the water at all.

When it reaches the city walls, a reservoir is to be built, and adjoining the reservoir a triple tank for receiving water. Three pipes of equal bore are to be installed in the reservoir, leading to the receiving tanks, which are connected in such a manner that when the two outside tanks overflow, they pour into the middle tank. Pipes run from the middle tank to all the basins and fountains, from the second to the baths, that they might provide an annual public income, and from the third to private homes. In this way water for public use will not be lacking, for private parties will not be able to draw it off, since each has its own separate supply from the source. I have set up these divisions so that those who draw water off to their homes for private use might by their rents help the maintenance of the aqueducts by contractors.

But if there are hills along the course between the city and the water source, the following procedure is used. An underground channel is to be dug with the uniform slope described above. If the bedrock is tufa or hard stone, the channel is to be cut directly in it, but if it is earth or sand, a vaulted channel with floor and walls is to be built in the tunnel and the water carried through it in this manner. Vertical shafts are to be cut from the surface every 120 feet. . . .

If from the source there is an even slope to the city without any higher intervening hills capable of interrupting it, but with low spots, it is necessary to build it up to an even slope as with the flow in channels. And if the way around these depressions is not long, a detour is made, but if they are unbroken, the water course will be directed along the sunken area [that is, in an "inverted siphon"]. When it comes to the bottom, it is carried on a low substructure to give it as long a level course as possible: this, then will be the *venter* ["belly"], which the Greeks call *koilia*. Then when it comes up against the hill, the long stretch of the *venter* prevents a sudden burst of pressure: the water is forced up to the height of the hilltop. . . .

But if we wish to incur less expense, we must proceed in the following manner. Terracotta pipes with walls no less than two digits thick are to be made in such a way that they are flanged at one end, so that one pipe can slide into and join tightly with another. . . . Aqueducts employing terracotta pipes have these advantages: first, that if some defect occurs, anyone can fix it; secondly, that the water from terracotta pipes is much more healthful than that from lead pipes. Lead seems to make water harmful for this reason, that it generates lead carbonate, and this substance is said to be harmful to the human body. So if what is generated by it is harmful, it cannot be doubted that it is itself not healthful. Lead workers can provide us with an example, since their complexions are affected by a deep pallor.

DOCUMENT 18
Rome's Urban Water Supply

> *The Romans were justifiably proud of their achievements in hydraulic engineering. Here, Pliny (Natural History 36.121–123) gives a brief but impressive list of the practical and decorative elements of the system that supplied Rome, while Frontinus (On the Aqueducts of Rome 1.16), always the practical bureaucrat, compares the utility of a good water supply to the achievements of Rome's cultural predecessors.*

But we must speak of marvels a true evaluation will find unsurpassed. Quintus Marcus Rex, when ordered by the senate to rebuild the channels of the Appia, Anio, and Tepula aqueducts, brought to Rome within the term of his praetorship a new aqueduct named after himself, driving underground channels through the mountains. Agrippa, too, while aedile, after adding the Virgo and repairing and putting in order the other aqueducts, constructed 700 basins, along with 500 fountains and 130 reservoirs, many of them magnificently decorated, and added 300 bronze and marble statues to these works, and 400 marble columns: all this in the space of a year. In the report of his aedileship, he himself adds that he celebrated games for 59 days and that admission to all 170 baths was made free: these are now infinitely more numerous at Rome. . . .

Now if someone shall carefully appraise the abundance of water in public buildings, baths, pools, channels, houses, gardens, and suburban villas, the distance the water travels, the arches which have been built up, the mountains tunneled, and the level courses across valleys, he will acknowledge that nothing more marvelous has ever existed in the whole world.

With such numerous and indispensable structures carrying so many waters, compare, if you please, the idle pyramids, or even the indolent but famous works of the Greeks.

DOCUMENT 19
Roman Public Baths

An essential element of Roman hydraulics, and indeed of Roman culture, was the construction of huge public bathing facilities, called thermae *because of their use of heated water (*aquae thermae*), in cities throughout the empire. Vitruvius (*On Architecture *5.10) describes their layout and the complexity of the heating systems, including multiple hot-water tanks, the double-flooring system (*hypocausts*) that artificially warmed the bathing rooms with radiant heat, and even the harnessing of passive solar heating through the orientation of the building.*

First of all, a site as warm as possible must be chosen, that is, turned away from the north and east. Further, hot and warm bath areas are to receive their light from the direction of the winter sunset—or if the configuration of the site does not allow it, in any case from the south—because the favorite time for bathing is fixed between noon and evening. And one likewise must see to it that women's and men's hot baths are adjoining and have the same orientation: for in this way it will be brought about that there is a common heating system for both of them and their fittings. Three bronze tanks are to be installed over the furnace, one for the hot bath, another for the warm bath, a third for the cold bath, and so arranged that the amount of hot water which flows from the warm tank into the hot will be replaced by the same amount flowing from the cold tank into the warm. The vaulted ducts are to be heated from a common furnace.

The hanging floors [hypocausts] of the hot rooms are to be made as follows: first, the ground is to be paved with tiles 18 inches on a side, sloping towards the furnace in such a way that when a ball is thrown in it cannot stop inside but rolls back to the furnace door by itself. In this way the heat will more easily spread out beneath the floor. On this surface piers of bricks eight inches square are to be built in such a pattern that tiles two feet square can be placed above them. These piers are to be two feet high, put together with clay kneaded with hair, and the two-foot tiles are to be placed on them to carry the pavement. . . .

Let the dimensions of the baths suit the size of the crowd. They should be planned in the following manner. Let the breadth be two-thirds of the length, not counting the room with the basin and tank. The basins should be placed below the light source so that those standing around it might not darken it with their shadows. The rooms containing the basins ought to have enough space that when first comers have taken their places around the basins those waiting their turn might be able to stand in order. The width of the tank between the back wall and the front edge should be no less than six feet, of which the lower step and the seat occupy two.

The *laconicum*, or sweat room, should be adjacent to the warm room. The dome should spring at a height equal to the width of the room. A window is to be left in the centre of the dome and a bronze disk hung from it by chains: raising and lowering this disk allows adjustment to the sweating.

SHELTER AND SECURITY

DOCUMENT 20
The Ingredients for Roman Concrete

> *Vitruvius* (On Architecture *2.4.1–5.1*) *describes the components of Roman concrete in considerable detail; in the second passage, Pliny* (Natural History *35.166*) *draws attention to pozzolana, a special ingredient from the neighborhood of Mount Vesuvius that allowed concrete to set underwater.*

In cement structures it is necessary first to enquire concerning the sand, that it is suitable to mix into mortar and that it does not have earth mixed in with it. The following are the types of quarried sands: black, grey, red, and carbuncular. Of these, the one that makes a crackling noise when rubbed in the hand or struck is best; while the one that is earthy will not be rough enough. Likewise if it is covered up in a white cloth, then shaken up or pounded, and it does not soil the cloth and the earth does not settle into it, then it is suitable. But if there are no sandpits from which it can be dug, then it must be sifted out from riverbeds or from gravel or even from the seashore. But these have the following defects when used in buildings: the wall dries with difficulty and this type of wall does not allow continuous loading—it requires interruptions in the work—and it cannot carry vaults. But even more, when seashore sand is used in walls and stucco is applied onto them, a salty residue leaches out and destroys the surface. But quarried sand dries quickly in the buildings, the plaster coating is permanent, and it can carry vaults. Here, however, I am speaking of sand that is recently taken from the sandpits. For if it is taken out and lies too long, weathered by the sun and moon and hoar frost, it breaks down and becomes earthy. As a result, when it is thrown into the masonry it is not able to bind the rubble, but the rubble sinks and falls down because the walls cannot support the loads. But freshly quarried sand, although it exhibits such great excellence in buildings, is not so useful in plaster, because with its richness the lime mixed with the straw cannot dry without cracking on account of the strength of the sand. River sand, on the other hand, although useless in *signinum* [waterproofing work] because of its fineness, attains a solidity in plaster when worked by polishing tools.

After considering the account of the sources of sand, one must be careful that, in regard to lime, it is burned from white rock, whether [hard] stone or [softer] silex. The lime from close-grained, harder stone will be most useful in structural forms, while that made from porous stone will be best in plaster. Once it has been slaked, then let the mortar be mixed three parts quarried sand to one of lime; or if river or marine sand is thrown in, two parts sand to one of lime. These will be the proper proportions for the composition of the mixture. Furthermore, if anyone adds a third part of crushed and sifted burnt brick into the river or marine sand, he will make the composition of the material better to use.

But other creations belong to the Earth itself. For who could marvel enough that on the hills of Puteoli [Pozzuoli] there exists a dust—so named because it is the most insignificant part of the Earth—that, as soon as it comes into contact with the waves of the sea and is submerged, becomes a single stone mass, impregnable to the waves and every day stronger, especially if mixed with stones quarried at Cumae.

DOCUMENT 21
The Need for Fortification Walls

We saw earlier the almost simultaneous development of settled life and defensive fortifications at Neolithic sites like Jericho. Here, Aristotle

(Politics 7.10.5–8 [1330b–1331a]) gives a fourth-century B.C.E. *explanation for why such walls were still necessary.*

As for fortification walls, those who contend that cities laying claim to valor need not have walls hold a quite outdated opinion, particularly when it is clear that those cities that make such a display of vanity are, in practice, proved wrong. While it is not honorable to use the strength of one's wall to try to protect a city against a foe of equal or only slightly greater numbers, yet it is possible that the superiority of the attackers may happen to prove to be too much for the valor of a few defenders. If in this case the city is to be saved and not suffer harm or humiliation, the greatest possible security and strength of the walls must also be considered the most suitable for warfare, particularly in light of recent inventions that improve the accuracy of the missiles and artillery used in sieges. . . .

It is not enough just to put walls around a city: care must be taken to make them aesthetically pleasing for the city and at the same time appropriate for their military functions—keeping in mind those newly invented machines.

DOCUMENT 22
The Construction of a Circuit Wall and Towers

As always for works of civil engineering, we turn to Vitruvius (On Architecture 1.5) for a concise and accurate description of how the ancients constructed their defensive fortifications.

The foundations of the towers and circuit wall are to be laid in the following manner. The trenches should be dug down to bedrock, if it can be reached, and as extensively along the surface of the bedrock as seems reasonable given the scope of the work. These foundation trenches should be wider than those parts of the walls that will be above ground, and should be filled with structural material that is as solid as possible.

The towers are to project outside the wall, so that the enemy who is determined to approach the wall in an assault will be vulnerable to missiles from the towers, since both his left and right sides will be exposed. Extraordinary care must be taken, it seems, to avoid any easy approach for storming the wall; the roads ought to be led along the contours and be so contrived that the lines of travel do not lead straight to the gates but come from the [defenders'] left—a design that will place nearest the wall the right side of those who are climbing up, the side that is not protected by a shield.

Walled towns should not be laid out in a square shape or with prominent angles, but rather with a circular plan to give a more unobstructed view of the enemy. Those towns with salient angles are hard to defend, because the angle affords greater protection to the enemy than to the population inside.

I do believe that the wall should be made broad enough to allow armed men meeting on the top to pass one another without getting in each other's way. Through the whole thickness, splines of charred olive wood should be set as closely together as possible so that both faces of the wall, bound together by these long thin boards as if by pins, should be permanently stable—for neither rot nor weather nor time can harm this material. . . .

The interval between two towers should be set so that one is no further than a bow shot from the other, which will ensure that, no matter what section is attacked, the enemy can be repulsed by the scorpions and other missile-shooting devices from the towers on the right and the left. On the inner side of the towers there should be a gap in the wall as wide as the tower, spanned by wooden gangways that give access into the towers along joists with no iron reinforcements. This way, if the enemy captures any part of the wall, the defenders can cut these joists away and (if they work quickly) the enemy will not be given the chance to make his way into any other parts of the towers and wall—unless he is prepared to take a plunge.

The towers should be built round or polygonal, since siege-engines very quickly weaken square towers, the constant beating by rams shattering their corners. When it comes to round structures, however, the pounding is directed into the centre, like wedges, and cannot do any damage.

Likewise the defensive works involving curtain wall and towers are especially safe when used in tandem with earth ramparts because they cannot be harmed by rams, tunneling, or any other machines. Still, it is not reasonable to build an embankment in all places, but only where outside the wall there is a high stretch of ground and level access for attacking the defenses. In places like this, first trenches should be dug. . . .

As for the materials that should be used for the core or outer skin of the wall, it is impossible to make specific prescriptions since not everywhere can we find the supplies that we might want. Where squared stone is available, or flat stone, rubble, fired or unbaked brick, use it. . . .

DOCUMENT 23
The Invention of Catapults

*Diodorus of Sicily (History 14.42.1, 43.3, 50.4) rightly attributes
the invention of such offensive siege machines as the catapult to fourth-
century Sicily.*

As a matter of fact, the catapult was invented at this time [399 B.C.E.]
in Syracuse, for the greatest technical minds from all over had been
assembled in one place. . . . Catapults of all sorts were built, as well as a
great number of other missiles. . . . The Syracusans killed many of their
enemies by shooting them from the land with catapults that shot sharp-
pointed missiles. In fact this piece of artillery caused great consternation,
since it had not been known before this time.

DOCUMENT 24
The Onager

*Among the Roman contributions to siege machinery was the "wild ass,"
described here by Ammianus Marcellinus (History 23.4.4–7). He makes
a bit of a muddle of his description in the third sentence: the sides were in
fact held together by cross-posts, whereas the ropes were twisted to give
tension to the throwing arm that he describes in the next sentence.*

On the other hand the scorpion (which they now call the onager or
"wild ass") follows this design. Two beams are hewn out of oak or holm
oak, slightly curved [in the middle] so that they seem to rise up like
humps. These are joined together in the manner of a bow-saw: each side
piece is pierced by a rather large hole, through which durable ropes are
passed and bound between the beams, holding the framework together so
that the engine does not break apart. From the middle of the ropes a
wooden arm rises obliquely, pointing upwards like the pole of a chariot
[unhitched]. The arm can be raised higher or drawn downwards by cords
that are wrapped around it [near the top end]. To the tip of this arm are
attached iron hooks, from which hangs a sling made of hemp or [?] iron.
A large cushion of goat's hair stuffed with fine bits of straw is placed in
front of this wooden arm, bound on [a cross-brace] with strong
fastenings. . . .

In battle, then, a round stone is placed in the sling and four young men
on either side, turning the bars [of the windlass] to which the ropes are

fastened, bend the arm nearly horizontal. Then at last the soldier in charge, standing close above the machine, uses a sharp blow from a hefty mallet to strike out the bolt that holds in position the tethered rope of the device. The swift blow releases the arm, which then smacks into the soft cushioning and hurls the stone, which will crush whatever it hits.

The machine is called a *tormentum* because all of the released energy is first created by twisting [for which the Latin stem is *tor-*] the ropes; or a scorpion since it has an upraised stinger; or recently an onager because, when wild asses [*onagri*] are attacked by hunters, they stay at a distance and kick rocks behind them, splitting open the chests of their pursuers or breaking their bones and bursting apart their skulls.

DOCUMENT 25
An Early Example of Siegecraft

> *Dozens of famous sieges figure in the narratives of historians from Thucydides to Ammianus. We begin with one of the earliest, the Spartan siege of Plataea in 430 B.C.E., at the beginning of the long war between Athens and Sparta (Thucydides, The Peloponnesian War 2.75–76), before the invention of elaborate siege engines.*

First the Spartans hedged the Plataeans in with a palisade of stakes made from the trees they had chopped down, so that no one could escape; then they began to raise an earthen ramp towards the city, hoping that the great size of their army engaged in this labor would make this the quickest possible way of taking the place. They cut timbers from Mt. Cithaeron and constructed a lattice-work, which they placed along either side of the ramp instead of a solid wall, to keep the ramp from spreading horizontally too much. They brought wood and stones and earth, and threw them into the ramp together with anything else that might fill up the mound. For seventy days and nights they kept piling up earth without stopping, divided into reliefs so that, while some were carrying earth, others slept or ate, supervised by Spartan commanders of the auxiliary troops from each city, who kept them at their work.

When the Plataeans saw the mound rising higher, they put together a wooden crib and set it on top of their city wall where the enemy was mounding earth against it, then built into it bricks that they removed from the nearby houses. The timbers served as a binding-frame for the bricks so that the construction did not become weak as it rose higher, and they had coverings of skins and hides that kept the workers and framework safe by protecting them from being hit by flaming arrows. Yet while the height of the wall was being raised considerably, the ramp outside was growing at an equal pace.

But the Plataeans had another idea. They breached their wall where the ramp abutted it and set about removing the earth into the city. When the Peloponnesians discovered this, they packed clay into wicker mats and threw this clot into the breach, to prevent the enemy from breaking it up and carrying it off as they had the loose earth.

Frustrated in this ploy, the Plataeans changed their plan and instead dug a tunnel out from the city and, when they calculated that they were under the ramp, began once again to remove the accumulated earth from underneath. And for a long time the Spartans outside the city, who had no idea what the Plataeans were up to, kept throwing material onto the mound, but it came no closer to completion since it was being hollowed out from underneath and was continually settling into the cavity that was emptied.

But fearing that even with this strategy their small number would not be able to hold off so many, the Plataeans came up with this additional plan. They stopped working on the high parapet opposite the ramp and, starting on either side of it from the bottom of the wall, began building a crescent-shaped barrier on the inside, curving inward towards the city, so that, if the main wall were taken, this one could hold out, forcing the enemy to build a second ramp against it—not only would they have to repeat their whole effort, but as they advanced into the arc of the new barrier they would be more exposed to attack from both sides.

At the same time as they were raising their ramp, the Peloponnesians brought siege-engines up to the city. One of them, moved up to the high defensive parapet opposite the ramp, knocked down a large part of it and struck fear into the Plataeans; but other engines at a different part of the wall were snared in nooses by the defenders and snapped off. The Plataeans also prepared large beams with long iron chains fixed at either end and hanging from two yard-arms tilted forward and jutting over the wall. Whenever an engine was about to attack some section of the wall, they would draw the beam up crosswise [over the enemy ram], and then drop it while letting the chains run loose. The beam would plummet down and break off the head of the ram.

DOCUMENT 26
The Defense of Syracuse

Our second example of an ancient siege in progress is especially in-teresting because of the marvelous technological inventions developed by

Archimedes to withstand the attack of the Romans in 213–211 B.C.E.
(Plutarch Marcellus *14.9–17.3).*

The king persuaded Archimedes to build for him machinery for every type of siege, both defensive and offensive. Because he had lived most of his life in peacetime and amid civic affairs, Archimedes had not himself made use of such engines before, but in the present circumstances his apparatus proved especially beneficial to the Syracusans. . . .

When the Romans began their attack from both the land and the sea, the Syracusans were struck dumb with fear, thinking that nothing could hold out against such a powerful assault. But when Archimedes let loose his engines, he launched on the Roman forces missiles of every description and stones of immense mass, which fell with a whiz and speed that one would not believe, mowing down those who stood in their path and throwing the ranks into confusion: nothing could withstand their weight.

As for the Roman navy, yard-arms unexpectedly emerged from the walls, sinking some of the ships by dropping great weights from above, and hoisting others bow-first straight up out of the water in iron claws or beaks shaped like those of cranes, and then plunging them back stern-first. Other ships were turned around and spun about by means of guy ropes and windlasses inside [the city], and then dashed against the steep promontories jutting out just under the wall, causing great loss of life among the crews on board, who were crushed. Again and again some ship would be lifted out of the water up into the air, then whirled back and forth—a horrible sight as it hung there, until its crew fell out and were hurled in all directions and the ship, now empty, would fall onto the walls or slip away once the grip was removed. . . .

After deliberating, the Romans decided to come close up to the walls, under cover of darkness if they were able, thinking that the tension cords Archimedes was using imparted such force that the missiles they discharged would fly right over their heads and be thoroughly ineffectual at close quarters, the distance not being right to score a hit. Archimedes, it seems, had long ago prepared for just such an eventuality by making the ranges of his instruments adaptable to any distance and by using compact missiles. There was a line of many small apertures through the wall, which allowed the short-range weapons to be placed so as to hit nearby targets while remaining invisible to the enemy.

So when the Romans came up close, unnoticed as they thought, they again were met by a barrage of missiles that hit their mark: rocks plummeting almost straight down on them, and arrows shot out of the whole line of the wall. So they fell back.

In the end, Marcellus saw that the Romans had become so terrified that, if a small cord or bit of wood was seen poking slightly over the wall, they would spin around and flee, shouting "There it is! Archimedes is aiming one of his engines at us!" So he discontinued all frontal assaults and set up a protracted siege for the duration.

TRANSPORTATION

DOCUMENT 27
Sailing Season in the Mediterranean

Though the Greeks and Romans both relied heavily on the Mediterranean as their principal commercial highway, the small size of their vessels and their rudimentary navigational techniques combined with the common winter storms to limit almost all sailing to the calmer half of the year (Hesiod Works and Days 618–634).

But if you conceive a desire for stormy seafaring, when the Pleiades flee the mighty strength of Orion and dive into the misty sea [late October to early November] is the time when gales blow from all directions. And from that moment no longer keep ships on the wine-dark sea, but think to work the land, as I advise you. Haul your ship out on dry land, surround it with stones to keep out the force of the winds that bring damp, and remove the drain plug so that the rain of heaven may not rot it. Stow all the tackle and fittings in your house, repairing the sail—the wings of a sea-roving ship—and hang the well-shaped steering-oar over the smoke from the hearth. You yourself wait for the proper sailing season to arrive, and then drag your ship to the sea and load a suitable cargo in it.

DOCUMENT 28
The Difficult Voyage of the Apostle Paul

The harrowing experience of St. Paul on his voyage to Rome (Acts 27.13–44) was not an unusual one.

When a light south wind began to blow, [the sailors] thought that they had obtained what they wanted and, raising anchor, they coasted along the shore of Crete. But not long afterwards the northeasterly wind struck us from the shore and, since the ship was caught by the wind and could not make way against it, we gave way to it and were carried along. Running up behind a small island called Cauda, we were able with great difficulty to secure the ship's boat and, after hoisting it up, they passed cables under the ship to hold it together. Fearing that they might be driven on to the Syrtes, they let down a sea anchor and so were carried along. Since we were being badly tossed about by the storm, the next day the sailors began to jettison the cargo, and on the third day, with their own hands they cast overboard the ship's tackle....

When the fourteenth night had come and we were being carried along in the Ionian Sea, the sailors suspected that they were nearing land and, casting the sounding-weight, they found 20 fathoms. A short distance along they sounded again, and found 15 fathoms. Afraid that we might run up on some shoals, they let out four anchors from the stern and prayed for daylight. The sailors lowered the ship's boat into the sea under the pretence of setting anchors from the bow, but in reality scheming to escape from the ship. But Paul said to the centurion and his soldiers, "Unless these sailors remain on the ship, we cannot be saved," and the soldiers cut the rope holding the boat, and let it go. We were in all 276 souls on the ship.

When day came they did not recognize the place, but saw a bay with a sandy beach, to which they planned to bring the ship, if they were able. They cast off the anchors, losing them in the sea, and at the same time untied the lashings that fixed the steering-oars; they spread the sail to the wind and made for the beach. But they struck some shoals and ran the boat up on them; the bow remained stuck fast, and the stern was broken up by the force of the waves. The centurion . . . ordered those who could swim to throw themselves overboard first and head for land, the rest to use planks or some pieces of the ship. And in this way it happened that all came safely to land.

DOCUMENT 29
The Sea Battle at Salamis

Accurate descriptions of naval battles are less plentiful than those of sieges. In this famous (but simplified) example, Herodotus (Histories 8.84–96) describes one of the most significant sea battles of antiquity, when the outnumbered Athenians defeated the Persian allied fleet in 479 B.C.E.

Then the Greeks put all their ships out to sea, and the Persian forces set upon them immediately as they put out.... Since the Greeks fought with order and in the proper array, while the foreigners did nothing either in an orderly manner or rationally, it was right that they should come to such an ends as befell them. . . . The majority of the foreigners perished in the sea, since they did not know how to swim. When the [Persian] ships in the front rank were turned to flight, at that moment most of them were destroyed. For the captains in the ranks behind, trying to advance in their ships in order to demonstrate to the king some accomplishment on their part, ran up against their comrades' ships as these fled. . . . A ship from Samothrace rammed an Athenian ship but, as the Athenian ship was sinking, a ship from Aegina attacked and sank the Samothracian ship. The Samothracians, though, being javelin-throwers, swept the marines from the deck of the ship that had sunk theirs, boarded it, and captured it. . . . When the sea battle broke off, the Greeks towed to Salamis such of the wrecks as still happened to survive.

DOCUMENT 30
The Harbor and Lighthouse of Alexandria

> *The Hellenistic harbor at Alexandria in Egypt, described here by Strabo (Geography 17.1.6–8), was—along with Rome's Ostia, Carthage, and the Piraeus of Athens—one of the four principal harbors of the ancient Mediterranean; it also boasted the largest lighthouse of antiquity.*

Pharos is a small, oblong island, quite close to the mainland and with it, creating a harbor that has two entrances. The shoreline has the form of a bay framed by two headlands that project seaward, and the island is located between them, closing off the bay: for it lies lengthwise, parallel to the shore. The eastern of the extremities of Pharos is closer to the mainland and the promontory opposite (which is called Lochias) and gives the harbor a narrow entrance. In addition to the narrowness of the passage, there are rocks—some below the water, others projecting above it—that continually break up the swell that rolls in on them from the open sea. This end of the island is a rock, washed on all sides by the sea, that has on it a tower marvelously constructed of white stone in many storeys, and carrying the same name as the island. Sostratus of Cnidus, a friend of the kings, dedicated this, as the inscription says, for the safety of those who sail the sea. Since the coastland was low lying and harborless in both directions, and also had reefs and some shoal water, those who sailed in from the open sea had need of some elevated and conspicuous sign in order to set a good course for the harbor entrance. . . .

As for the great harbor, in addition to being beautifully enclosed by the mole and by natural topography, it is deep close inshore, so that the largest ship can tie up by the steps of the quay. It is also divided up into several harbor basins.

DOCUMENT 31
Constructing a Harbor

Vitruvius (On Architecture 5.12.1–7) has given us generic instructions for situating and constructing a commercial harbor.

I must not omit the proper arrangement of harbors, but rather explain by what techniques ships are protected in them from stormy weather. Harbors that have an advantageous natural location, with projecting headlands or promontories that form naturally curved or angular recesses, seem to be the most useful. Colonnades or shipyards are to be constructed around the circumference, and entrances from the colonnades to the markets. Towers are to be built on either side [of the harbor entrance], from which chains can be drawn across by means of winches.

If, however, we have no natural harbor situation suitable for protecting ships from storms, we must proceed as follows. If there is an anchorage on one side and no river mouth interferes, then a mole composed of concrete structures or rubble mounds is to be built on either side and the harbor enclosure thus formed. Those concrete structures that are to be in the water must be made in the following fashion. Earth is to be brought from the region that runs from Cumae to the promontory of Minerva [i.e., pozzolana], and mixed into the mortar used in these structures, in the proportion of two parts earth to one part lime. Next, in the designated spot, formwork enclosed by stout posts and tie beams is to be let down into the water and fixed firmly in position. Then the area within it at the bottom, below the water, is to be leveled and cleared out, [working] from a platform of small crossbeams. The construction is to be carried on there with a mixture of aggregate and mortar, as described above, until the space left for the structure within the form has been filled. Such is the natural advantage of the places we have described above.

But if, because of waves or the force of the open sea, the anchoring supports cannot hold the forms down, then a platform is to be built out from the shore itself or from the foundations of the mole, made as firm as possible. This platform is to be built out with a level upper surface over less than half its area, while the section towards the shore is to have a sloping side. Next, retaining walls 1.5 feet wide are to be built towards the sea and on either side of the platform, equal in height to the level surface described above. Then the sloping section is to be filled in with sand and brought up to the level of the retaining walls and platform surface. Next, a mass of the appointed size is to be built there, on this leveled surface, and when poured is to be left at least two months to cure. Then the retaining wall that holds in the sand is cut away, and in this way erosion of the sand by the waves causes the mass to fall into the sea. By this procedure, repeated as often as necessary, the breakwater can be carried seaward.

But in locations where the land is not naturally configured, one must use the following procedure. Let double-walled formwork [that is, cofferdams] be set up in the designated spot, held together by close-set planks and tie beams, and between the anchoring supports have clay packed down in baskets made of swamp reeds. When it has been well tamped down in this manner, and is as compact as possible, then have the area bounded by the cofferdam emptied and dried out using installations of water screws and water wheels with compartmented rims and bodies. The foundations are to be dug there, within the cofferdam. If the foundations are to be on a rocky, solid bottom, the area to be excavated and drained must be larger than the wall that will stand above, then filled in with a concrete of aggregate, lime, and sand. But if the bottom is soft, the foundations are to be covered with pilings of charred alder or olive wood and filled in with charcoal, as described for the foundations of theatres and city walls. Then raise a wall of squared stone with joints as long as possible, so the stones in the middle may be well tied together by the joints. The space inside the wall is to be filled with rubble packing or concrete, so it will be possible to build a tower upon it.

When all this has been finished, the shipyards must be considered, and in particular that they be laid out facing north; for a southern exposure, on account of its heat, leads to dry rot, wood worms, ship worms, and other pests, and nourishes and maintains them. Furthermore, because of the danger of fire, these buildings should be constructed with as little wood as possible. There should be no restriction on their size, but they should be built to the dimensions of the largest ships, so that even these will have a roomy berth when they are drawn up on shore.

DOCUMENT 32
The Persian Royal Road

In the first passage Herodotus (Histories 5.52–53) gives the technical details of the world's first state-organized highway and postal system; then

Xenophon (Cyropaedia 8.6.17–18) describes its operation; and we end with a quotation from Herodotus again (Histories 8.98), adapted as the motto of the U.S. Postal Service.

The nature of the road is as follows. All along it are royal rest stops and excellent lodgings, and the entire road runs through inhabited and safe country.... In all there are 111 stages, with as many rest stops, on the road going up from Sardis to Susa.... For people traveling at a rate of 150 *stadia* [= 20 miles] each day, just 90 days will be consumed.

In regard to the magnitude of his empire, we have also discovered another device of Cyrus, by which he learned more quickly the state of affairs at any distance. For after examining how long a journey could be finished in a day by a horse that was ridden hard, he established posting stations at just such distances and equipped them with horses and men to look after them. And at each of the places he stationed the proper men to receive and pass on the dispatches, and to take charge of the exhausted horses and men, and to furnish fresh ones. [Sometimes riders traveled by day and night.] This is undeniably the fastest travel by land possible for humans.

There is no mortal man who can accomplish a journey faster than these Persian messengers.... Not snow, not rain, not heat, not night hinders these men from covering the stage assigned to them as quickly as possible. The first rider passes the dispatch to the second, the second to the third, and so on along the line.

DOCUMENT 33
An Example of Roman Road Building

Though the Romans were as renowned for their highways as for their aqueducts, we unfortunately lack a comprehensive ancient account of how they built them. This passage from the biographer Plutarch (Gaius Gracchus 7.1–2) gives a general sense of the technique, though it of course varied according to the terrain.

Gaius Gracchus was especially anxious about road building, paying attention to utility as well as to what benefited grace and beauty. For the roads were carried straight through the country without wavering, were paved with quarried stone, and were made solid with masses of tightly packed sand. Hollows were filled up and bridges were thrown across whatever wintry streams or ravines cut the roads. And both sides were an equal and parallel height, with the result that the road for its entire course had a level and beautiful appearance. Besides these things, he measured the whole road mile by mile—the mile is a bit less than eight *stadia*—and set up stone columns as distance indicators. He also placed other stones on either side of the road at lesser intervals, so that it would be easier for those people who had to mount horses to get on them from the stones without requiring a groom for help.

DOCUMENT 34
A Law of Caesar Restricting Wheeled Traffic in Rome

> *Because Rome had developed haphazardly, by the first century* B.C.E. *its urban road system was incapable of handling the traffic—both vehicular and pedestrian—of a city of perhaps 900,000 inhabitants. As we see from this inscription* (Corpus Inscriptionum Latinarum 1.593.56–66 = Inscriptiones Latinae Selectae 6085), *the Dictator Caesar tried to resolve the problem by restricting access for wheeled vehicles to the hours of darkness, to protect pedestrians during the day.*

On those roads that are or shall be within the city of Rome among those places where habitation shall be continuous, no one, after the first day of next January, shall be permitted in the daytime—after sunrise or before the tenth hour of the day—to lead or drive any freight wagon except when it is necessary to bring in or transport material for the sake of building the sacred temples of the immortal gods, or for the sake of building public works, or where, in carrying out a public contract for demolition, it shall be necessary for the good of the public to carry material out of the city and out of those places, and in situations for which specified persons shall be allowed for specified causes to drive or lead freight wagons by this law.

On those days when the Vestal Virgins, the *Rex sacrorum*, and the flamens shall be required to ride in wagons in the city for the sake of the public sacrifices on behalf of the Roman people, and when wagons shall be necessary for the sake of a triumph on the day someone will have the triumph, or when wagons shall be required for games publicly celebrated at Rome or within one mile of the city of Rome, or for the procession at the Circus Games,... for the sake of those causes and on those days nothing in this law is intended to prevent wagons from being led or driven in the daytime in the city.

DOCUMENT 35
Caesar's Bridge over the Rhine River

The Romans in particular were adept at throwing bridges across streams and rivers that previously had to be forded. Exceptional examples of their multi-arched stone structures can still be seen crossing the Tiber River in Rome; and this example of a complex wooden bridge built and described by Caesar (Gallic War 4.17–18) is a testament to Roman engineering.

Caesar had decided to cross the Rhine for the reasons given earlier; but to cross by boats he deemed not safe enough and ruled it worthy for neither himself nor the Roman people. And so, even though he was confronted by the greatest difficulty for making a bridge because of the river's width, swiftness, and depth, he nevertheless decided that he had to make the effort or else not lead his army across.

He used the following method for the bridge. At intervals of 2 feet, he joined pairs of timbers that were 1.5 feet thick, sharpened a bit at their bases, and measured for the depth of the river. Having lowered these into the river with machines, he fixed them and rammed them down using pile drivers,... leaning forward and sloping so that they inclined with the natural flow of the river. In addition, he planted two piles opposite these at in interval of 40 feet downstream, fastened together in the same manner but turned into the force and flow of the river. These two rows were kept firmly apart by inserting into their tops 2-foot-thick beams of the same length as the distance between the piles and supported with pairs of braces at the outer side of each pile. As a result of this combination of holding apart and clamping together, so great was the stability of the work and its character that the greater the force of the water rushing against it, the more tightly its parts held fast together.

These beams were interconnected by timbers laid at right angles, and then these were floored over with long poles and wickerwork. In addition, piles were driven at an angle into the water on the downstream side, which were thrust out underneath like a buttress and joined with the entire structure, to take the force of the river. Others were similarly placed a little bit above the bridge so that if tree trunks or vessels were sent by the barbarians to knock down the structure, the force of those objects might be diminished by these defenses and the bridge protected from harm.

Ten days after the timber began to be collected, the bridge was completed and the army led across.

DOCUMENT 36
The Barter System of Trade

*Though speaking of the late Bronze Age, Homer (The Iliad 7.465–
475) here betrays his own society in eighth-century Greece, just before
the invention of coinage, when even iron was still precious enough to be
used as a medium of exchange.*

The sun set, and the work of the Achaeans came to an end. They
slaughtered oxen throughout their encampment and took their meal. A
fleet of ships had arrived from Lemnos with a cargo of wine, sent by
Euneus, . . . son of Jason, who had included in the shipment a separate
gift of a thousand measures of wine for Agamemnon and Menelaus, the
sons of Atreus. From these ships the long-haired Achaeans bought
themselves wine by barter, some giving bronze in exchange and others
flashing iron, some hides or live cattle and others slaves. And then they
laid out a bounteous feast. . . .

DOCUMENT 37
Early Coinage

*Here Herodotus (Histories 1.94) and Strabo (Geography 8.6.16)
recount the traditional (and slightly conflicting) attributions of the invention of coinage and of the first silver denomination.*

The Lydians were the first people we know who used currency coined
from gold and silver, and they were also the first to engage in retail trade.

According to Ephorus, silver was coined first on the island of Aegina
by Pheidon, because the place was a center of trade, its agricultural
poverty having encouraged its inhabitants to earn their livelihood as
merchants at sea—whence, Ephorus adds, minor goods are called "Aeginetan merchandise."

RECORDKEEPING AND TIMEKEEPING

DOCUMENT 38
The Nilometer

*The requirements of intensive agriculture and irrigation were the
motivations behind the development of writing in early-Bronze-Age*

> Egypt: to keep accounts of produce and taxation and, as this passage from Strabo (Geography 17.1.48) indicates, to maintain annual records of the Nile's flood.

The nilometer is a well built of ashlar masonry on the bank of the Nile, in which are indicated the highest, lowest, and average inundations of the Nile. For the water in the well rises and sinks along with the river. In consequence, there are signs on the wall of the well shaft to designate the height of the complete and of the other inundations.... For [by comparing] these marks and dates [to those of past years], they know far in advance what the inundation will be and make predictions. This is helpful not only to the farmers with respect to the division of water, to embankments, canals, and other such things, but also to the authorities with respect to the public revenues.

DOCUMENT 39
Egyptian Scripts

> Diodorus of Sicily (History 3.4.1–4, 3.3.5) gives us a comprehensive description of the pictographic and ideographic elements of Egyptian hieroglyphs.

To complete our discussion of the Egyptians' antiquities, mention must be made of their script, which is called "hieroglyphic" by the Greeks. It turns out that the shapes of their characters correspond to animals of every sort, to the extremities of the human body, and to tools (especially those used by carpenters). For it is not through a combination of syllabic sounds that their script expresses the underlying meaning, but rather from the allusion latent in the objects represented and their metaphorical meaning that practice has impressed on their memory.

They draw, for example, pictures of a hawk and a crocodile, a snake and elements of the human body: an eye, a hand, a face, and so on. In this case the hawk, because it is pretty well the swiftest winged creature, signifies to them anything that happens swiftly. Then, with apt metaphorical allusions, this sense can be applied to all swift creatures and whatever else conforms closely enough to the nature of those thus identified. The crocodile is symbolic of everything that is evil, the eye is the guardian of right behavior and protector of the whole body. As for the bodily extremities: the right hand with fingers splayed connotes the acquisition of resources, while the left hand with fingers clenched suggests the defensive protection of property. The same reasoning holds for the other characters, whether parts of the body or tools or anything else. For by tracing closely the allusions that are implicit in any given object and by exercising their minds through long practice and memorization, they learn to read fluently everything that has been written.

There are two [other] scripts used by the Egyptians: one, labeled "popular," is learned by everyone; the other, called "sacred," is understood only by the priests of the Egyptians, who learned it from their fathers as one of the things that should be kept secret.

DOCUMENT 40
The Greeks Adopt the Phoenician Script

*Herodotus (Histories 5.58–59) here passes on the traditional iden-
tification of Kadmos as the transmitter of the Phoenician alphabet to the
Greeks. He also describes the use of skins as a writing surface, some three
centuries before the "invention" of parchment in Pergamon.*

These Phoenicians who accompanied Kadmos...and settled in Boeotia taught the Greeks many things, but their greatest lesson was the alphabet, which as far as I can tell was unknown to the Greeks before this time. At first they used the standard Phoenician script, but with the passage of time they changed both the sound and the shape of the letters.

Most of the land in their neighborhood at that time was occupied by the Ionian Greeks, who learned their letters from the Phoenicians and, after making a few changes in their forms, put them to their own use. And they called the script that they used "Phoenician," which was only right since it had been the Phoenicians who had introduced it to Greece. So, too, the Ionians call papyrus sheets "skins," a holdover from antiquity when a scarcity of papyrus had them using the skins of goats and sheep; and even in my own day many non-Greeks use such skins as a writing surface.

I have personally seen Kadmean letters carved on some tripods in the Temple of Ismenian Apollo at Thebes in Boeotia, and they are essentially the same as the Ionian alphabet.

DOCUMENT 41
The Emperor Claudius Adds New Letters
to the Latin Alphabet

*The efforts of the scholarly Emperor Claudius to supplement the Latin
alphabet with new symbols for common sounds, as described here by*

Tacitus (Annals 11.13.3–14.5), proved futile. Today, the simplified spelling and emoticons of computer texts proves that sometimes the cavaliers do win out over the puritans.

Once he learned that the Greek alphabet, too, had not been invented from beginning to end at a single stroke, the Emperor Claudius added new letter forms [to the Latin alphabet] and promoted their use in public....

In Italy the Etruscans were taught the alphabet by Demaratus from Corinth, while our earliest ancestors learned it from Evander the Arcadian. And the forms of the Latin characters are the same as the oldest letters of the Greeks. But, like the Greeks, we had a small number of letters to begin with, to which later additions were made. Claudius used this as a precedent for adding three more letters,[1] which remained in use while he was emperor but disappeared afterwards—though they can still be seen in public inscriptions set up in fora and on temples.

DOCUMENT 42
Papyrus as a Writing Surface

Pliny (Natural History 13.68–72, 74, 77, 81, 89) describes the cultivation and treatment of papyrus, the principal writing surface of antiquity.

The character of papyrus will also be discussed, since it is on the use of paper especially that civilized life, or at least its historical memory, depends.... Papyrus grows in the swamps of Egypt or where the Nile's still waters have spread beyond their banks and formed pools less than 3 feet deep.... Paper is made from papyrus by splitting it with a needle into strips that are extremely thin but as wide as can be managed. The best papyrus comes from the middle of the plant, the quality declining with each subsequent layer that is split off....

Whatever the quality, paper is woven together on a board that has been moistened with water from the Nile, the sludge providing the binding force of a glue. After both of its ends are trimmed, each strip of papyrus is first plastered onto the table flat and straight, then other strips are laid across them to form a lattice, which is pressed between beams. The sheets are dried in the sun and then joined together,... though never more than 20 to a roll.... Any unevenness is smoothed off with an

---

1. One to stand for the consonantal *u* (our *w*), another for the Greek double consonant *y* (*ps*, also Latin *bs*), the third to represent the *y* sound halfway between *i* and *u*.

ivory tool or a shell, though the text is liable to fading because the polishing makes the page less absorbent and more glossy.

DOCUMENT 43
The Oddities of the Roman Calendar

The evolution of calendars in all societies was slow and deeply rooted in ancient traditions. In the first passage, Pliny (Natural History 7.212) comments on the simplicity of timekeeping in early Rome; in the second, Censorinus (The Natal Day 20.4–11) reveals the irregularities that had separated the civil calendar from the solar year, and describes Caesar's plan to bring them into permanent alignment.

In the Twelve Tables [451–450 B.C.E.] only sunrise and sunset are listed. After a few years, midday was added, which the consul's attendant announced when, from the Senate, he saw the sun between the speakers' platform and the ambassadors' waiting area. He also announced the last hour of the day when the sun retreated from the Maenian Column to the prison, but only on clear days. . . .

Afterwards, [one of Rome's early kings] established the 12 months and 365 days [as the period of a year]. . . . At last, when it had been decided to add an intercalary month of 22 or 23 days in alternate years, so that the civil year corresponded to the natural [solar] year, it was intercalated best in the month of February between the festivals of the Terminalia [23 February] and Regifugium [24 February]. This was done for a long time before it was perceived that the civil years were somewhat longer than the natural years. The duty for correcting this fault was given to the pontiffs along with the power for them to intercalate at their own discretion. But most of these men further distorted the matter entrusted to them to correct by wantonly intercalating longer or shorter months in accordance with their hatred or favoritism, by which some men left office more quickly and some served longer. . . .

The calendar was so out of step that Gaius Julius Caesar, the *pontifex maximus*, in his third consulship with Marcus Aemilius Lepidus [46 B.C.E.], in order to correct the earlier defect, inserted two intercalary months, totaling 67 days, between November and December although he had already intercalated 23 days in February. This made that year 445 days long. At the same time he provided that the same mistakes would not occur in the future, for once he abolished the intercalary month he regulated the civil year according to the course of the sun. And so he added 10 days to the

355, which he divided among the seven months of 29 days. . . . In addition, on account of the quarter day that is known to complete a true year, Caesar decreed that after a cycle of four years a single day (where once there had been a month) should be intercalated after Terminalia [23 February], which is now called *bissextus* ["double," our 29 February].

DOCUMENT 44
The Origin of Sundials

> *In the first two passages, Diogenes Laertius (Lives of Eminent Philosophers 2.1) and Herodotus (Histories 2.109) give two accounts of how the Greeks developed sundials, . . . and there is truth in both; in the third, a character from the comic poet Plautus (The Boeotian Women = Aulus Gellius Attic Nights 3.3.5) expresses a view of the tyranny of clocks that now seems remarkably contemporary.*

Anaximander was the first man to invent the gnomon and to set it up as a sundial in the territory of Sparta to mark the solstices and equinoxes. . . . He also built clocks.

The Greeks learned the sundial, the gnomon, and the 12 divisions of the day from the Babylonians.

May the gods destroy that man who first discovered hours and who first set up a sundial here, and who cut up my day into pieces and made me wretched. It's a fact that when I was a boy, my only sundial was my stomach, by far the best and truest of all clocks. When it advised you, you ate, unless there was no food. Now, even when there is food, it isn't eaten unless the sun allows it. Indeed, the whole town is so full of sundials these days that the majority of its people crawl about all shriveled up with hunger.

DOCUMENT 45
How to Construct a Water Clock

> *Vitruvius (On Architecture 9.8.2–7) gives a precise and accurate description of Ctesibius' water clock, which remarkably could accommodate the seasonal hours of variable length.*

The methods of making water clocks have also been examined, . . . first of all by Ctesibius of Alexandria. . . . He began by making a hollow opening in a piece of gold or by piercing a gemstone, since these materials are not worn by the action of water, nor do they collect grit and become clogged. The water flowing in at a regular volume through that opening raises an inverted bowl, which is called the cork or drum by the craftsman. A bar and revolving drum are attached to this apparatus, and both are fitted with regularly spaced teeth that, when meshing into one another, make measured rotations and movements. Other bars and other drums, toothed in the same manner and driven by the same motion, cause various effects and movements by their turning: figures are moved, cones revolve, pebbles or eggs fall, trumpets sound, and other peripheral actions happen. On these clocks the hours are marked either on a column or a pilaster; a figure raised from below points them out with a rod through the entire day.... [To accommodate] the shortening and lengthening of the days, [tapering lines for] the hours are to be marked off horizontally around a small column facing the analemma, ... and this column is to be made to revolve so that, as it turns continuously beneath the rising figure's rod, which points out the hours, it thus accommodates the shortening and lengthening hours according to the month of the year.

CRAFTS

DOCUMENT 46
Sluicing for Gold

> *Placer gold was harvested and worked long before the metal ages began, because it occurs naturally in a pure form and is malleable enough to be worked without special tools or techniques. Here, Pliny (Natural History 33.66) and Strabo (Geography 11.2.19) reveal where and how this gold was obtained.*

Gold in our part of the world—passing over Indian gold dug up by ants, or among the Scythians by griffins—is found in three ways: first, in river deposits, as in the Tagus in Spain, the Po in Italy, the Hebro in Thrace, the Pactolus in Asia Minor, and the Ganges in India. No gold is more refined, for it is thoroughly polished by the very flow of the stream and by wear.

It is said that among them [some tribes of Colchis on the Black Sea] mountain torrents swollen by melting snow carry gold down, and the locals catch it with perforated troughs and fleecy hides, and that this is the origin of the myth of the golden fleece....

DOCUMENT 47
The Horrors of Mining

Mining was the most dangerous occupation in antiquity, as Diodorus of Sicily (History 3.12.1–13.1) makes clear in this disturbing passage.

Around the frontiers of Egypt and the adjoining territory of both Arabia and Ethiopia there is a region that possesses many large gold mines, where much gold is gathered up with great suffering and expense. For while the earth is black by nature, it contains seams and veins of a white stone [quartz] distinguished by its brightness, surpassing in its radiance all the stones that by nature have a bright gleam. Those who oversee the work in the mines extract the gold by means of a multitude of workers, for the kings of Egypt gather up and hand over for gold-mining men who have been convicted of crimes, those taken prisoner in war, along with those who have fallen prey to unjust accusations and been thrown into prison through spite—sometimes only themselves, sometimes all their relatives too. At one and the same time the kings exact punishment from those who have been condemned and receive great profit from their labors.

Those who have been handed over, a great number in all, and every one of them fettered with chains, keep busy at their work without ceasing, both by day and all through the night without receiving any rest, carefully guarded against any attempt at flight. For garrisons of foreign soldiers who speak languages different from theirs guard them, so that no one can through conversation or some friendly communication corrupt any of those set over him. After burning the hardest of the gold-bearing matrix with a great fire and making it friable, they carry on the process of production by hand. Thousands of the unfortunate creatures crush with a quarrying hammer the rock that has been loosened and is capable of being worked with moderate effort. The workman who assays the ore is in charge of the whole operation and gives instructions to the workers. Of the men chosen for this misfortune, those individuals of outstanding physical strength break up the quartz rock with iron hammers, applying to the work not skill, but force, not cutting tunnels through the rock in a straight line, but wherever there is a vein of the shining rock. These men, then, spending their time in darkness because of the twists and turns in the galleries, carry lamps tied to their foreheads, and after shifting the position of their bodies according to the specific character of the vein, they throw down to the gallery floor the fragments of rock they dig out. And they keep up this work incessantly under the hard supervision and blows of an overseer.

Boys who have not yet reached puberty crawl through the tunnels into the galleries hollowed out in the rock and with great effort collect the ore that has been thrown down bit by bit and carry it back to a place outside the mouth of the mine in the open air.

DOCUMENT 48
The Mythical Smithy of Hephaestus

In this passage from Homer's The Iliad *(18.468–482), the poet describes how the god Hephaestus (the Roman Vulcan) made preparations in his workshop for manufacturing a new set of armor for Achilles, at the request of the hero's mother Thetis. The items in the last sentence belong to the working of iron—another example of Homer including contemporary technology in a poem about the past.*

So saying he left her there and went to his bellows. These he turned towards the fire and ordered them to work. And the bellows, twenty in all, blew on the crucibles, blasting forth strong wind in all degrees of strength to fan the flames, and were at his service as he hurried about here and there; wherever Hephaestus wished them to blow they did, and the work went forward. On the fire he put stubborn bronze, and tin and precious gold and silver. Then he set a great anvil on the anvil-block, and in one hand he grasped his mighty hammer and in the other hand he grasped his tongs.

DOCUMENT 49
Making Glass

Pliny (Natural History 36.190–193) here gives a summary of the materials and techniques for manufacturing glass vessels in the first century C.E.

In the portion of the province of Syria that is called Phoenicia and borders on Judaea, among the foothills of Mt. Carmel, there is a swamp called Candebia. The Belus River is believed to flow from it and in five miles reaches the sea by the colony of Ptolemais. . . . It is muddy and deep, and the sand is not visible except at low water. These deposits are rolled by the waves and gleam once the impurities have been rubbed away. Then also, it is believed, they are made astringent by the salty bite of the sea, and ready for use. The beach is no more than half a mile long, but for many centuries this sand alone was used for the production of glass. There is a story that soda [natural sodium carbonate] merchants were driven here in their ship. While they were scattered along the shore preparing a meal, not finding any stray stones to set their pots on, they instead put beneath them lumps of soda from the ship. When these were heated and mixed with the beach sand, streams of an unknown translucent liquid flowed out, and this was the origin of glass.

Soon, since man's skill is ingenious, he was not content to mix just soda, but magnetite, since it is believed to attract to itself the melted glass just as it does iron. In the same way, shining stones came to be added to the melt in many places, then shells and pit sand. There are authors who state that the glass in India is incomparable. The heating is done with light, dry wood, and copper and soda (preferably Egyptian) are added to the melt. Like bronze, glass is melted in a series of furnaces, and dull blackish lumps are formed. Molten glass everywhere is so sharp that before any pain is felt it cuts to the bone whatever part of the body it strikes. The masses are melted again in the workshops and colored, then some of the glass is shaped by blowing, some ground on a lathe, some engraved like silver. Sidon was once renowned for these workshops, since indeed she even invented glass mirrors.

ATTITUDES

DOCUMENT 50
Aristocratic Prejudice Against Artisans

Xenophon (Estate Management 4.2–3) here expresses bluntly the attitude of the wealthy landed class of Greek states toward the crafts and manual labor.

To be sure, the so-called banausic arts are spoken against and—quite rightly—held in contempt in our states, for they ruin the bodies of those practicing them and those who supervise, forcing them to sit still and pass their time indoors, some even to spend their day at a fire. As their bodies are softened, so too their minds become much more sickly. As well, the so-called banausic arts leave no leisure time for paying attention to one's friends or state, with the result that the persons who practice them have the reputation of treating their friends badly and being poor defenders of their homeland. In some states, particularly those with a warlike reputation, it is forbidden for any citizen to practice the banausic arts.

DOCUMENT 51
A Roman Aristocrat's View of Occupations

Cicero (On Duty 1.42) here reflects a Roman attitude that mirrors that of Xenophon, but recognizes the importance of agriculture as the foundation of Roman culture. The glory of working the land was expressed in political as well as social terms: the wealth of Roman senators could include only landed property, the majority of it in Italy.

Now as to which crafts and other means of earning a living are suitable for a gentleman to practice and which are degrading, we have been taught more or less the following. First of all, those occupations that stir up people's ill will—such as the tax gatherer or moneylender— are condemned. Also vulgar and unbecoming to a gentleman are all the jobs taken on by hired workers, whose labor is purchased rather than their skill, for their very salary is the remuneration for their servitude. Also to be considered vulgar are those who buy from wholesale merchants in order to sell immediately, for they do not make any profit without significant deception—and there is nothing more base than misrepresentation. All craftsmen spend their time in vulgar occupations, for no workshop can have anything liberal ["befitting a free man"] about it. The lowest esteem is accorded those occupations that service the sensual pleasures: "fishmongers, butchers, cooks, and poulterers," as [the comic poet] Terence writes. . . .

But the professions that require a greater degree of intelligence or from which a significant social benefit is derived—such as medicine, or architecture, or the teaching of liberal subjects—these are honorable for those to whose social rank they are appropriate. . . . However, of all the gainful occupations, none is better, none more profitable, none more pleasant, none more worthy of a free man than agriculture.

DOCUMENT 52
The Technical Gifts of Prometheus

*Mythology credits the divine Prometheus with giving the human race
fire, as well as instructing them in many inventions, for which a jealous
Zeus punished him. As is clear from this monologue by Aeschylus
(Prometheus Bound 442–506), the Greeks saw Prometheus as the great
benefactor of humankind.*

What I, Prometheus, did for mortals in their misery, hear now. To
them, at first mindless, I gave mind and reason. . . . I showed them the
risings and settings of stars, hard to interpret till now. I also invented for
them numbering, the supreme skill, and how to set words in writing, to
remember all things, the inventive mother of the Muses. I was the first
to harness beasts under the yoke, enslaving them with a trace or saddle,
to take man's place under the heaviest burdens; I put the horse to the
chariot, and made him obey the rein and be an ornament to wealth and
greatness. No one before me discovered the sailor's wagon, the flax-
winged craft that roam the seas. Such tools and skills I discovered for
humans. . . . As for those benefits to humans that lay hidden in the
earth—the bronze, iron, silver, and gold—who other than I could claim
to have been the first to find them? . . . Learn the whole matter in a brief
phrase: all the arts [*technai*] possessed by mortals come from Prometheus.

DOCUMENT 53
Hostility toward Innovation

*While probably anecdotal rather than real, these two stories well illus-
trate the sort of suspicion of the changes that inevitably result from innovation. Both Suetonius (Vespasian 18) and Petronius (Satyricon 50–
51) relate incidents from the first century C.E.*

To an engineer who promised to transport some heavy columns to the
Capitoline Hill at a low cost, the Emperor [Vespasian] gave a significant
reward for his scheme, but refused to put it into operation, saying "You
must let me feed the poor folk."

There was once a craftsman who made a glass bowl that was un-
breakable. He was given an audience with the Emperor [Tiberius],
bringing along his gift. He had the Emperor hand it back, and then threw

it on the floor. The Emperor was as frightened as could be, but the man picked up the bowl from the ground—and it was dented just like a vessel made of bronze! He took a little hammer from his shirt and fixed it perfectly without any problem. By doing so he thought he had made his fortune, especially after the Emperor said to him, "No one else knows how to temper glass this way, do they?" Now just see what happened. After the man said "No," the Emperor had his head chopped off, because if this invention were to become known, we would treat gold like dirt.

DOCUMENT 54
The Five Ages of Humankind

Hesiod (Works and Days 107–178) gives us our earliest description of how the Greeks viewed the decline of the human race, from the Age of Gold to the present. That attitude is a pessimistic and sobering contrast to our contemporary belief in continuous progress and the improvement of life, and it undoubtedly contributed to the generally negative view of technology and innovation.

I beg you to consider seriously that gods and mortals are born from the same source. First, the immortal gods dwelling in Olympian homes made the Golden race of people who lived in the time when Cronus ruled the heavens. They lived like the gods, carefree in heart and free from labor and misery; ... all good things were theirs: grain-giving earth spontaneously bore her copious and ungrudging fruit, and in pleasant peace they lived off their lands in pleasant abundance. ... Then the immortal gods dwelling in Olympian homes made the second race, the Silver one, much worse than the previous, unlike the Golden in either thought or appearance. Each child was reared for a hundred years by its noble mother, a complete simpleton in its own home; and when they finally grew up and reached maturity, they survived only a brief time. ... The Father Zeus made the third race, the Bronze race of mortals, not at all like the Silver race, from ash trees, terrible and mighty; they loved the wretched works of Ares [god of war] and acts of arrogance; ...their armor and weapons were bronze, bronze their houses, and with bronze tools they worked: dark iron did not yet exist. And, overcome by their own hands, they went into the dank and dark house of cold Hades, leaving no name. ... Then Zeus, the son of Cronus, made another race, the fourth on the bountiful earth, better and more just, the divine race of heroes who are called demigods, the race before ours on the boundless earth.

Some were destroyed by grim war and terrible battle [at Troy and Thebes]; . . . to others Father Zeus gave the gift of a home and means of living, and settled them at the end of the earth apart from everyone. . . . Fortunate are these heroes, since the grain-giving Earth produces a honey-sweet harvest three times a year for them. Oh, that I were not living among the fifth race, but had either died before or been born afterwards! For now is the Iron race, when humans will never cease from labor and sorrow by day, and from suffering at night, since the gods will give only grievous concerns. And Zeus will destroy this race of mortals, too. . . .

GLOSSARY

The following list includes those terms used in the text that are not defined there but might be unfamiliar to readers.

Amphora: A pottery container used throughout the Mediterranean for shipping and storing grains and liquids. Generally about 1 m tall, with a narrow neck to prevent spillage and evaporation, two vertical handles for lifting and carrying (the Greek *amphi-phoros* means "carried by both sides"), a swelling body for greater capacity, and a pointed bottom that could be pressed into the dirt floors of storerooms.

Atrium: The first large and central room in a Roman house, used by the owner to receive guests, but also surrounded by small, windowless bedrooms for family members. A large square opening in the roof, its four corners supported on columns, supplied indirect illumination; the opening also served to let smoke out, and to allow rainwater from the roof to fall into a reflecting pool below, often with a storage cistern beneath.

Automaton: A machine or gadget operating without human intervention; an early form of robotics.

Balneum: A small Roman bath, either for the public or fitted into a house of the well to do.

Banausia: A Greek term for "craftsmanship," perhaps derived from the word for "furnace." Over time it assumed pejorative overtones; hence our classical authors apply it to manual labor, to working with one's hands rather than mind, and to physical labor that is inherently incompatible with a free citizen and thus demeaning.

Barbarians: To Greeks, any race other than their own, people who did not speak Greek; to the Romans, the tribes that lay beyond the boundaries of the empire. The term generally (but not always) is used dismissively.

Basilica: A Roman building designed originally as a law court, with an apse at one end for the presiding judge, and often lined with shops along the street frontage. Compare the Greek stoa. Its large capacity (juries numbered in the hundreds) and association with the much-admired Roman legal system made it an obvious choice of design for early Christian churches, which took over the name.

Castellum: In hydraulic engineering, the water distribution chamber at the urban end of an aqueduct line.

Censor: The highest office of the Roman political system, to which two prominent citizens were elected every five years to serve for eighteen months. Their duties included letting public contracts and organizing the quinquennial census of citizens. Since membership in the upper social classes was governed by expectations of wealth and morality, the censors would examine their fellow citizens' qualifications and demote them if found wanting; it is this power that we now associate with the title.

Circus: The Roman stadium used for chariot racing; the track was not banked, and chariots had to turn an abrupt 180 degrees at either end as they raced the traditional seven laps, all of which made for an exciting and bloody spectator sport.

Corbelled arch, vault, dome: A Bronze-Age technique for covering spaces with large stones held in place by the weight of the stones above; often called a pseudo-arch, since it does not make use of the keystone that is the essential element of a true arch.

Domus: A Roman private house, limited to the very wealthy; the inward-looking design served to remove the family physically from the noise and dangers of the urban environment outside. Best known from the excavations of Pompeii and Herculaneum. In the oldest style, the rooms were arranged around a central hearth (the Latin word for which is *focus*), which was tended by the young girls of the family in a tradition that was to be applied to the state itself, whose everlasting fire in the (central) Forum was tended by the Vestal Virgins.

Dorian: Pertaining to tribes of northern Greeks who did not migrate into the peninsula with their Mycenaean cousins around 1900 B.C.E. Before the millennium was out, they had learned ironworking from itinerant Hittite craftsmen and began to move southwards, often displacing the Mycenaeans and eventually settling largely in the Peloponnese.

Insula: An apartment building in Roman times, the antithesis of the traditional *domus*, accommodating many families in small units in a single building of multiple storeys. Best known from the excavations of Ostia, but present throughout the empire in densely populated urban areas (e.g., Ephesos).

Klepsydra: "Water thief," a simple gravity-fed water clock invented by the Greeks to measure the relative passage of time and used to limit courtroom speeches, for example.

Megaron: The central suite of rooms in Mycenaean Greek palaces, consisting of a shallow porch with a pair of columns supporting the roof, giving access to an interior vestibule, which itself leads to the main chamber with a round hearth at the center and an elevated portion of roof above resting on four columns.

Metope: The (usually) sculpted stone panels of a Doric Greek temple, located between the triglyphs on the architrave block above the columns.

Nymphaeum: A Greek or Roman public fountain house that supplied urban dwellers with their water for drinking, cooking, and washing.

Peristyle: An open courtyard surrounded by columns supporting a protective roof, and with windowless outside walls; a Greek tradition in domestic architecture that found its way to Rome, and became an essential element in the design of a *domus*, where it was located at the rear of the dwelling to afford the family a private area to spend the day.

Piscina: A pool, either in Roman baths or as an element of urban hydraulic systems, where it served as a settling tank.

Polis: An independent Greek city-state; that is, an urban center (like Athens) and its surrounding farmland (Attica), forming a single unified state with its own economic, legal, political, and social institutions.

Qanaat: An underground channel, common in the arid areas of the Near East, that carried water down a gentle slope from a spring to a town or farms; often discernible on the surface from the regular vertical shafts that were used during construction and for maintenance.

Quern: A simple, hand-operated mill for grinding grain, often consisting of no more than one stone superimposed on another and moved back and forth over the whole grain to produce flour.

Roman Empire: Geographically, the territory controlled and governed by Rome, which by the first century C.E. included all lands bordering the Mediterranean Sea. Historically, the period from Augustus (27 B.C.E.) to the barbarian invasions of the fifth century C.E.

Stoa: A covered market, usually a row of separate shops opening onto a covered and colonnaded portico to provide relief from the sun and protection from rain.

Thermae: Large Roman bathing structures, typical of the imperial period, and found throughout the Empire; usually comprised of a series of large, variously heated rooms grouped symmetrically around an axis, often capable of accommodating hundreds of bathers, elaborately adorned, and with shops, small theaters, and brothels appended.

Tholos: A round building with a domed roof; in Bronze-Age Greece, covered by a corbelled vault and used for burial (often termed a "beehive" tomb); in classical Athens, the public building in the Agora where citizens could always find a member of the Council.

Triclinium: The dining room of a Roman house, so called because it contained three couches (*tri-kline* in Greek), arranged in a U-shape, on each of which reclined three diners.

Triglyph: A marble panel with three vertical bands inserted between the metopes of a Doric Greek temple, and representing the terracotta plate attached to the end of the wooden beam that supported the roof in the primitive prototype.

Warp: The vertical threads on a loom, usually attached to strings that allowed them to be raised or lowered in any combination. Sometimes called the web.

Weft: The horizontal thread that was attached to a shuttle and passed between the raised and lowered warp threads to create a pattern.

ANNOTATED BIBLIOGRAPHY

This bibliography, organized by the chapters of the text, is designed to give the interested reader a route to discovering more about the tools and techniques of antiquity, as well as the social, cultural, and intellectual setting in which they were invented and exploited (or, in some cases that we have seen, ignored).

The list is far from exhaustive: in the first place, I have limited it to works in English; second, I have tried to select volumes that stand a good chance of being available, either through bookstores or, more likely, in public and college libraries; and last, I have emphasized those works that are, in general, academic while still being intelligible to the general reader. For those wishing more detail, I can do no better than to direct you to the first item in this bibliography, where you will find listed everything that was worth reading two decades ago.

Finally, in case my very brief comments do not make it obvious, I have indicated with an asterisk those volumes that most scholars would agree are both the stars of the discipline and at the same time of interest to the nonspecialist.

Reference Works

*J. P. Oleson. *Bronze Age, Greek and Roman Technology: A Select, Annotated Bibliography*. New York: Garland, 1986. Though in need of updating, given the burgeoning academic interest in ancient technology in the last two decades, this is still an essential volume for anyone wanting to dig more deeply into any aspect of the discipline than is possible in the surveys that follow. The book lists 2,030 monographs and articles written in most European languages; annotated entries are arranged by technology, and are thoroughly cross-referenced; there are brief summaries of the contents of each work, and short critical comments on their value.

R. J. Forbes. *Studies in Ancient Technology*. 9 vols. Leiden: Brill, 1964–1972. A monumental and often groundbreaking work that includes chapters on different technologies from the Bronze Age to medieval times, based principally on ancient texts rather than artifacts, and with exhaustive bibliographies. Of particular interest: volume 2 on irrigation, power, and transportation by land; volume 3 on food and diet; volume 4 on textiles; volume 7 on mining and quarrying; and volumes 8 and 9 on metals and metallurgy.

S. Hornblower and A. Spawforth, eds. *The Oxford Classical Dictionary*. 3rd ed. Oxford: Oxford University Press, 1996. This is an invaluable work that covers all aspects of the ancient Mediterranean world in short encyclopedic articles written by scholars and supplemented by brief bibliographies. General articles like "Technology" are cross-referenced to more specific ones on (for example) "Water Supply," then "Aqueduct," and finally "Iulius Frontinus."

General Studies

*K. D. White. *Greek and Roman Technology*. Ithaca: Cornell University Press, 1984. Perhaps the best attempt, at least until recently, to relate ancient technology closely to the economies and cultures of Greece and Rome. The author is an admired expert, and he cleverly manages to introduce even novices to the topic while still presenting some detailed examples. Thoroughly illustrated, excellent bibliographies, and sixteen appendices on the details.

C. Singer, E. J. Holmyard, A. R. Hall, and T. I. Williams, eds. *A History of Technology*, vol. 1: *From Early Times to the Fall of Ancient Empires ca. 500 B.C.*; vol. 2: *The Mediterranean Civilizations and the Middle Ages*. Oxford: Oxford University Press, 1954 and 1957. These are the first two of a series of volumes that present the history of technology largely in the western world. Each chapter on an individual technology has been contributed by a specialist author, which gives the volume authority if not consistency. Little use of documentary evidence; good bibliographies for their time.

T. K. Derry and T. I. Williams. *A Short History of Technology from the Earliest Times to A.D. 1900*. London: Oxford University Press, 1960. A brief but comprehensive and reliable study of technology and its social implications, from the beginnings to the end of the nineteenth century, of which roughly the first 40 percent covers everything up to the Industrial Revolution. This is a more accessible and shorter version of the preceding, from which it was partly derived.

H. Hodges. *Technology in the Ancient World*. Harmondsworth: Penguin, 1970; reprinted Barnes & Noble, 1992. A chronologically arranged study of the evolution of technologies with a focus on the archaeological record of the Near East and Egypt; extensively illustrated, easy to read, and factually reliable, though Hodges' interpretation of the technological "stagnation" of later antiquity is now much disputed.

J. G. Landels. *Engineering in the Ancient World*. Reprint. Berkeley: The University of California Press, 2000. A standard work for a generation, though the revised edition regrettably adds little to the original. A reliable account of selected technologies—energy, hydraulic engineering, siege machinery, and sea and land transportation—firmly based on the ancient documentary accounts and the author's own practical experiments.

M. Daumas. *A History of Technology and Invention, I: The Origins of Technological Civilization*. New York: Crown Publishers, 1969. This is a wide-ranging and readable account of most technological developments in world cultures until the pre-modern period. Well illustrated, and generally reliable.

V. G. Childe. *What Happened in History*. 3rd ed. New York: Penguin Books, 1964. An intriguing if now dated Marxist account of the interaction between technology and society from the origin of humans to the end of antiquity. It was Childe who proposed the concept of the three "popular and democratic" inventions of the archaic period: the Greek alphabet, coinage, and iron working.

L. S. De Camp. *The Ancient Engineers*. New York: Ballantine Books, 1974. A popular overview of technologies subdivided by time period from the Bronze Age to late medieval Europe, including a chapter on the Far East. While easy reading, it is generally unoriginal and with insufficient (and often unclear) illustrations. Long available in paperback.

*B. M. Fagan. *The Seventy Great Inventions of the Ancient World*. New York: Thames and Hudson, 2005. A lavishly illustrated survey of the evolution of all technologies from the Paleolithic to the end of antiquity, emphasizing the Mediterranean world but including a few forays into the Americas and the Far East. Each two- to five-page essay is written by a recognized authority on the topic. Too superficial to satisfy most readers, but a first-rate introduction with some stunning photography and clear reconstructions.

P. James and N. Thorpe. *Ancient Inventions*. New York: Ballantine Books, 1994. A popularizing and somewhat breathless account of hundreds of ancient inventions, from rocket cars to computers and umbrellas to aphrodisiacs, by a pair of enthusiastic historians devoted to proving to the contemporary world that just about everything we think of as modern was actually invented by our ancient ancestors. Well researched and illustrated, if a bit uncritical and often somewhat misleading.

K. Greene. *The Archaeology of the Roman Economy*. Berkeley: The University of California Press, 1986. A study of the material evidence used to interpret the technologies of transportation, coinage, agriculture, metals, and pottery. Well documented, though without reference to ancient texts; good bibliographical essays at the end of each chapter; richly supplied with maps, images, and diagrams.

D. Hill. *A History of Engineering in Classical and Medieval Times*. London: Croom Helm, 1984. One of the few studies of engineering that pays appropriate attention to the Arab contributions following the end of the ancient world, by a practicing engineer with an advanced degree in Arabic studies. Not a comprehensive treatment of the author's three themes—civil engineering, mechanical engineering, and clocks and instruments—but most useful for its extension beyond European antiquity.

Sources of Information

*J. W. Humphrey, J. P. Oleson, and A. N. Sherwood. *Greek and Roman Technology: A Sourcebook*. New York: Routledge, 1998. A wide-ranging, if not exhaustive, collection of ancient documents that describe the technologies of the Greeks and Romans, translated into English and with brief introductions and explanatory notes. A useful adjunct to modern studies that often neglect the written evidence in favor of the archaeological. A companion volume covering the physical evidence—contemporary depictions, artifacts, and comparative anthropology—was contemplated but shelved because of the complexities (and expenses) of copyright.

J. F. Healy. *Pliny the Elder on Science and Technology*. Oxford: Oxford University Press, 1999. A perceptive analysis of Pliny's chapters on science and technology, combining excerpts from the original *Natural History* with modern commentary on his (mis)understanding of natural and mechanical principles. The emphasis is on the sciences rather than technology, but the author has much useful to say about metals, glass, papyrus, timekeeping, and the like.

P. MacKendrick. *The Greek Stones Speak*; and *The Mute Stones Speak*. 2nd ed. New York: W.W. Norton & Company, 1981 and 1983. A pair of standard and long-lived popular accounts of the history of archaeological excavation in the Greek world and the Roman Empire, respectively. Engagingly written and well illustrated; now quite dated, but a pleasant and informative read.

Energy and Machines

*A. G. Drachmann. *The Mechanical Technology of Greek and Roman Antiquity. A Study of the Literary Sources*. Copenhagen: Munksgaard, 1963. This classic study combines literary analysis and redrawn manuscript illustrations (including those from Arabic translations of the originals) to explain the simple machines of antiquity and how they were combined into complex devices. It is an excellent and scholarly account of Hero's *Mechanics*, Vitruvius, siege engines, and basic machines.

A. P. Usher. *A History of Mechanical Inventions*. Revised edition. New York: Dover Publications, 1988 (1954). An enduring work from the 1920s that, remarkably for its time, attempts to integrate the evolution of technologies with their social and economic context, from antiquity to the early-modern period, relying in part on Gestalt psychology. Despite that, a well reasoned account not to be overlooked.

*B. Cottrell and J. Kamminga. *Mechanics of Pre-Industrial Technology*. Cambridge: Cambridge University Press, 1990. This is an essential survey, by an engineer and an archaeologist, of the basic mechanics involved in tools and machines employed around the world before the coming of industrialization. A practical (and sobering) introduction to basic engineering principles that many archaeologists find difficult to comprehend: the behavior of fluids and solids in hydraulic systems; the stresses of beams, trusses, and arches in civil engineering; torsion and the motion of projectiles; friction of wheeled vehicles and buoyancy of ships. Required reading for anyone working in the history of technology.

Food and Clothing

*K. D. White. *Roman Farming*. Ithaca, NY: Cornell University Press, 1970. The standard work on all aspects of farming in the Roman world by the recognized authority, who uses documentary and archaeological evidence to illustrate everything from the farmstead in general to soil types, fertilizers, crops, and domesticated animals. Well illustrated.

K. D. White. *Country Life in Classical Times.* London: Paul Elek, 1977. An attractive collection of translated descriptions by classical authors who had a passion for farming and the rural life. A useful antidote to the urban focus that is common in ancient history; the Younger Pliny would have loved this slim volume.

M. S. Spurr. *Arable Cultivation in Roman Italy, c. 200 B.C. to c. A.D. 100.* London: Journal of Roman Studies Monograph 3, 1986. A scholarly and detailed description of the agricultural environment, the crops and the tools used to cultivate and harvest them, animal husbandry, and rural labor forces.

K. D. White. *Agricultural Implements of the Roman World*; and *Farm Equipment of the Roman World.* Cambridge: Cambridge University Press, 1967 and 1975. A pair of indispensable catalogues of the myriad of Roman tools used in cultivation and domestication: plows, forks, sickles, reapers, baskets, and storage vessels, even the dibble stick. Scholarly discussions of the uses of these tools, illustrating the frequent difficulty of matching the ancient literary references (quoted in abundance) with known artifacts. Useful line drawings.

L. A. Moritz. *Grain-Mills and Flour in Classical Antiquity.* Oxford: Oxford University Press, 1958. A comprehensive study of all aspects of the processing of grains, including every known type of mill. After half a century, still a standard reference.

*J. J. Rossiter. "Wine and Oil Processing at Roman Farms in Italy." *Phoenix* 35 (1981), 345–361. A scholarly but accessible description of the processing of grapes and olives based on a comparison of the literary and archaeological evidence. An admirable model for how to use a variety of evidence.

G. Rickman. *The Corn Supply of Ancient Rome.* Oxford: Clarendon Press, 1980. Analyzes thoroughly and accurately all aspects of the growing, importation, processing, and consumption of grains in the Roman world, with eleven detailed appendixes. Note that the word "corn" is used by the British to describe wheat.

E.J.W. Barber. *Women's Work: The First 20,000 Years. Women, Cloth, and Society in Early Times.* New York: Norton, 1994. A welcome treatment of all aspects of textile manufacture in pre-modern times, especially valuable in placing the technology in its social context.

Water

N. Smith. *Man and Water: A History of Hydro-Technology*. London: Peter Davies, 1976. A reasonably comprehensive survey of water use from the Bronze-Age Near East to modern times, with useful sections devoted to the ancient Mediterranean. A good introduction to the social and economic motivations behind the development of hydraulic engineering.

O. Wikander, ed. *Handbook of Ancient Water Technology. Technology and Change in History*. Brill Academic Publishers, 1999. Now the standard handbook to any study of ancient hydraulics, by one of the most respected experts.

*J. P. Oleson. *Greek and Roman Mechanical Water-Lifting Devices: The History of a Technology*. Toronto: University of Toronto Press, 1984. The standard work on the topic, relying on both documentary and archaeological evidence to present a coherent and reliable account of the evolution of wheels, chains, and pumps to raise water. Excellent bibliography.

*A. T. Hodge. *Roman Aqueducts and Water Supply*. London: Duckworth, 1992. The standard study, already a classic, by one of the world's most respected students of Roman water supply. A treasure trove of information from determining reliable sources to flushing public latrines, and all the urban manipulation of water in between.

*F. Yegül. *Baths and Bathing in Classical Antiquity*. Cambridge, MA: MIT Press, 1992. A comprehensive, extraordinarily well illustrated, and award-winning treatment of Greek and Roman private and public baths, with an especially useful appendix on the water supply and heating of *thermae*. The author, a respected scholar and professor of the history of architecture, is better known to most as the builder of a model Roman bath building outside ancient Sardis in modern Turkey, captured by the *Nova* television series.

M. Lang. *Waterworks in the Athenian Agora*. Princeton: American School of Classical Studies at Athens, 1968. A brief but useful and authoritative description of the various hydraulic elements excavated in the agora, including pipes and drains, wells and fountains, and even toilets.

H. B. Evans. *Water Distribution in Ancient Rome*. Ann Arbor: University of Michigan, 1994. An almost unique study of what happened to the aqueduct waters after they entered the city of Rome, based principally on a close analysis of Frontinus (physical remains being scarce). The author traces through the city the course of each of the major lines, identifying where possible *castella* and fountains. A remarkable effort of sleuthing, but woefully short of maps and illustrations.

*A. T. Hodge. "A Plain man's Guide to Roman Plumbing." *Classical Views* 26 (1983), 311–328. An outstanding brief introduction to the aqueduct and distribution systems of Rome, by a respected scholar who would later produce the standard reference work on the subject (see above).

Shelter and Security

J. M. Camp II and W. B. Dinsmoor Jr. *Ancient Athenian Building Methods.* American School of Classical Studies at Athens, 1984. Another of the admirable booklets published by the excavators of the Athenian Agora, this one profiling briefly (but with plentiful illustrations) all the major aspects of civil engineering: preparation of the site, the labor force, building materials and their transportation, and the structural elements including doors and windows, floors, and roofs.

M. Korres. *The Stones of the Parthenon.* Los Angeles: J. Paul Getty Museum, 2000. A short and semipopular description of every stage in the construction of the Parthenon, from the quarrying of marble to the transportation, erection, and finishing of the blocks. Each of the twenty-three stages in the process is given a brief description accompanied by a clear and informative pen-and-ink drawing by the author.

R. E. Wycherly. *How the Greeks Built Cities.* 2nd ed. New York: W.W. Norton & Company, 1962. A readable and reliable account of how the classical Greeks laid out their urban centers, including fortification walls, the agora, public buildings, and waterworks. Well illustrated with photographs and plans.

*J. B. Ward-Perkins. *Roman Imperial Architecture.* 2nd ed. Harmondsworth: Penguin Books, 1981. This classic and profusely illustrated chronological account of the evolution of Roman architecture from Augustus to the end of the empire incorporates many plans and useful descriptions of engineering techniques.

O. F. Robinson. *Ancient Rome. City Planning and Administration.* London: Routledge, 1992. An outstanding survey of the practical elements of town planning, including building controls, public works, sanitation and public health, policing and public order. A fascinating treatment that includes much relevant to the application of technologies to urban survival.

H. de la Croix. *Military Considerations in City Planning: Fortifications*. New York: George Braziller, 1972. This is a thin but useful outline of the history of urban fortifications from prehistory to the Renaissance. The fifty-page interpretive essay is, by necessity, fairly superficial, but it is supplemented by ninety-one illustrations and drawings that bring the material alive.

*F. Winter. *Greek Fortifications*. Toronto: University of Toronto Press, 1971. The most comprehensive and respected study of all aspects of Greek defensive walls, including design, construction, tactics, and sieges. The author's familiarity with the physical remains throughout the Greek world is astounding. Profusely illustrated, and with admirable line drawings.

A. W. Lawrence. *Greek Aims in Fortification*. Oxford: Clarendon Press, 1979. A standard and thoroughly illustrated reference for all the literary and archaeological evidence concerning fortifications and sieges.

I. A. Richmond. *The City Wall of Imperial Rome*. Oxford: Oxford University Press, 1930.

M. Todd. *The Walls of Rome*. London: Paul Elek, 1978. Two complementary and reliable studies of the defensive walls of Rome, the first a more exhaustive treatment of the wall first erected by the Emperor Aurelian in 270 C.E. and reworked for centuries thereafter, the second a more concise account of the imperial wall and its republican predecessor.

S. Johnson. *Late Roman Fortifications*. Totowa, NJ: Barnes & Noble, 1983. This welcome study of the defense of the empire in the troubled third and fourth centuries relies largely on the physical remains of urban and frontier fortifications. Useful comments on design and construction techniques as well as strategy. Thoroughly illustrated.

P. B. Kern. *Ancient Siege Warfare*. Bloomington: Indiana University Press, 1999. This chronological recapitulation of the history of sieges from the Near East to the Romans is based principally on the ancient texts. While there is some technical discussion of the machines themselves, the author is more interested in the social and moral aspects of sieges: the brutality, the devaluation of the traditional warrior, the presence of women in warfare, and so on.

*E. W. Marsden. *Greek and Roman Artillery, I: Technical Treatises*; and *II: Historical Development*. Oxford: Clarendon Press, 1971 and 1969. The most accessible and reliable study of the topic, from the classical origins of the catapult to the fall of the Roman Empire, relying on both literary and archaeological evidence, by a scholar who experimented extensively with reconstructed models; well illustrated, comprehensive (but now dated) bibliography.

Transportation

*L. Casson. *Travel in the Ancient World*. London: Allen & Unwin, 1974. A standard and reliable work about all forms of transportation in the ancient Mediterranean, on both land and water, written by an academic expert who manages to reach both scholarly and popular audiences at the same time.

L. Casson. *The Ancient Mariners. Seafarers and Sea Fighters of the Ancient Mediterranean in Ancient Times*. 2nd ed. Princeton: Princeton University Press, 1991. As with all of Casson's works, a scholarly but very readable account, this time of sea travel and warfare from the Bronze Age to the end of the Roman Empire.

L. Casson. *Ships and Seamanship in the Ancient World*. Revised edition. Princeton: Princeton University Press, 1986. A volume devoted entirely to the vessels themselves: construction, rigging, crews, and speed of travel; based on an exhaustive study of the literary and material evidence, and richly illustrated.

L. Casson. "The Mystery of the Trireme." *Horizon* 14.1 (1972), 110–113.

V. Foley and W. Soedel. "Ancient Oared Warships." *Scientific American* (April 1981), 148–163.

P. Lipke. "Trials of the Trireme." *Scientific American* (March/April 1988), 22–29.

*J. S. Morrison and J. F. Coates. *The Athenian Trireme. The History and Reconstruction of an Ancient Warship*. 2nd ed. Cambridge: Cambridge University Press, 2000. Four studies that give a useful perspective on how our understanding of ancient technologies evolves: the first two, good attempts to understand the structure and operation of an oared warship based on thin literary and physical evidence; the third and fourth, an intriguing account of the reconstruction of a trireme and the practical experiences of those who took her through sea trials. The last is especially recommended for both its careful detail and its underlying sense of discovery.

C. M. Kraay. *Archaic and Classical Greek Coins*. London: Methuen, 1976. This standard reference for the origins and early history of Mediterranean coinage, by a reputable scholar, includes examples of all the coins discussed in this volume.

C. C. Vermeule. "Minting Greek and Roman Coins." *Archaeology* 10 (1957), 100–107. This is a short and popular, but accurate and nicely illustrated, description of the minting techniques for ancient coins.

F. Meijer and O. van Nijf. *Trade, Transport and Society in the Ancient World. A Sourcebook*. London: Routledge, 1992. A collection of translated ancient documents—literary, papyrological, and epigraphic—illustrating all aspects of the transportation of goods by land and sea throughout the Mediterranean world. Short but useful annotations.

Recordkeeping and Timekeeping

J. F. Healey. *The Early Alphabet*. Berkeley: University of California Press, 1990.

E. A. Havelock. *The Literate Revolution in Greece and its Cultural Consequences*. Princeton: Princeton University Press, 1982. These two standard works on the evolution of literacy in archaic and classical Greece each includes a study of the origins of the alphabet. The authors may disagree on details, but their overall assessments of the impact of literacy on ancient society are similar.

L. H. Jeffery. *The Local Scripts of Archaic Greece. A Study of the Origins of the Greek Alphabet and its Development from the 8th to the 5th Centuries B.C.* Oxford: Clarendon Press, 1961. The standard reference for the now widely accepted theory that the Greek alphabet originated in the middle of the eighth century at a trading site on the eastern Mediterranean coast, where all the necessary participants were active; based on an exhaustive study of relevant inscriptions.

W. V. Harris. *Ancient Literacy*. Cambridge, MA: Harvard University Press, 1989. This scholarly but readable study of the impact of the invention of the alphabet on the political, social, and even religious life of a previously oral culture is a model study of the unpredictable cascading effects of a technical invention on an entire civilization.

N. Lewis. *Papyrus in Classical Antiquity*. Oxford: Clarendon Press, 1974. A useful and sound survey of the cultivation of papyrus and its conversion into a writing surface.

S. L. Gibbs. *Greek and Roman Sundials*. New Haven: Yale University Press, 1976. The only accessible and reliable account of various designs of sundials, from both physical and documentary evidence, which are often difficult to interpret and sometimes downright mysterious.

Crafts

*D. E. Strong and D. Brown. *Roman Crafts*. New York: New York University Press, 1976. An admirable collection of chapters, written by experts, devoted to various aspects of the material production of the Roman world, including the working of metals and the manufacture of jewelry; wood-working; textiles and leather; pottery, lamps, and terracotta figurines; glass; and the minting of coins. An essential reference for anyone inter-ested in ancient technology.

*A. Burford. *Craftsmen in Greek and Roman Society*. Ithaca, NY: Cornell Uni-versity Press, 1972. A superb description of the life and occupations of artisans in antiquity, based on every sort of primary evidence, and well illustrated.

*J. F. Healy. *Mining and Metallurgy in the Greek and Roman World*. Ithaca, NY: Cornell University Press, 1978. A thorough and reliable account of all aspects of metals and metallurgy in antiquity, from basic geology and mining through smelting. Well illustrated.

J. V. Noble. *The Techniques of Painted Attic Pottery*. 2nd ed. London: Thames & Hudson, 1988. A superb analysis of the complex techniques used to produce the Black-Figure and Red-Figure pottery of the late archaic and classical period, from the choice of clays to the wheel, decoration, and firing procedures.

J. W. Hayes. *Handbook of Mediterranean Roman Pottery*. Norman, OK: Uni-versity of Oklahoma Press, 1997. A useful, brief introduction to the production, shapes, and functions of both fine and coarse Roman wares, by the acknowledged expert. Helpfully illustrated.

R. H. Brill. "Ancient Glass." *Scientific American* 209 (1963), 120–131. A useful and understandable survey of the origins of glass working in the ancient Mediterranean.

Technology, Innovation, and Society

R. S. Brumbaugh. *Ancient Greek Gadgets and Machines*. New York: Crowell, 1966. A popular description of the various machines and automata of the Hellenistic and Roman period.

D. J. de S. Price. "Automata and the Origins of Mechanism and Mecha-nistic Philosophy." *Technology and Culture* 5 (1962), 9–23. A classic analysis of the beginnings of mechanistic philosophy in antiquity, and its reappearance in the Renaissance. Useful discussion of clocks in particular.

*D. J. de S. Price. *Gears from the Greeks. The Antikythera Mechanism: A Calendar Computer from ca 80 B.C.* Transactions of the American Philosophical Society 64.7 (1974). The painstaking reconstruction of a set of badly corroded bronze gear wheels and dials recovered from the Mediterranean Sea, dated by the author to the first century B.C.E. and convincingly identified as a "computerized" calendar. A fascinating story of sleuthing, though recent reexamination of the artifact suggests that Price may not have gotten it all right (see Internet Resources below).

S. Bedini. "The Role of Automata in the History of Technology." *Technology and Culture* 5 (1964), 24–41. An intriguing catalogue of the manufacture of automata down to early modern times, and their function as an imitation of natural phenomena. Rightly acknowledges the significance of mechanical principles employed in useless devices.

M. I. Finley. "Technical Innovation and Economic Progress in the Ancient World." *Economic History Review* 18 (1965), 29–45.

K. Greene. "Technological Innovation and Economic Progress in the Ancient World: M. I. Finley Re-considered." *Economic History Review* 53 (2000), 29–59. The first is a scholarly but readable analysis of the reasons why innovation (and progress) was generally scorned in antiquity; a literate and widely influential presentation of the social attitudes of the wealthy, but should now be read in conjunction with Greene's reconsideration, which rightly questions the assumption of technological "stagnation" in the Roman Empire.

Internet Resources

The following list, far from comprehensive, includes reputable websites that deal substantially with the themes of this volume. Readers are invited to report inactive links or additional sites to the author: humphrey@ucalgary.ca.

Map Room. The Interactive Ancient Mediterranean Project, University of North Carolina at Chapel Hill. http://iam.classics.unc.edu/map/map_room.html. A series of downloadable maps that illustrate all geographical areas of the ancient Mediterranean.

Sextus Julius Frontinus: The Aqueducts of Rome. B. Thayer, University of Chicago. http://penelope.uchicago.edu/Thayer/E/Roman/Texts/Frontinus/

De_Aquis/text*.html. The complete text of Frontinus' *de Aquis*, in Latin and English translation, with promised links to the original manuscript. A welcome contribution to technology studies.

The Pneumatics of Hero of Alexandria. University of Rochester. http://www .history.rochester.edu/steam/hero/index.html. An online copy of the only complete English translation of this important work, by Bennet Wood-croft and published in 1851. Includes useful line drawings.

**Perseus Digital Library*. Gregory Crane, ed. Tufts University. http://www.perseus .tufts.edu/. This website has, in addition to images and secondary sources on a variety of topics, 489 primary source texts from authors such as Plato, Aristotle, and Pliny the Elder. It is a valuable resource for the study of all areas of antiquity.

**Greek and Roman Science and Technology*. Created by T. E. Rihll, Department of Classics and Ancient History, The University of Wales, Swansea. http:// www.swan.ac.uk/classics/staff/ter/grst/HomePageG&RS&T.htm. An excellent website on general science and technology, providing a "Who's Who" of ancient scientists, a glossary of terms, a list of works on scientific topics written by authors in the ancient world, brief introductions to specific topics, and links to online texts and translations.

**Ancient Roman Technology*. Directed by G. Houston, Department of Classical Studies, University of North Carolina, Chapel Hill. http://www.unc.edu/ courses/rometech/public/frames/art_set.html. A valuable electronic handbook of ancient Roman technology, created and maintained by faculty and students at the University of North Carolina at Chapel Hill. Contains sections on the following topics: survival, clothing, food, arts and crafts, mines, quarries and stone working, transport, construction and engineering, spatial organization of towns and cities, and other areas of technology and science such as medicine. These areas are in various stages of completion and work is ongoing.

Index of Mathematicians. School of Mathematics and Statistics, University of St Andrews. http://www-groups.dcs.st-and.ac.uk/~history/Mathematicians/. Biographies of mathematicians throughout history, with good surveys of the work of Aristotle, Archimedes, and Hero.

Archimedes. C. Rorres. http://www.mcs.drexel.edu/~crorres/Archimedes/contents .html. "A collection of Archimedean miscellanea under continual development." Contains links to images and descriptions of several inventions by Archimedes such as the "claw" and the water screw.

Archimedes' Death Ray: Idea Feasibility Testing. D. R. Wallace, Massachusetts Institute of Technology. http://web.mit.edu/2.009/www/lectures/10_ArchimedesResult.html. An intriguing attempt by MIT students to re-create the alignment of mirrors said to have been designed by Archimedes to concentrate the sun's rays and ignite enemy ships.

An Ancient Greek Computer. D. J. de S. Price. http://etl.uom.gr/mr/Antikythera/price.htm. An online version of an article published in *Scientific American* in 1959. The "Back" link at the bottom of the website page will connect you to other information on this device. A recent reevaluation of Price's interpretation is described at http://www.economist.com/displaystory.cfm?story_id=1337165.

The Antikythera Mechanism Links. R. Russell. http://www.giant.net.au/users/rupert/kythera/kythera5.htm. A long list of weblinks to dozens of sites (not all scholarly) that discuss the mysterious device.

Agricultural Revolution. Washington State University. http://www.wsu.edu/gened/learn-modules/top_agrev/agrev-index.html. An online course module about early agriculture and settlement, with brief notes, some graphics, and questions to consider.

The Nilometer. Eternal Egypt. http://www.eternalegypt.org:80/EternalEgyptWebsiteWeb/HomeServlet?ee_website_action_key=action.display.element&story_id=&module_id=&element_id=30559&language_id=1. A useful description of the device invented in the early Bronze Age to track the annual flood of the Nile and predict its height. The site's home (http://www.eternalegypt.org/) offers many texts and graphics about all aspects of Egypt in antiquity.

A Taste of the Ancient World: an exhibit about Greco-Roman eating and drinking, farming and starving. Created by students for the Kelsey Museum of Archaeology at the University of Michigan. http://www.umich.edu/~kelseydb/Exhibits/Food/text/Food.html. This site contains information on all areas of ancient food production, and includes images and descriptions of tools used in farming and food production in antiquity. Material based on excavations by the University of Michigan at Karanis, a farming town in Roman Egypt.

Ancient Greek Dress. Metropolitan Museum of Art, New York, N.Y. http://www.metmuseum.org/toah/hd/grdr/hd_grdr.htm. Information about Greek clothing includes images from vase paintings and sculpture.

Roman Clothing. VRoma Project, Co-Directors S. Bonefas and B. F. McManus. http://www.vroma.org/~bmcmanus/clothing.html. Provides information on

Roman clothing and its link to social status. Its parent site, www.vroma.org, is an excellent source for all areas of Roman history.

Water Wheels. R. D. Hansen. http://www.waterhistory.org/histories/waterwheels/. Provides information on the use of water wheels by the Romans.

The History of Plumbing—Pompeii & Herculaneum. http://www.theplumber.com/ pom.html. An online version of the article that appeared in *Plumbing and Mechanical Magazine*, July 1989. This article is part of a collection of articles on the history of plumbing at theplumber.com.

Roman Aqueducts. http://www.inforoma.it/feature.php?lookup=aqueduct. This site contains basic information on Roman aqueducts, with images and schematic drawings. Its parent site, www.InfoRoma.it, is useful for other topics as well.

Some Hydraulics of Roman Aqueducts. Myths, Fables, Realities. A Hydraulician's Perspective. H. Chanson, University of Queensland. http://www.uq.edu.au/ ~e2hchans/rom_aq.html. This site, constructed and maintained by a professor of civil engineering, contains much detailed information on aqueducts, as well as good photographs and links to other sites.

Olynthos. http://www.macedonian-heritage.gr/HellenicMacedonia/en/C1.7.html. Details the ancient Greek city of Olynthos and its building plan, with links to sites with information on housing in ancient Greece.

Ostia: Harbour City of Ancient Rome. http://www.ostia-antica.org/. Images of Roman urban housing, and plans and reconstructions of this ancient port town.

Greek Hoplites. HistoryforKids.org. http://www.historyforkids.org/learn/greeks/ war/hoplites.htm. Contains information on Greek military tactics and technology. Though intended for a younger audience, it contains quality information at a basic level.

Ancient Greek Methods of Boating and Shipping. K. McMahon, N. Chadha, and P. Hotchkiss. http://www-adm.pdx.edu/user/sinq/greekciv2/war/kenny.html. Information on several areas of maritime life in ancient Greece, including trading by sea and naval warfare.

The Roman Calendar. http://www.roman-britain.org/calendar.htm. Provides detailed information on the Roman calendar, timekeeping, and the calendar reforms of Julius Caesar.

Wonderous Glass: Reflections on the World of Rome. M. C. Root, Kelsey Museum of Archaeology, University of Michigan. http://www.umich.edu/~kelseydb/

Exhibits/WondrousGlass/MainGlass.html. Information on all areas of the craft of Roman glass making.

The Technique of Bronze Statuary in Ancient Greece. Metropolitan Museum of Art, New York. http://www.metmuseum.org/toah/hd/grbr/hd_grbr.htm. Contains information on how bronze statues were created in the ancient world, including a description of the "lost-wax" technique.

Ancient Metallurgy. D. K. Jordan, University of California at San Diego. http://weber.ucsd.edu/~dkjordan/arch/metallurgy.html. Detailed information on various aspects of ancient metallurgy includes the different types of metals available, their uses, and ways of working with them.

Video Resources

The following comprise just a small selection of titles available on VHS and/or DVD. All are designed for the nonprofessional, but the ones here at least show an acceptable level of scholarship and reliability. All come from the Discovery Channel Store: http://shopping.discovery.com/product-58059.html#desc.

What the Ancients Knew. The technological history of the ancient Egyptians, Romans, and Chinese. Three DVDs, 50 minutes each.

Unsolved History: Trojan War. A combination of archaeologists and engineers examine Homer's *The Iliad* and the site of Troy in northwest Turkey, in an attempt to understand the function and construction of the famous horse. One DVD, 86 minutes.

Seven Wonders of Ancient Egypt. Computer graphics help reconstruct seven engineering achievements of early Egypt, including the pyramids, the tombs in the Valley of Kings, and the Sphinx. One DVD, 50 minutes.

Seven Wonders of Ancient Greece. A study of the engineering behind seven important structures from the ancient Greek world: the theater of Epidaurus, the statue of Zeus at Olympia, Apollo's Temple at Delphi, the Colossus of Rhodes, the Bronze-Age settlement at Akrotiri on Thera/Santorini, the Palace of Knossos, and the Parthenon. One DVD, 50 minutes.

Seven Wonders of Ancient Rome. Seven examples of Roman engineering expertise, illustrated with digital reconstructions: The Pantheon, aqueducts, the Appian Way, the Baths of Caracalla, Trajan's Market, the Circus Maximus, and the Colosseum ("the ancient world's Rose Bowl"!). One DVD, 50 minutes.

Super Weapons of the Ancient World: The Ram. Engineers, timber framers, and blacksmiths try to create functioning, life-size replicas made entirely out of authentic materials, and then put them to the test under battle conditions. A team of engineers from the U.S. Military Academy at West Point struggles to recreate a Roman tortoise ram. One DVD, 50 minutes.

Building the Impossible: The Roman Catapult. An attempt to construct a replica of the Roman stone-throwing ballista, with an emphasis on the materials used to build the machines and how Roman military engineers were able to coax considerable force out of what is really a simple device. One DVD, 50 minutes.

INDEX

Figure numbers are indicated in italics; page numbers of Primary Documents are in boldface.

About the Author

JOHN W. HUMPHREY is a Roman historian and archaeologist at the University of Calgary. He is co-author of *Greek and Roman Technology: A Sourcebook* (1998), a volume of translated and annotated ancient texts that describe the technical history of the Greeks and Romans. He has excavated at four sites in Greece and Turkey, and has traveled extensively throughout the Mediterranean, studying and photographing contemporary examples of ancient technologies.